COMMUNICATING FOR FUTURE BUSINESS PROFESSIONALS

· ·

MICHAEL GREENE
JONATHAN G. RIPLEY

Prentice Hall
Upper Saddle River, NJ 07458

Library of Congress Cataloging-in-Publication Data

Greene, Michael
    Communicating for future business professionals/Michael Greene,
    Jonathan G. Ripley.
        p.   cm.
    Includes index.
    ISBN 0–13–157736–0
    1. Business communication. 2. Business writing. 3. Résumés
(Employment) 4. Career development. 5. College graduates—
Employment. I. Ripley, Jonathan G. II. Title.
HF5718.G74   1998
808′.06665—dc21   97-18315
                                                        CIP

Acquisitions Editor: Elizabeth Sugg
Director of Production and Manufacturing: Bruce Johnson
Managing Editor: Mary Carnis
Editorial/Production Supervision and Interior Design:
    Tally Morgan, WordCrafters Editorial Services, Inc.
Cover Design: Miguel Ortiz
Manufacturing Buyer Ed O'Dougherty
Marketing Manager: Danny Hoyt

 © 1998 by Prentice-Hall, Inc.
Simon & Schuster/A Viacom Company
Upper Saddle River, New Jersey 07458

Printed in the United States of America

10   9   8   7   6   5   4   3   2   1

ISBN 0-13-157736-0

Prentice Hall International (UK) Limited, *London*
Prentice Hall of Australia Pty. Limited, *Sydney*
Prentice Hall Canada Inc., *Toronto*
Prentice Hall Hispanoamericana, S.A., *Mexico*
Prentice Hall of India Private Limited, *New Delhi*
Prentice Hall of Japan, Inc., *Tokyo*
Prentice Hall of Southeast Asia Pte. Ltd., *Singapore*
Editora Prentice Hall do Brasil Ltda., *Rio de Janeiro*

CONTENTS

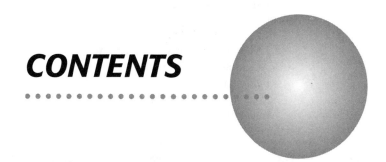

PREFACE

This textbook was designed and written with several purposes in mind. Among the multiple functions of our text is the notion that it should serve as a career planning tool and a desktop reference. We wanted to produce a text that would help students prepare the documents that would help them gain employment, and we wanted to supply students with a comprehensive and practical guide to accomplishing the wide variety of writing and speaking tasks they could expect to encounter in the workplace. Accordingly, we have provided step-by-step, detailed instructions for producing well designed business documents, preparing effective presentations, and participating productively in a number of business settings.

TEXT FOCUS

Task-focused, *Communicating for Future Business Professionals* provides practical advice and answers for people who need to communicate in writing, at a meeting, or in front of a group. The text is organized by career steps. If readers work through the chapters, they will encounter a variety of tasks in the order they will likely experience them as they move from school into the workplace.

DESIGNING DOCUMENTS

One of the features we include is the document design process, a set of general procedures for designing business communications, whether they are spoken words in a face-to-face situation or written words faxed-to-fax across cities and continents. Whatever the communication situation, readers can use the document design process to help them create clear, direct messages.

EXERCISES

The exercises deal with a variety of business situations, so that a context is provided for communication. We expect that those who use the book are already familiar with a good deal of business vocabulary and that they are aware of common roles, tasks, and functions in a typical business organization.

Many of the exercises and examples involve a small business firm, Pascal Business Systems, engaged in the sales, distribution, and installation of business software and office automation systems. We provide short applications in areas like quality and inventory control, human resources, marketing, and customer correspondence, in order to supply a recognizable business context.

STUDY SUPPORT

Finally, we provide an on-line internet site which contains further resources, including:

- Downloadable Powerpoint slideshow to support individual chapters.
- A set of links to download language arts shareware/freeware programs with our reviews and teaching suggestions.
- Interactive case studies with links to sites on the World Wide Web and followup electronic homework which will be e-mailed to registered instructors.

You can reach us at **CLS@TIAC.NET.** Files can also be accessed from **www.prenhall.com** (search for greene) or **www.prenhall.com/business_studies.**

ACKNOWLEDGMENTS

There were so many people who helped us that it is impossible to thank everyone. Some people who offered assistance, advice and support along the way:

Contributors
John Buettner
Mark Fontanella
Bob "Flash" Fraser
Bob Gundersen
Owen Harris
Patrick Hetherton
Bonnie Jean Kern
Raymond Lawless
Brad Miller
Sean Murphy
Carol Twigg
Marilyn Stern

Staff
Russ Bramhall
Mike Carter
Mike Feller
Dick Goller

Gary Ham
Phyllis Harris
June Joseph
Barbara Karanian
Marty Kemen
Paul Lazarovich
Sandy Pascal (the real one)
Mark Schuh
Gary Simundza
Kathy Spirer
Joanne Tuck
Les Welter

Students
Majalia Ansel
Roberto Bagu
David Betz
Jeffrey Comeau
Paul Comendul

Kristen Delbuono
Jessica Despres
John Donnellan
Chuck Frisbie
Ralph Goodwin
Francis Henderson
Richard Holland
Anne Lavallee
Gary McCarthy
Christine Randall
Bob Raymond
John Ruehrwein
Janet Rustin
John Squillace
Brian Solomon
Scott Tamosunas
Bruce Ward
James Watkins

We would like to thank all of the students who have taken our Professional, Technical, and Oral Communications courses at Wentworth throughout the years. They offered a wealth of valuable feedback. The staff of the Wentworth Alumni Library was always there to lend a helping hand.

To Tally Morgan at WordCrafters Editorial Services, and Dana Smith at Pine Tree Composition, we offer our sincere thanks.

Michael wants to thank Bob Dylan, the Jayhawks, and Wilco for letting him sing along as he was writing.

Finally, we dedicate this book to Hillary, Joshua, Rebecca and Jared, and to Elizabeth, Jennifer, and Kristen. And to Edie, who knows her contributions.

Jon Ripley
Michael Greene

section 1
APPLYING FOR WORK

. . . .

Welcome to *Communicating for Future Business Professionals*. We've tried to make this book readable and clear so that you can learn from us and enjoy what you read. We have organized the chapters to correspond to the steps you might follow as you progress toward your career goals. For this reason, we are starting with this section, titled "Applying for Work," so that you can focus on who you are and what you want to do in the future. Chapters in this section offer an introduction to the material covered in the text and guidelines for conducting a self-assessment, preparing your résumé, and interviewing for a job. Once you realize what you want to do, you will find that you have a variety of reasons to improve your communication skills.

Chapter 1   *Looking Ahead*

Chapter 2   *Assessing Yourself*

Chapter 3   *Creating Your Résumé*

Chapter 4   *Interviewing*

LOOKING AHEAD

Processing and Managing Information

Surveying Your Time Horizon

Making Good Use of This Book

What This Book Is About

How This Book Is Organized

Discovering a Context for Your Communications

Examining What Your Future Holds

This chapter has several purposes. One of them is to explain how this book works, or rather how you can make this book work for you: how you can use the book to anticipate and prepare for the communication tasks you will encounter when you finish school and begin work.

We want you to be able to look ahead a few years after your graduation to a point where you are involved in the daily life of a business, where you are writing and speaking not for a teacher's approval and college credit, but for a way to earn your living, to achieve success, and to accomplish the goals you set for yourself. This text approaches business communications through your own perspective, emphasizing skills, techniques, and methods that a business professional at the entry level (and beyond) will find useful.

Our book is intended to be a practical introduction to many of the situations you will face in your business career and the types of tasks you will need to accomplish. Whether you are looking for a comprehensive guide to the kinds of communication responsibilities you will likely meet in your profession or a quick review of how to do a particular task, we have designed this book to help you.

We hope you will find this book useful enough to keep when you leave school, and that you will bring it to the office with you as a reliable assistant for the day-to-day communication tasks you will encounter.

PROCESSING AND MANAGING INFORMATION

When you graduate from school and enter the business world, you will quickly discover how much of your time is spent managing information. You may be surprised at how closely the business cycle resembles an information cycle.

Whether you are processing customer transactions or summarizing data periodically, the information you communicate is essential to your company's decision-making. Successful businesspeople are able to gather, analyze, create, and distribute information.

Organizations large and small need to process data and turn it into information. Records must be kept for taxes, inventory, customer transactions, ordering, and marketing. Decision making depends upon the analysis, reporting, and presentation of this information. The management of information is crucial to the functioning of all modern organizations and businesses. Companies use information to gain competitive advantages.

Whatever product or service your business offers, good information provides the basis for on-time delivery, quality control, and satisfied customers. Your business success will depend on your ability to process and manage information efficiently in order to meet the needs of your clients. Most of what you will need to know about business communication is logical, interesting, and essential to a successful business career, and can be connected in practical ways to what you are learning and have already learned about business and organizations.

Managing the flow of information should not be a new and unfamiliar process to people interested in business. Much of what you will need to do is governed by common sense and traditional business practices. For example, every business has an available inventory of information. This information about products and services needs to be current, accurate, readily available, and convenient to use. Information inventory provides a competitive advantage to companies that utilize it efficiently.

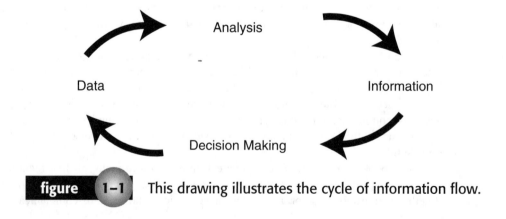

figure 1–1 This drawing illustrates the cycle of information flow.

The global marketplace and new technologies mean that business opportunities have become more and more time sensitive. Orders for goods and payment for these orders can be transmitted globally and confirmed within minutes. *When* you provide information is increasingly important. New technologies such as fax machines, cellular phones, and satellite transmissions have increased the speed of business information.

Many other business principles apply to the management of information. An immediate example is quality control. You will need to develop the ability to sort out useful information from the ever-growing quantities of data and noise that business communication systems produce. The quality of information will determine whether it is used. The availability of different types and greater quantities of information makes business communication skills even more important.

If you develop your communication skills so that you can manage information effectively, you will have increased time for the parts of the job that you will enjoy the most: creative planning and development tasks.

SURVEYING YOUR TIME HORIZON

One of the concepts that we use in this book is the idea of a *time horizon*. This concept asks that you expand your perspective on the world by looking ahead as well as around yourself. You are probably accustomed to thinking of the horizon as a physical distance, the farthest point away from you that you are able to see. Your time horizon is the interval of your future that you can clearly and realistically imagine.

One of the mental perspectives that successful people develop is an expanded time horizon. This means that instead of thinking about tomorrow or next week or next month, you can develop the capacity to look even further ahead, to imagine yourself a year from now or two years from now, and to anticipate what you will be doing and what you will need to know. In other words, we want you to imagine your future and be ready for when it arrives.

Getting ready to graduate from college, finding a job, and changing roles from student to employee are important transitions in your life; you want to be prepared to accomplish these changes smoothly. In this book we want to help you look ahead to the next two or three years after graduation, to help you imagine the kinds of jobs you will be doing, the challenges you will face, and the types of preparation that will make you successful.

We also would like you to expand your geographical and cultural horizons and consider the challenges and opportunities involved in international and intercultural communications. Whatever business you become involved with, you will need all of the customers you can find. The ability to communicate effectively with people from different cultures and perspectives will be a valuable asset to you and your employers.

MAKING GOOD USE OF THIS BOOK

We have designed this book with several purposes in mind. First of all, we want it to be a planning tool that will help you imagine the next few years of your life as a business professional and to prepare for the communication tasks you will face. In other words, you can use the book to look ahead. We assume that this is also *your* main purpose: to famil-

time horizons	
What year is this? How old are you now?	
Add four years. What year is this? How old are you now?	
Have you changed physically in the last four years? How?	
Are you married or single? Describe your living arrangements.	
What kind of car are you driving? Describe your car.	
What kind of clothes do you wear to work? Describe your hair.	
Are you working?	
If yes, describe the organization. What is your role in the organization? How much do you get paid? What are your job duties? Are you happy? If no, describe what you are doing with your time. How do you support yourself? Are you happy?	

iarize yourself with your future as a business professional and to develop the specific communication skills you will need to have. The primary focus is on you and your own personal development and career planning.

Second, we want to supply you with a comprehensive and practical guide to accomplishing the wide variety of writing and speaking tasks you can expect to encounter. Different chapters provide detailed step-by-step instructions for producing well-designed business documents, preparing effective presentations, and participating productively in a number of business settings. If you need to get something done—design a business document or a presentation, for example—you will find useful suggestions and directions for immediate application. If you need practical advice, you can go directly to it. Whether you use this book as a career planning tool that will help prepare you for your eventual entry into the workplace, or as a desktop reference guide that will help you complete a pressing business task, you will find what you need.

When you enter the business world you will discover that promotions and salary increases will frequently reflect how well you communicate; generally, the higher you go in the company, the more you will be expected to communicate formally. As you move into supervisory and decision-making positions, more and more of your time will be spent at a desk and at meetings. You will communicate to groups of people who will be judging you and your ideas by three things:

- the way you use words
- the way you organize your ideas
- the attitude they perceive in you

You can use this text to improve in each of these areas.

What This Book Is About

This book is about you and your future. It is designed to help you prepare for your business career by anticipating and practicing many of the communication tasks you can expect to encounter in your professional life. Your business success will depend greatly on your ability to communicate quickly and responsively in the context of a business environment. Learning to write and speak in a professional manner while you are in school makes sense in a time when companies want their new employees to be prepared and ready to participate and contribute as soon as they join the company. Your abilities to communicate will create the connections you need to achieve your own career goals.

This book is not designed to help you with college compositions, essays, poetry, or creative fiction. For these tasks you need other resources and tools. This handbook is for business professionals who need to communicate effectively in a work setting.

How This Book Is Organized

The overall structure of this text is meant to be clear and apparent. We begin from your viewpoint: that of a college student who is studying some aspect of business and preparing to begin a job search. We then move through the next two or three years of work experience in terms of your growing responsibilities and communication challenges. If you work through the chapters from beginning to end, you will encounter a variety of tasks in the order in which you will likely experience them as you move from school into the workplace.

On the other hand, you may want to go directly to a particular task that you need to complete now. The index, the table of contents, and the headings are all designed to help you locate what you need to complete an immediate task. We have organized this book with multiple entry points so that you can begin at various locations and find the information and help you need quickly and easily. At some future time, for example, you may need a quick refresher on how to write a long report. You can go directly to the appropriate part of the book.

Parts of this book explore different types of business communication: employment, face-to-face, interoffice, customer, and team/collaborative communications. The parts are distinguished by their focus on different purposes, audiences, and situations. Still, there is a common core to all of these types of communication. This is the *document design process,* a set of general procedures for designing communications, whether they are spoken words in a face-to-face situation or written words faxed across cities and continents. Whatever the communication situation, you can use the document design process to assist you in creating clear, direct messages.

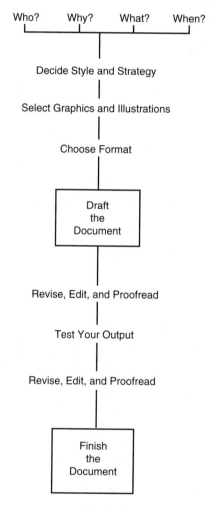

figure **1–2** The document design process.

learning about document design

The *document design process* is a basic underlying set of procedures you can use whenever you have a document to write, whether it is a résumé, a memo, a business letter, a report, a marketing proposal, or an office manual. Once you have some practice, you can incorporate the process into any communication task, including oral presentations. (In Chapter 14 we modify the process slightly to become the *presentation design process*.) As you become more familiar with the process, you will find that you need spend only a few minutes going through the early stages before you begin your draft.

Why? The first question you need to ask is, "Why am I creating this document?" You may want to *propose* a course of action or behavior for the future; *report* on behavior that occurred in the past; *document* or record information for future reference; *persuade* other people concerning your ideas, qualifications, and products; or *instruct* them on how to follow procedures or processes. You may have a primary and a secondary purpose, or you may have multiple purposes. Write down your purpose: The purpose of this document is to _____. My secondary purpose is to _____. When the reader finishes reading this document, I would like the reader to _____.

Who? You need to develop a profile of your audience. Here are five questions to get you started:

> Who is my audience? (What do I know about my audience?)
> What is my relationship to this person or these people?
> Under what circumstances will this document be read?
> What are the expectations of my audience?
> What does my audience need to know?

What? When you approach any communication task, you either (1) know all you intend to communicate or (2) need to find out something to include. If you know all of the message, you simply have to make sure all of it is included in your document. If you need to find out something, you have to conduct research. This research may mean gathering information in a variety of ways: conducting experiments, interviewing people, conducting a survey, searching through company records, or utilizing all of the different reference options available in a library.

When? You need to schedule your time to complete a task successfully. Deadlines actually help us by establishing limits. First, discover exactly how much time you have, then work backward, leaving enough time for each step in the document design process. Develop an outline for long documents. Contact all of the people—collaborators, artists, your sources, and so forth—who will be involved in the preparation of the document. Develop a time chart and let everyone know their deadlines. Stick to your schedule.

(Continued)

Decide Style and Strategy *Style* refers to the ways you express your message, or the specific words and phrasing you use to convey your ideas. Opt for a professional style—cautious, deliberate, and concerned about the audience. Clarify your message; choose words that will convey your message precisely. *Strategy* refers to the approach you take to a communication situation and the way your readers understand and react to the context of the situation. You want to skillfully manage the reactions of your audience to your message.

Select Graphics and Illustrations New technology allows us to enhance our documents with strong visual images. We cover how to create tables, charts, graphs, drawings, and other visuals in Chapter 13, "Designing Graphics and Illustrations."

Choose a Format Organize your information by enhancing the design of your pages. Follow standard formats, but add creative touches to make your document distinctive. As you read through this text, you will see standard formats for many different kinds of documents.

Draft the Document A draft is more than a rough sketch of a document; it is a nearly complete version that needs polishing. Very important documents may require multiple drafts. All of the decisions you have made should be reflected in your draft.

Revise *Revising* refers to the process of examining and improving the content and design of your document; *editing* refers to the process of examining and improving grammar, mechanics, and style; and *proofreading* refers to the process of eliminating typographical and other errors from your document. You need to do all three processes, at times simultaneously, as you work to create the best possible document.

Test Your Output The more important and the more complex the document, the more you need to get feedback from others, even if this means asking others to evaluate what you have written. You need readers who can offer constructive criticism, and you need to respond to this feedback positively; don't be defensive, but hear what your test audience has to say.

Revise Make sure you do a final check of your document just before you produce the final version. Errors may creep into your document as you rewrite your draft.

Finish the Document In the final stage of the document design process, you are assembling all of the pieces of the document, preparing the final copy, and delivering the document. Given the many possible forms your document may take—hard copy, electronic mail, fax, and so forth—you need to consider how your audience will receive your message.

Section 1, "Applying for Work," is concerned with the job search and employment applications; it demonstrates that this material has an immediate, practical value for you. The earlier you begin preparing for the job market, the more successful you will be. Credentials and qualifications can be reverse-engineered by looking ahead to see what employers are seeking and using your time in school to build an attractive résumé.

Section 2, "Discovering Your Role in an Organization," is designed to help you investigate your company systematically and discover the culture and customs of your particular organization. We show you how to improve your reading and telephone skills by organizing more effectively. We encourage you to make maximum use of powerful electronic tools for writing and presenting information. Meetings, large and small, are discussed in some detail because your effective participation or leadership may be an important element in your business success.

Section 3, "Communicating in Your Organization," which discusses how to create interoffice and business correspondence, contains sensible advice on writing memos and letters that accomplish their purpose. You'll learn how to organize short reports for effective decision making and favorable attention. Practical tips on presentations that persuade audiences are given; considerable attention is paid to graphic design and illustration as support elements for written and oral presentations.

Section 4, "Working on Team Projects," deals with complex communications where cooperation, collaboration, and coordination become important elements in a team project–based context. Many business documents and presentations, such as manuals, marketing proposals, and annual reports, are the result of group efforts. Your ability to work effectively with teams to produce complex documents and presentations will be valued in most business settings.

The final section, "Looking Down the Road," once again urges you to prepare for your future very carefully. The skills, information, and techniques you acquire now will serve you in whatever career path you choose. Your imagination and active interest in your own prospects will prepare you for success.

DISCOVERING A CONTEXT FOR YOUR COMMUNICATIONS

When you become part of any new business environment, you need to discover a good deal of information. You do this by observing everything around you very carefully.

You need to find out how people act in this organization, what is the usual way of doing things, who makes decisions about what, and how you can make yourself personally effective. You need to study how people communicate, how they write and say things, how phone and fax messages are handled, how meetings are run, how information is shared or not shared, and what the customary procedures are. All of these background details make up the *context* for business communications.

The exercises in this text deal with a variety of business situations, so that we can introduce you to some of the common contexts of business communications. We expect that you are already familiar with a good deal of business vocabulary and that you are aware of common roles, tasks, and functions in a typical business organization. We provide short applications in areas like quality control, inventory control, human resources, production, marketing, and accounts payable and receivable in order to supply a recognizable business context.

Many of the exercises and examples in this text involve a small business firm, Pascal Business Systems, engaged in the sales, distribution, and installation of business software and office automation systems, and specializing in ergonomics. This company uses computers to automate the routine tasks found in a typical business environment and frequently provides training and sales support for its customers. You will find a more complete description of Pascal Business Systems in Appendix A.

We want you to remember that you will be communicating within an organizational environment and that you must design your messages for this context. By becoming acquainted with this company and the way it operates, you will gain a context for your writing, a feel for the situation in which you are designing your messages.

You may be assigned to various tasks within Pascal Business Systems. Your assigned role defines who you are within the company. Your task defines what you must do. The different situations you face will require different communication solutions. These short application cases are intended to help you experience realistic simulations of what you can expect in your future career.

time horizons	
What year is this? How old are you now?	
Add four years. What year is this? How old are you now?	
Have you changed physically in the last four years? How?	
Are you married or single? Describe your living arrangements.	
What kind of car are you driving? Describe your car.	
What kind of clothes do you wear to work? Describe your hair.	
Are you working?	
If yes, describe the organization. What is your role in the organization? How much do you get paid? What are your job duties? Are you happy? If no, describe what you are doing with your time. How do you support yourself? Are you happy?	

EXAMINING WHAT YOUR FUTURE HOLDS

Forecasting and preparing for the future are standard business practices, ones we believe you should apply to yourself and your own career. You need to build up an inventory of skills, techniques, references, and experiences, which will enable you to communicate effectively. Whatever your business situation, you will find that preparation is essential.

Throughout this text we will stress the advantages of an expansive time horizon. Your ability to imagine yourself in the future, coupled with a realistic assessment of your skills and talents, will prepare you for career success.

LOOKING AHEAD EXERCISES

1. What is your major? If you are unde-cided, what possible careers are you con-sidering? What do people do who major in these career paths? Prepare to partici-pate in a class discussion of exactly what it is that people do on the job in a variety of careers.

2. Complete the "Time Horizons" question-naire shown on page 12. Write down your answers and be prepared to share them with your classmates.

3. Perhaps the most interesting way of learn-ing about time horizons is to talk to some person near the end of his or her business career, someone with a wide-reaching his-torical view. Set up an interview, and ask this person questions such as:

   What events have most surprised you?

   What technological changes did you least anticipate?

   How did business approaches, compe-tition, financing, and regulations change during your career?

   What stayed the same?

   What do you recommend for me to learn while I am in school?

4. Where will you be one, five, ten years from now? How can you get there? Today's business environment is marked by office automation technology, vigor-ous competition within a global economy, increased customer expectations, and a rapid pace of change. Expecting change

Capability	Rating (circle the appropriate number: 1 = low, 5 = high)				
Vision	1	2	3	4	5
Creativity	1	2	3	4	5
Flexibility	1	2	3	4	5
Strategic planning	1	2	3	4	5
Written communications	1	2	3	4	5
Oral communications	1	2	3	4	5
Common sense	1	2	3	4	5
Mechanical ability	1	2	3	4	5
Persistence	1	2	3	4	5
Leadership	1	2	3	4	5
Add your own capability:	1	2	3	4	5

and recognizing your need to prepare for it is a major challenge for people entering the business world. You will need vision, creativity, flexibility, and, above all, planning. Using the chart on page 13, prepare a personal capability profile for yourself in which you estimate your resources for the future.

5. This is a group exercise. Everyone in the group takes a piece of 8½-by-11-inch paper and draws two lines on it, creating three zones. The space in each zone should represent the relative values you give to these three areas of business and personal satisfaction: autonomy, affiliation, and achievement. In other words, divide your paper into three zones that represent the importance you give to self-determination, friendship, and accomplishment. The size of these zones may vary greatly within your group, but the drawings should provide a very interesting basis for discussion.

Show your drawing to the other members of your group and compare and contrast their responses to your own. You will realize that different people expect to fill different needs through their working lives. What do these differences suggest for people who will need to work together? What can you learn about yourself in relation to others? (See chart at bottom of page.)

6. Find an assignment—an essay, a research paper, a homework assignment, a lab report—that you have submitted for a grade in one of your courses. Now apply the document design process to this assignment. Answer the following questions:

Why did you prepare the assignment?

Who was the audience?

What was your message?

What was your deadline?

Now, as well as you can, describe the style of your document.

What strategies have you employed to get your message across?

Describe the format of your document.

What graphics and illustrations did you include?

After you answer these questions, suggest changes you can make to improve the design of the assignment.

Lourdes Santiago

Sandy Pascal

Robert Bonner

ASSESSING YOURSELF

Evaluating Your Interests and Abilities
Learning What Employers Are Seeking
Building a Network
Understanding How Organizations Work
Beginning Your Investigation

In the previous chapter, you discovered some concepts—time horizons and the document design process—that you can use for the rest of your life. As you move through all of the expected and the unexpected events of your working life, you will gain the ability to project further into the future. Instead of days, weeks, months, semesters, or years, you will be able to look decades down the road.

In this chapter we will begin a self-assessment process that will start you on your career path. Some of you may have very little idea about what you want to do with your life. Now is the time to consider your future. You need to gain perspective now so that you can prepare yourself while you are in college. In this chapter you will be encouraged to analyze what you are capable of doing, what you would enjoy doing, and how to increase your chances of getting where you want to be.

EVALUATING YOUR INTERESTS AND ABILITIES

Before beginning your job search, you need to conduct a rigorous and realistic inventory of your skills, abilities, and qualifications. A careful evaluation of what you are qualified to do and what you want to do will help you with every stage of your career planning, from résumé preparation through the interview process. Knowing what you want is very important. Too many people make the mistake of trying to channel their own objectives into whatever vacancies happen to exist at the moment. You may have to take temporary jobs, but you should try to decide what you would enjoy doing, what you would like for a career. Then you need to determine if you have the credentials and qualifications.

This means comparing your work experience, education, and training to the requirements of the jobs you want. Unless you have persuasive substitutions, there is little sense in applying for jobs that require credentials or experience you simply do not have.

Now is the time to acquire the skills and qualifications you will need. For example, do you feel that you are unable to articulate your ideas well? That your shyness will prevent you from reaching your goals? You may want to take a public speaking class that forces you to speak in front of groups. Do you write well? You may want to take more courses that require intensive writing. Do you plan to start your own company some day? What kind of background and experiences will you need for your company to be successful? Will you need to meet with people daily and convince them of your qualifications? In addition, don't overlook computer skills and the ability to speak in a language other than English as selling points when you enter the job market.

LEARNING WHAT EMPLOYERS ARE SEEKING

You will be hired for your potential. You cannot possess all of the attributes and skills you will need during the entire course of your career; much of the technology hasn't been invented yet and so you will need to be trained and retrained. Organizations, therefore, are vitally concerned with such things as how quickly you learn, how flexible you are, how well you listen, and how curious you are. Organizations also assess how well you get along with others. After all, you will be working with others. No matter how much you know, you will have to share it. The ability to collaborate with others on a project is essential.

> The tighter the job market gets, the more emphasis there is on thinking clearly, on sizing up changing circumstances, on dealing with situations where the answer isn't written out for you.
>
> Elizabeth Coleman, president of Bennington College (Powers 1993, 40)

What are employers looking for? They want organized, conscientious, composed, neat, well-groomed, enthusiastic, self-motivated individuals with good communication skills. In many cultures, including the predominant one in the United States, there is a fine line between being self-confident and bragging; the trick is to achieve the right balance, to let potential employers know that you are sure of yourself without appearing overbearing.

In other words, you need to think in terms of what you can bring to an organization; even if you cannot bring sophisticated skills, you can bring a positive attitude and a willingness to learn.

BUILDING A NETWORK

You need to be familiar with the current job market. This means establishing an information network, which will keep you up-to-date on job qualifications, employment trends, and sudden opportunities. When you are aware of what employers require, you can focus your coursework, work experience, and credentials to meet their needs.

---

job search sites on the web

Job listings on Yahoo
http://www.yahoo.com/Business/Employment/Jobs/
Rensselaer Career Resources Homepage
This list provides access to online job databases and other employment related information found on the Internet.
http://www.rpi.edu/dept/cdc/homepage.html
Professional Societies/Federal and State Agencies/Nonprofit Organizations
http://www.rpi.edu/dept/cdc/society.html
Employer's Direct
Job databases or information servers maintained by various employers.
http://www.rpi.edu/dept/cdc/employer/

Use all of the resources available to you. Browse through the "Help Wanted" pages in your Sunday newspaper and become familiar with local salary levels and job qualifications. Use the library in your hometown or at your school or company to help in your job search. Occupational handbooks, professional journals, and government publications all provide information about work opportunities.

Another important source of information for your job search is expert advice. Join the local chapter of a professional organization in your field of interest. Attend their meetings and talk to people who are doing what you would like to do. Practical advice and inside job leads are only two of the benefits you will receive. A third benefit is that membership in these groups looks good on your résumé. Here are some business groups for you to consider:

AIESEC (Association Internationale des Etudiants en Sciences Economiques et Commerciales)

American Management Association

American Marketing Association

Association of Collegiate Entrepreneurs

Business Professionals of America

Foundation for Student Communication

National Association of Business Economists

National Student Business League (Minority Business)

$tudent Investment $ociety

Don't forget to use the placement services at your school or the human resources department where you work. Placement offices can provide useful counseling and suggestions about the job search process. Campus interviews provide an opportunity to meet company representatives in a comfortable setting. Human resources personnel have a strong interest in promoting and training individuals from within the organization, so if you are currently working part time, take advantage of their help.

UNDERSTANDING HOW ORGANIZATIONS WORK

Almost all organizations in the United States and Europe are organized according to a *hierarchy*. Hierarchies are most often arranged in a pyramid-like structure, with more and more employees represented at each level as you look down the pyramid. (Most large organizations have prepared an organizational chart that displays their particular hierarchy.)

Most likely, you will be hired to fill an entry-level position somewhere near the bottom of the pyramid. In time, as you prove your value to the organization, you will be promoted upward. Each higher level of the organization represents a higher degree of power, authority in decision making, income, and benefits; the top level would represent the company president, the chief executive officer, or the head of a branch of government where the rewards and obligations are very high. In theory, the intense competition for the relatively fewer positions at each step up the ladder results in only highly qualified individuals rising to the top.

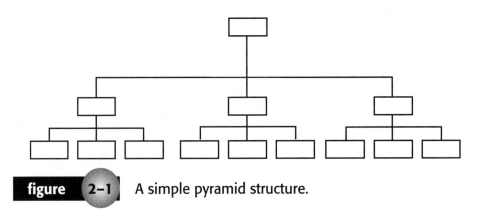

figure 2-1   A simple pyramid structure.

Your understanding of how your organization works can guide you to success, helping you avoid potential pitfalls and make the decisions that will enhance your career. (This does not imply that you should burn with ambition to reach the top or be disappointed if you do not reach the highest levels of the hierarchy.) What we are advocating is a clear vision of how organizations work.

In reality, most organizations are more complex than a straight pyramid. The organizational structure represents a complicated web. Even in these more complicated systems, there is a hierarchical structure, though it may be more difficult to recognize.

At each level, there may be certain *protocols,* or norms—accepted behaviors or ways of conducting yourself when communicating with other members of the organization. For example, it may be inappropriate within some organizations for an entry-level employee to make suggestions about policy at a meeting attended by high-level staff. In other organizations, it may be inappropriate to call someone by his or her first name in a meeting, but it would be perfectly acceptable to do so in a casual conversation by the water cooler.

Note that not all organizations work this way. Some are much more democratic. Many organizations use a *cluster model,* wherein networks of small teams operate as independent units, forming when needed and then breaking apart when a task is completed. (Morrison and Schmid, 197) Projections about organizations of the future suggest that the average company will employ fewer people and will be organized in a variety of ways, including networks of specialists. In such cases, organizational charts may be ever-

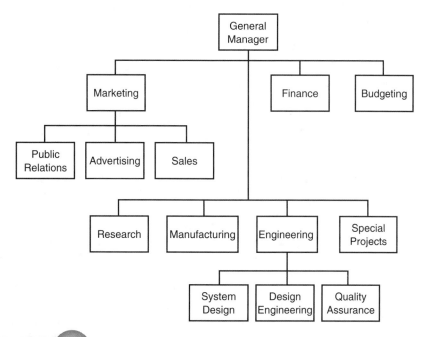

figure 2-2 The hierarchical structure of a large research and development company.

changing. (Kiechel, 39–40) Such institutions may be much more flexible and democratic, but even these cannot function efficiently unless they are organized in some hierarchical form. After all, someone must make the key decisions that provide direction for the organization, and someone must be held accountable.

When you apply for a job, you should attempt to make a quick evaluation of the organizational structure and your future position within this structure. Your standing within this structure will influence how you behave and, specifically, how you communicate: the words you choose and in some cases the amount of information you divulge to your audience.

How does knowing the organizational structure benefit you? Easy. You gain confidence. You can frame intelligent questions at your interview. You possess a sense of realism about how you fit into an organization. Finally, you avoid embarrassing, costly errors.

Also be aware that besides the formal hierarchical structure, organizations also have informal structures. Key personnel may not have a management job title, but they may have specific knowledge that gives them power. All but the smallest organizations have a *grapevine,* an informal information network that passes on information—management decisions, facts, rumors, and gossip—in indirect ways.

Beginning Your Investigation

Even if you are not scheduled to graduate for a number of years, it is time now to begin planning your future. What kinds of jobs appeal to you? What are your strengths? How creative are you? What kinds of work do you find fulfilling? What sparks your curiosity? Do you want to be self-employed some day?

Specifically, how are your math skills? Your design skills? Your communication skills? You may have already chosen a major. Do you have a good understanding of the field you are studying in college? Do you know what is involved in doing the job? Do you have any skills that a business organization would want to pay for?

Speak with the faculty in your field; speak with recent graduates; speak with family friends. Attend meetings and conferences in your fields of interest. Ask faculty members for suggestions on meetings and conferences.

Many schools have career counselors who are willing to work with you as you begin your investigation. Make an appointment, and do your homework before you meet. Prepare a list of specific questions and requests for information. Career counselors can provide valuable information if they know what you want.

You may discover that the career you desire is nothing like what you had thought. You may be able to take courses or gain information now that will be crucial later on. You may be able to combine fields that will allow you to create your own job. A general observation may help as you begin your self-evaluation: technology advances. The fields of today vanish and are replaced by new fields. You and your peers may have three or four distinct careers as one growth area begins to decline and another technology comes to the fore. The ability to retrain and the flexibility to adjust to change will always pay off.

Be honest as you begin your self-evaluation. Each of us has strengths and weaknesses. As you identify your strengths, don't overlook the areas where you need to improve. Consider your reasoning skills, your cross-cultural skills, and your ability to col-

fields of the future

It is impossible to predict with complete accuracy what fields will be hiring in the future, but according to *The 100 Best Job$ for the 1990s & Beyond* by Carol Kleiman (Dearborn Financial Publishing, Inc., 1992), the following areas are likely to show growth:

- Health care
- Computer graphics
- Biotechnology

- Robotics
- Information technology
- Laser technology

Services will remain the fastest growing major industry division.

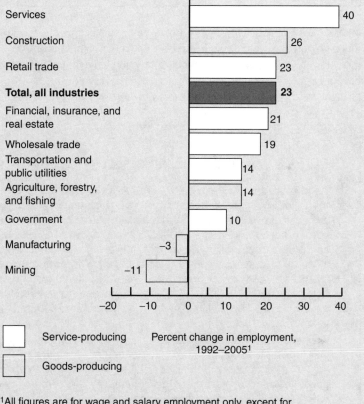

Services	40
Construction	26
Retail trade	23
Total, all industries	**23**
Financial, insurance, and real estate	21
Wholesale trade	19
Transportation and public utilities	14
Agriculture, forestry, and fishing	14
Government	10
Manufacturing	−3
Mining	−11

□ Service-producing   Percent change in employment, 1992–2005[1]
□ Goods-producing

[1]All figures are for wage and salary employment only, except for agriculture, forestry, and fishing, which includes self-employed and unpaid family workers.

Reprinted with the permission of the Bureau of Labor Statistics.

(continued)

Kleiman suggests that a degree in the humanities will be desirable for many positions in the future: "Liberal Arts majors will be vigorously recruited by employers who previously went after business majors." (24) Holders of MBAs (Master of Business Administration), however, will continue to possess a key educational credential. There will be demand for engineers, lawyers, paralegals, health care specialists, corrections officers, and computer analysts.

Fifty percent of all new jobs created in the 1990s will require some education beyond high school, and almost one-third will be for college graduates only. (Today 22 percent of all occupations require a college diploma.)

We'd like to add the following fields to the list: waste management, environmental engineering, graphic design, telecommunications, multimedia, video production, fiber optics, information gathering and distribution, primary and secondary education, and city planning and space utilization.

laborate with others. How many times have you been outside the United States? How much do you know about the lifestyles of people in other cultures?

If you have read this chapter carefully and have thought about what it says, now you have a target. You know what you need to do. This doesn't mean that your target won't change over time. It will. And it doesn't mean that your life will follow a smooth, arrow-

examples of self-assessment strategies

An Li moved to the United States from Thailand five years ago. Although she has made significant progress with the English language, she knows that she has to improve her communication skills before she can achieve her career goal to become a certified public accountant. She has excellent math skills and always does well in the courses in her major. She decides that she needs to enroll in a speech course and an English composition course offered by her college. She will also seek tutoring at the learning center on campus to help her master the English language. Every day she will read the local newspaper. Finally, she will encourage her friends and family to speak English whenever possible.

Robert Beauregard is certain that he will need computer skills when he begins looking for a job in the real estate industry. Although he is intimidated by his lack of knowledge, he decides that he will enroll in an elective course entitled "Introduction to Computers" offered by the community college he attends. He will go to the college library and read as many monthly magazines and journals related to computers as he can find. He will choose one of these magazines to subscribe to on a regular basis. Some of his friends own computers, and he decides to seek their advice.

like path straight to where you want to go. Ask a variety of successful people, including your teachers; very few of them could have predicted where their lives would take them. You may find that they had a very difficult time finding the right job for them, and they may have been through some rough waters. They may also be surprised to find themselves where they are today.

ASSESSING YOURSELF: EXERCISES

1. Make a list of your interests, abilities, and experiences. Now write down three types of jobs you would like to have. Compare the two lists. Do your interests, abilities, and experiences match up with the jobs you would like? What do you need to do to create a match between the two lists?

2. This exercise requires the formation of small groups. In groups of three or four, discuss your plans for the future. What is your ideal job? Where do you see yourself in 5 years? 15? 25? Go around the group to discover what work experiences each individual has had. Were they happy in their jobs? What were the rewards?

3. Find three successful individuals. (You may define *successful* by your own criteria.) Interview them and discover how they arrived where they are today. Write a brief synopsis of their career histories.

4. Write a profile of your ideal organization. It can be public or private. What does it do? Where is it located? How big is it?

Now picture yourself working for this organization. Are you in an office? If yes, describe the office. If no, describe where you are. Do you have a desk? Describe it. Now consider such things as vacation time, work hours, benefit packages, working conditions, the use of a company car, or any other detail that fits your ideal job.

5. Make a list of all of the people who are in your network. Write their names and their affiliations (where they attend school, where they work, and so forth) in a chart similar to the one shown below.

6. Work with the librarian at your school to conduct a search of material about your chosen career field. Try to find books, articles, encyclopedia entries, videotapes, and whatever other recent references you are able to access. Write a one-page summary of what you have learned from your search.

7. Assess your strengths and weaknesses. Make a list of five key strengths and three key weaknesses. Now write down a strategy for overcoming your weaknesses. Share your list with someone you

Name	Relationship	Phone #	Affiliations

Self-assessment

My long-term goal is:

My strengths are:
-
-
-
-
-

My weaknesses are:
-
-
-

To obtain my goal, this is what I should do:
-
-
-
-

trust. To help you get started with this task, complete the table above.

8. Use the World Wide Web address

   http://www.yahoo.com/Business_ and_ Economy/

   to search for sites that correspond to your business interests. Save the interesting sites as *bookmarks* and bring them to class for others to use.

9. Use the U.S. Department of Labor's *Dictionary of Occupational Titles* or the Bureau of Labor Statistics' *Occupational Outlook Handbook* to learn about your profession's entry-level positions, average salaries, employment projections, and job descriptions. (Make sure you find recent editions.) Copy the titles and job descriptions of three jobs you expect to be qualified for after you graduate.

10. Consult the *Business Periodicals Index* (H.H. Wilson Company) to find professional magazines in your field. Find three specific articles in these magazines that discuss business issues relevant to your career path. Summarize these articles and list your sources.

CREATING YOUR RÉSUMÉ

3

Now that you have conducted a self-assessment, you should have a somewhat more focused view of what kinds of career possibilities you desire. In this chapter you should try to apply this view in the creation of a résumé as you begin the job application process. Please note: there may be holes or gaps in your qualifications. The self-assessment you conducted in Chapter 2 should help you identify these potential problems. You have the opportunity to use your time in college to fill in these gaps and improve in the areas where you are weak.

SELLING YOUR SERVICES BY RÉSUMÉ

Your *résumé*—also called a *curriculum vitae* or a *work history*—is a sales document that needs to be designed for a quick sale. On average, the reader will spend less than 30 seconds before deciding whether you will be interviewed. Another person will narrow the selection of applicants to those who meet specific qualifications. Your résumé needs to persuade this limited audience that you should be considered. Keep this audience in mind.

These busy readers want information quickly, so use conventional formats. Your audience is familiar with these standard formats and can go right to the particular information they want to find.

DESIGNING YOUR RÉSUMÉ

Almost all résumés use the same parts, but the arrangement and focus is shifted to emphasize your strong points. In general, there are three types of résumés: the chronological résumé, the functional résumé, and the targeted résumé.

Traditional or *chronological résumés* list your education and work experience beginning with your present situation and moving backward. Time is the organizing principle. Many reviewers prefer this style because they can go right to the information they need.

Functional résumés arrange work experience by function rather than time. In other words, you list the functions you have performed rather than the order or length of time you have done them. This is a useful style for people who want to focus on what they can do, rather than where they have worked.

Targeted résumés incorporate elements from both chronological and functional résumés. Using a traditional organization pattern, you target a specific job by focusing on skills and abilities related to that job. All of the information you provide is aimed to this end. Work experience, education, and personal activities are all used to support your interest in a particular position.

Parts of the Résumé

Whichever type of résumé you select to present yourself to employers, you will include the same categories of information:

- heading (name, address, and phone number)
- career objective
- educational background
- work experience
- awards, achievements, and special skills

GWENDOLYN BROWN
211 Robinson Way
Tulsa, OK 74103
918-555-3872

Employment Objective

Employment with an organization where I could work with a Training and Development team or an Occupational Safety and Health team.

Education

Bachelor of Science, December 1997
Industrial Education and Technology
Iowa State University, Ames, IA

Relevant Coursework

Total Quality Improvement
Industrial Training Program Development
Industrial Training Needs Assessment
Handling of Products and Hazardous Materials
Legal Aspects of Occupational Safety and Health
Principles of Accident Prevention
Introduction to Occupational Safety

Work Experience

Sexual Harassment Awareness Facilitator, 1994–Present
YWCA, Tulsa, OK

Facilitated sexual harassment awareness to middle-school-aged children
Reorganized training curriculum to promote audience interaction
Demonstrated the correlation between harassment and common middle-school behavior
Developed a method of program evaluation

Office Assistant, Summer 1993–1994
Murphy Temporary Agency, Tulsa, OK

Researched organization information
Organized and compiled organization information packets
Assisted in customer relations
Maintained company filing system

Professional Affiliations

American Society of Training and Development
American Society of Safety Engineers
National Society of Black Engineers

References

Available on request

figure 3-1 A traditional résumé.

LOURDES SANTIAGO
1510 Andrews Drive
Houston, TX 77002
713-555-5789

EMPLOYMENT HISTORY

Freelance Graphic Design, Desktop Publishing
Through independent contracting and temporary assignments, designed and produced graphics, presentations, and print materials on Macintosh and PC systems in a variety of industries, including educational publishing, service bureau/slide houses, consulting firms, and marketing firms.
March 1994–Present

Publishing Specialist—The Coil Corporation, Houston, TX
Designed and produced overhead sales presentations, color slide presentations, and large-scale training program materials using Macintosh graphic illustration and page layout software. Systems demands included maintenance of local and bridged networks; software installation, updating, and instruction; and hardware purchase research, recommendation, and installation.
June 1994–Present

Publication Manager—Houston Business Journal
Responsible for accounting, processing, and updating of subscriber files of two monthly trade publications; client billing for all publications; installation, maintenance, and instruction of software, including organization and supervision of local computer network; design of publication ads; and general office duties.
1993–1994

EDUCATION

Houston Community College
   Associate Degree in Business Information Systems, September 1998
   Internship: Pascal Business Systems, Spring 1997
COMPUTER SKILLS

Programming/Prototyping
WWW site design and server setup, WWW page design, HTML coding. Storyboarding/prototyping experience with HyperCard and SuperCard.

Macintosh
Adobe Photoshop, QuarkXPress, Adobe Illustrator, Adobe, Aldus PageMaker, Adobe PageMaker, Microsoft PowerPoint, Fractal Design Painter, MacDraw II, MacDraw Pro, Microsoft Word, Microsoft Excel.

PC
All cross-platform graphics, presentation, and publishing programs mentioned above, in addition to most other Windows graphics, presentation, and publishing programs.

References: Furnished on request.

 **figure** **3-2** A functional résumé.

ROBERT BONNER
41 Bridge Road
Costa Mesa, CA 92628-5005
714-555-5067

PROFESSIONAL PROFILE

A hands-on, goal-oriented professional with diversified experience in finance
and accounting. Highly motivated, detail-oriented, concise, and well
organized. A self-starter with excellent time management, interpersonal, and
communication skills, promoting the development of strong working
relationships with individuals at every level.

SELECTED ACCOMPLISHMENTS

• Recommended actions that have led to improved corporate policies and
  procedures.
• Improved city budget monitoring process, resulting in decreased
  expenses.

PROFESSIONAL EXPERIENCE

Adams Bank • Costa Mesa, CA • 1995–Present • **Internal Auditor**

Responsible for planning and implementing bank-related audits. Functions
encompass the development of audit tools and subsequent audit testing.
Financial documents audited include Ginnie Mae, HUD, Freddie Mac, and
Fannie Mae, as well as commercial and conventional mortgages.

City of Costa Mesa • 1995–Present   **Assistant Deputy Treasurer**

Assist City Treasurer in a variety of tasks including monitoring and
overseeing town budget and expenditures, check signing, and interfacing with
taxpayers regarding town financial status. Act on the treasurer's behalf in
his or her absence.

EDUCATION

Orange Coast College, Costa Mesa, CA
Associate Degree in Accounting, 1998
Experience with Novell, Unix, and MS-DOS/Windows

CIVIC ACTIVITIES

Costa Mesa Rescue and Medical Service • Costa Mesa, CA
   Volunteer Emergency Medical Technician

Excellent references provided upon request

figure 3–3 A targeted résumé.

The *heading* should contain your name and address. This needs to be complete and accurate. Provide your ZIP code; your nine-digit ZIP code is even better. Include a telephone number where you can be reached, along with the area code and extension, if needed. Make sure that potential employers can reach you easily. Center the heading. Put your name in all caps and use boldface so that it will stand out. Don't center any other parts of the résumé; centered text is more difficult to read.

BONNIE J. KERN
237 Los Almadeiros Highway
San Pedro, CA 90731
(310) 555-7832

Your *career objective* should show a clear sense of purpose and a long-range focus. Your objective provides organization and coherence to the rest of the résumé. State your immediate objective and then what you would like to be doing in the next five to ten years. (If you have not read Chapter 2, "Assessing Yourself," and do not have a clear sense of your future, you may want to go there now.) Make your objective broad enough so you can be considered for more than one job, but specific enough to indicate your interests and aptitudes. One effective strategy is to state two goals: short-term and long-range. This can indicate thoughtfulness, ambition, and a defined career path:

Career Objectives
    Short-term goal: Initial employment in the field of accounting
    Long-term goal: A position in supervisory management

Your *educational background* will qualify you for many high-paying and vital, challenging jobs. List your education and training in reverse order, beginning with the most recent. Name the school; the city where it is located; the degree, certificate, or credits you earned; and the date you participated or graduated.

First-time applicants often include their high school and the dates attended. Include any details that may be impressive to a potential employer; if you were a member of the honor society, president of the student body, or captain of a sport, include this information. You will drop this part of your résumé as your background grows. Fifteen years after your high school graduation, employers will be more interested in your recent accomplishments.

Work experience, particularly if it relates to the job you are seeking, will provide strong support for your application. List job titles, employers, concise descriptions of your responsibilities and accomplishments, and dates of employment. Begin with your most recent employment, since that is what interests potential employers the most. The résumé is a brief reference sheet, so you need to focus attention on your ability to get things done. Use *action words,* which are verbs that emphasize the characteristics, skills, and abilities called for in the job description. See Gwendolyn Brown's résumé in Fig. 3–1 for an example of the skillful use of action words.

If you are designing a functional résumé, list the activities you have performed instead of listing the jobs. Use categories such as Management, Sales, and Training to group skills and functions for easy reference. This is a good arrangement if you want to emphasize your versatility and ability to do many different tasks.

---

ethical considerations

When people are looking for work, they may exaggerate their qualifications. Know that there is a difference between enthusiasm and dishonesty. You should describe your experience and background in positive terms, but you need to stick with the truth. It is unethical to misrepresent yourself.

It is a serious mistake to make up credentials. Even if you are not discovered during the hiring process, you are vulnerable later when attention is focused on your performance or records.

If you resort to false details and misleading information, you are violating the essential expectations of honesty that provide the basis for human interactions.

Listing *awards, achievements, and special skills* is an effective way to provide employers with a quick profile of your personal interests. Often your outside activities reveal management and leadership abilities. Use this section to include anything that will relate positively to the job you are seeking: professional involvements, additional skills, community participation, and so on.

If you possess specific skills that may land you a position by themselves, you may want to devote a separate section to them. Highlight languages you speak fluently. Include specific computer programs you have mastered. If you know how to operate specific equipment, list it here. Don't pad your résumé, but if you have relevant material, include it.

As a general rule, don't include your references. State that these are available on request. This way an employer will have to contact you to reach your references and you will be able to let them expect a call or letter. (See the section titled "Requesting References" later in this chapter.)

Format of the Résumé

Your résumé is many different things: an ad for your services, a summary of your experience and qualifications, a description of your skills, and a background sheet. Your résumé should be a persuasive document. It is designed to sell you and your skills and services to the employer. Since the résumé supplies the reader with a one- or two-page reference for you, it must be attractive and error-free. Mistakes, clutter, or misrepresentation tell the reader your document is not credible.

Your résumé must be attractive and readable. Highlight your main sections with headings, boldface, margins, and white space. Flush left and ragged right margins are the easiest to read. Single-space your text; double-space between sections. Try to keep your résumé to one page if it is at all possible. Readers should immediately understand your layout, so communicate your organization visually.

- Set important terms in boldface.
- Be consistent. Use a similar style throughout.
- Bullet items for emphasis.

At the very least, your résumé must be neatly typed, on good-quality paper, and free of spelling, mechanical, and grammatical errors. This document represents you during the

learning about typography

A typeface is a specific design of an alphabet, complete with other standard characters such as numbers and symbols. A *serif* typeface has short horizontal strokes extending from the end of the main stroke of a letter. This sentence is set in Times Roman, which is an example of a serif typeface. A *sans serif* typeface does not have these extensions. This sentence is set in Helvetica, which is an example of a sans serif typeface. Point size refers to a standard unit of measurement representing the height of a typeface. There are 72 points to an inch.

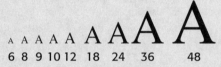

6 8 9 10 12 18 24 36   48

A *font* represents a complete alphabet, including numbers and symbols, of one point size of one typeface.

When you are creating your résumé, limit yourself to two typefaces, one for headings and one for the supporting text. Here are some possible combinations:

Headline Typefaces	Text Typefaces
Helvetica Bold	Times Roman
Palatino Bold	Helvetica
Palatino Bold Italic	Palatino

You may want to experiment with different combinations to enhance the visual appeal of your document. Résumés are generally set in 12-point type. Of course, you have some flexibility here if you have access to a laser printer with extended capabilities. If you are trying to fit extensive information on one page, try 11-point type. Conversely, if you are worried about not having enough text to fill a page, consider increasing the point size to 13 or 14. Don't, however, increase the point size to more than 14 because this will be viewed as too obviously filling the page.

Use tabs to indent rather than the spacebar. Your text will align precisely; if you change typefaces, the tabs will continue to align.

job search and it must be perfect. Technology has raised standards, so you might want to have your résumé typeset. Service bureaus will charge a set fee; with a good word-processing or page layout program and a laser printer with the capacity to print a variety of typefaces, you can produce your résumé by yourself.

Be aware that there may be different formats for different kinds of jobs. Résumés in the creative arts are much more imaginative than for the corporate business culture. Fit your design to the nature of the field. Format is culturally influenced, so try to find examples from your particular field to serve as models. While keeping to a format may feel confining, it is also liberating because it allows you to work within guidelines.

If you are using your résumé to apply for different types of jobs, use a word processor and a laser printer. This allows you to change your résumé and still have perfect copies. Many service bureaus provide laser output and advice on how to construct multiple versions of your résumé.

The Video Résumé

The latest in résumé production is the video résumé. Individuals who have access to high-quality video recorders can produce short, professional mixes of text and video to sell themselves to potential employers. If you decide to create a video résumé, write a complete script before you begin recording, rehearse often, and be prepared to re-record to produce a smooth, error-free video. Speak in a relaxed, conversational manner. You may want to read Chapter 14, "Delivering Presentations," for general guidelines.

If you film indoors, film a brief test of the lighting. Try to reduce shadows. Record in front of a muted backdrop or with plenty of space behind you. You may want to choose a location that is relevant to your career field. For example, for a job in industrial real estate, you could record in front of an industrial park.

---

learning about paper and printing

Choose good-quality paper for your résumé and cover letter. Bond paper of at least 25% rag content will create a professional look. Generally, it is best to stay away from flashy colors. We recommend a conservative off-white.

If you are using a laser printer, consider purchasing smooth, glossy, high-quality paper made especially for laser printers. (Recycled paper is now of sufficient quality that you can make an environmentally sound purchase without compromising your document.) Laser printers produce a resolution of at least 300 dpi (dots per inch), a number that is a minimum standard for professional documents.

Service bureaus, businesses where you can rent time or services on state-of-the-art computers and printers, offer the possibility of producing typeset documents at 1200 dpi or more.

---

who will read your résumé?
it may be a computer

Many companies, particularly large ones, have begun a process of scanning résumés with optical character recognition (OCR) software. The résumés, turned into digital data, are stored in special databases. These databases are searched for key words, based on the key words found in various job descriptions. This makes your résumé preparation even more important. Be sure to include key words that describe what you know and what you can do. If a computer is searching for "C++ " skills or "real estate license," it can find only what you have included.

Send a conventional résumé along with the video just in case your potential employer does not have a videocassette player available. And be careful; a video résumé may not be appropriate if you are seeking employment in many conventional, conservative business fields.

REQUESTING REFERENCES

Although you should not include the names, addresses, and telephone numbers of your references on your résumé, you should begin now, as you design your résumé, to assemble a group of individuals to serve as your references. Usually you will be asked for three individuals. Look first for people with whom you have a personal relationship. If you are in school, consider asking faculty you know well; it is better to be recommended by someone who gave you a B and considers you an excellent candidate than someone who gave you an A but will not recognize your name. People you have worked for and people in your community with whom you have had contact, including clergy, community leaders, athletic coaches, and neighbors, are all good sources for a recommendation. If you are fortunate enough to have a long list of potential references, choose people who know you best, people who are good communicators, and people who have a job title that most people associate with trustworthiness.

Obviously you cannot use people as references without obtaining their permission. When you approach them, ask them if they could give you a wholeheartedly positive recommendation. You can say, "Would you have any reservations about giving me a positive reference?" You want people to be honest in their response. You don't want someone who will say yes and then give you a lukewarm reference when he or she is called by a potential employer. You want the people who recommend you to say specific things, not make general comments, so provide your references with a list of your skills and achievements. You should give each reference a copy of your résumé.

Make a separate sheet of your references, printed on high quality paper. Make enough copies so that you can give one to each interviewer you meet.

SENDING YOUR APPLICATION PACKAGE

Once you have a résumé, you have completed the first step in the application process. You need to pay careful attention to the rest of the application package: the letter of application and the envelope.

The Application Letter

Letters of application—frequently termed *cover letters* because they literally cover the résumé within the envelope—are always sales letters. What you are selling is your ability to do a job. The letter is your sales representative. It speaks for you and represents you. If the letter catches the reader's interest and the résumé supports this initial response, you will get the interview.

Remember, potential employers will examine your letter carefully to see whether you can communicate effectively in writing. The quality of your application will indicate your ability to do the job. Always proofread and sign your letter.

When you write a letter of application, you are marketing yourself. You are trying to persuade the person who screens the résumés that you are qualified for serious consideration. Focus on what you can do for the organization to which you are applying. The purpose of the letter is to create enough interest to get you the interview. Your purpose is to make someone want to meet with you.

Keep your application letter short. Express your interest in the position, highlight any particular strengths on your résumé, and ask for an interview. This is all that the letter has to do. Three paragraphs, each with its own task, will accomplish your purpose.

A help-wanted ad and letter of application are shown below.

The Prospecting Application

A prospective employer is someone you have targeted to ask for employment. *Prospecting* means sending out unsolicited letters; you send out inquiries without being asked in the hopes that a job might be available. You are advertising for an interview. Large firms

---

Pascal Business Systems
Site support/training specialist
Box 43

Training is done at customer sites and focuses primarily on our application software. Knowledge of one or more of the following is required: Novell, Unix, TCP/IP, NFS, MS-DOS/Windows. The successful candidate will have a minimum of an Associate Degree in Accounting, Business Management, or Computer Science. Contact Herman Tannebaum. Résumés only.

41 Bridge Road
Costa Mesa, CA 92628–5005

October 19, 1997

Mr. Herman Tannebaum
Box 43

Houston Chronicle
Houston, TX 77002

Dear Mr. Tannebaum,

I would like to apply for the position of Site Support/Training Specialist that you advertised in this Sunday's Houston Chronicle.

Enclosed you will find my résumé, which details my work and educational background. You will notice that I have had extensive experience with networks and operating systems, including both Novell and Unix. I am confident that I can learn new applications quickly and reliably.

My uncle lives in the Houston area and I can be available for an interview at your convenience. Thank you for your consideration.

Sincerely,

Robert Bonner

Robert Bonner

enc.

receive many prospecting applications every day, so your letter and résumé need to be perfect for you to have a chance of success.

You need to start out with your central selling point, whether it is experience or education, and quickly explain how your abilities can benefit the company. Make it clear that you are looking for a specific job, not just work. Substantiate your abilities by pointing to accomplishments that can be verified. In other words, prove yourself.

One way to make a good impression is to demonstrate that effort and research have gone into your letter. Address your letter to the correct person within the organization if you can obtain this information. Show that you are aware of the organization's operations, products, services, and competitors. Your letter should highlight information in your résumé, not provide details. The letter is a first step, pointing to the résumé, not replacing it.

Use bullets to highlight crucial information. Here is one possible pattern, utilizing a three-paragraph structure:

• Explain why you are writing. If you are responding to a classified ad, say so.

- State what makes you stand out for this job. Highlight items on your résumé, but add the qualities you possess that are not mentioned on your résumé.
- Close your letter. State that you are available for an interview and that you will call at a specific time.

If you are sending your unsolicited résumé to a company in the hopes that they will find or create a position for you, then your best chance of success is to learn as much as

---

May 24, 1998

1510 Andrews Drive
Houston, TX 77002
(713) 555–5789

Ms. Sandy Pascal, CEO
Pascal Business Systems
Texas Commerce Tower, Suite 5A
600 Travis St.
Houston, TX 77002

Dear Ms. Pascal,

I would appreciate very much an opportunity to meet with you and demonstrate how my unique experience and education could be of particular advantage to your company's future growth.

My internship last summer at Pascal Business Systems helped me focus my academic and career goals. My fourteen weeks with your company involved me with a whole variety of sales support activities including preparing brochures and catalogs, coordinating trade shows, providing data and information to salespeople in the field, and interacting with customers.

During the past two semesters I have concentrated on developing my electronic publishing and business communication skills. I am confident that I can improve the ways in which Pascal Business Systems provides support for field marketing representatives. This would include designing and maintaining an online catalog which could be coordinated with current inventories.

I am available for an interview at your convenience and look forward to an opportunity to discuss ways to improve operations and communications with field locations and sales. Thank you for your kind consideration.

Sincerely,

Lourdes Santiago

Lourdes Santiago
(713) 555–5789

you can about that company and use this knowledge in your cover letter. On page 37, for example, is a letter from Lourdes Santiago to Pascal Business Systems, suggesting herself for a position as a sales support/administrative specialist.

Lourdes is not responding to an ad for an existing position; rather, she is describing the special skills she can bring to the company which will make it worthwhile to find a place for her. Notice that Lourdes has a special advantage. She worked for Pascal Business Systems as an intern. She knows the company well and the people in the company know her; they are familiar with her work and her ability to get things done.

Letters are well received when they are delivered to a specific person rather than a job title or "To Whom It May Concern." Always try to write to a specific individual. Call the organization and ask for a name; don't hesitate to ask for the correct spelling. If you are unable to find a name or if the classified ad lists only a job title, then it is acceptable to send your letter to a Personnel Officer, the Director of Personnel, or the Employment Administrator.

The Envelope

Pay careful attention to the look and feel of the envelope. Don't simply assume that it doesn't matter. Fig. 3–4 shows some guidelines for designing your envelope from the U.S. Postal Service.

BEGINNING NOW

Creating a résumé now may provide you with strategies and purposes for the rest of your time in college. You will benefit from designing your first résumé long before you enter the job market. If you do not have skills, you know you need to get some: gain some computer skills, enroll in appropriate training programs, join campus organizations. An important part of self-assessment is acting on the assessment.

Remember this: your résumé is successful if it gets you an interview. Very few people ever get hired because of a résumé. Organizations want to meet you. If you don't get an interview, redo your résumé. If you get the interview and not the job, reevaluate your interviewing skills. We have designed the next chapter to help you present yourself positively in an interview.

CREATING YOUR RÉSUMÉ: EXERCISES

1. The primary exercise for this chapter is for you to create an effective résumé and prospecting letter, one that you can use in your job search. Show your job search documents to other persons in your class or group and get their feedback.

2. Carefully review Gwendolyn Brown's résumé (Fig. 3–1). Do you think this document would be more effective if it were in another font? Is full justified or ragged right more effective? Should it be targeted for a specific job? What sugges-

How to make every address you type readable

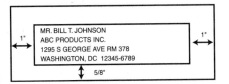

Make sure that:
- Left and right margins of address area are at least 1" from edge of envelope
- Bottom line of address area is at least 5/8" from the bottom of the envelope

The best ways to address.

- Typewrite or machine print all addresses using six lines per inch, if possible, But, if necessary, you may use up to eight per inch.
- Maintain a uniform left margin (flush left).
- Be sure characters are not too close together. They should not touch or overlap.
- Leave one to two spaces between words and between the state and ZIP or ZIP + 4 code.
- Make sure that the address lines are parallel with the bottom edge of the mail piece, especially if you are using address labels.
- Avoid using typefaces such as script, italic, artistic or other unusual typefaces, and dot matrix styles in which the dots do not touch.
- Use black ink on a white background for best results.
- Keep the address area (and space below) free of logos and other non-address information

Here's how you can be even more indispensable.

Follow these simple complete addressing guidelines to help your mail get where it's going faster.

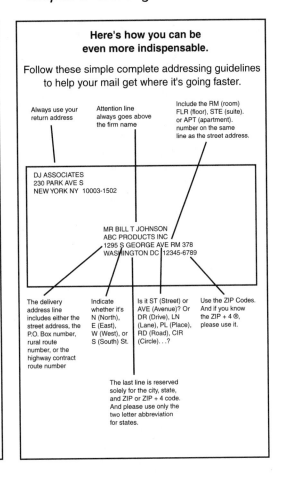

figure 3-4 ## Addressing guidelines.
Reprinted with the permission of the United States Postal Service.

tions can you come up with to improve it? Make a list of your suggestions and submit the list to your instructor.

3. Write an unsolicited letter which seeks to get Leslie Holmes of Pascal Business Systems to read your résumé and consider you for a position as an administrative assistant. Make sure you focus Holmes' attention on solutions to problems the company faces. See Appendix A for more information about Pascal Business Systems. On a separate sheet of paper, make a list of the strategies you

employ in your letter. Submit both the letter and the list to your instructor.

4. This exercise requires the formation of small groups. One member of the group is designated as the personnel director. The other group members should give their résumés to the personnel director and ask this person to rank the candidates seeking the job. Discuss the rankings, keeping in mind that the personnel director has a difficult task to do and is not criticizing you.

Now each of you can decide whether to make changes in your résumé.

5. This exercise also requires the formation of groups. You may want to keep the groups from Exercise 4. Look through the "Help Wanted" section of your Sunday newspaper. Circle any positions you think you might reasonably apply for. Choose one of the ads and write a letter applying for the job. Show the letter to your group for feedback.

6. Pascal Business Systems wants to hire a summer intern who will be able to work with a variety of temporary project teams. The company is looking for an individual with a wide range of interests and abilities, someone who is flexible and able to contribute to different types of projects.

   Look carefully at each of the three résumés in this chapter and decide which of these persons you would recommend for the position. Write a memo to your instructor in which you rank the three candidates. Provide brief explanations for your decisions. (See Chapter 9 for information about writing memos.)

7. If you were writing a prospecting application today, what would be your central selling point? Write down your response, carefully phrasing your selling point for your audience.

INTERVIEWING

Now that you have prepared a résumé, we will continue with the next step in the job application process. If successful, the résumé will get you interviews. Now you need to persuade your interviewers that you are the best candidate for the position.

Let's take an example. Suppose Pascal Business Systems lists a desirable job opening in the main newspaper in your area. It attracts 75 applicants, all individuals who have put time and effort into making their résumés appealing. The individual who receives the résumés, Leslie Holmes, immediately attempts to reduce the pile. She cuts the initial stack down to twelve. She calls each of the twelve; she is unable to reach two, three have already acquired another job, and three, for a variety of reasons, are not interested in the position. Leslie decides that she will interview the four candidates. One of them will get the job.

If you get a call in this case, you have improved your chances from one in 75 to one in 4. Your résumé has done tremendous work. Now it is up to you.

PREPARING FOR THE INTERVIEW PROCESS

Preparation for the interview involves three activities: research, anticipation, and practice. Begin by finding out everything you can about the organization. What does it do? What does it make? Who is the competition? The more you know about the organization, the more you will be able to relate your experience and skills to the needs of the organization. You also prepare by learning to anticipate. This means exercising your powers of imagination. Start with some questions that change your focus and point of view from your own perspective to that of the interviewer. What would you ask if you were in the position of hiring someone to do this job? What are you looking for? What qualities would make a candidate particularly valuable to the organization?

You can also prepare by anticipating the general types of questions that are common to many job interviews:

- What are your career goals?
- Why do you want to work for this company?
- How does your experience relate to this job?

Preparation means rehearsing by thinking about what you will say and imagining the response. If you are asked about your long-range plans or ability to work with a project team, your response should show that you have thought about the answer. If this is the first time you have ever considered your answer, your interviewer will know. Don't go to the other extreme and memorize your answer; people expect to interview a person, not a stage performer.

Finally, there is practice. Every interview builds your experience. Go to interviews even when you do not expect to get the position. You can be more relaxed if you do not expect success. Every interview is good practice if you are attentive and try to learn from your experiences.

> Many successful job candidates sign up for interviews with organizations that visit college campuses the year before they expect to graduate. You may build a contact that will land you a job the following year.

EVALUATING AND BEING EVALUATED

Many interviewees make the mistake of believing that the pressure is entirely on them to make a good impression and land the job. This is not true; you should approach the interview as your opportunity to evaluate the organization to decide whether you want to work there. (There is a side benefit to this approach: you will ask more intelligent questions if you are considering whether you want to join the organization.) An interview is not a one-way evaluation. You must decide whether the organization is right for you.

Imagine being an interviewer. You see a set number of candidates, sometimes one after another. All have adequate credentials. What will you look for? This is a difficult question to answer, since every organization is unique, but we can make some general assumptions. Organizations want people who are competent, willing to learn, enthusiastic about their future, secure with themselves, and without serious character flaws. Organizations want people who can work with others and who would be liked by their co-workers. As an interviewer, you want your questions to elicit information that will help you compare the candidates so that you can choose the best one. You would design your responses to bring forth this information. See Fig. 4–1 for a sample interview sheet showing some of the criteria an interviewer might consider.

Notice that up to this point we have not said anything about knowledge, about college grade point average, about what courses you have taken. These items are important, but in the eyes of most interviewers they are secondary to your appearance, your personality, and your willingness to learn. You may be asked about your credentials during the interview, but the focus of most of the interview will be how well you will fit into the organization. You will be hired if the "chemistry" is right, if you fit the goals and style of the organization. This is a hazy concept, we know, but it does adequately capture the tentative nature of the interview process.

Be aware that the interview may not begin when you meet with the interviewer. Some companies begin the evaluation process when you meet the receptionist. The behavior you exhibit while you are waiting—engaging in a conversation, shifting nervously, pacing around, smoking—may all be used to evaluate you. Remain calm and composed as you wait.

PREPARING FOR A SPECIFIC INTERVIEW

Employers interview you because they want to meet you face to face, to see what you are like and how you behave and interact. If credentials were enough, your résumé and references would provide enough information for potential employers to make a decision. Instead, your résumé serves as a focal point for a personal meeting, discussion, and possible negotiation.

Each interview is unique, and you should prepare for each one individually. Prepare for the interview by doing background research on the specific organization, dressing appropriately, and assembling a portfolio of work you have done. We will look at each of these three areas in turn.

Pascal Business Systems
Interview Sheet

Name of applicant _____

Relevant background and experience: _____

_____

Skills: _____

_____

Education: _____

_____

_____

Summary of references: _____

_____

_____

Personal factors: _____

_____

_____

Strengths: _____

_____

_____

Limitations: _____

_____

_____

figure **4–1** An example of an interview sheet.

	Superior	Good	Average	Poor
Appearance	☐	☐	☐	☐
Qualifications	☐	☐	☐	☐
Appropriateness for position	☐	☐	☐	☐
Social skills	☐	☐	☐	☐
Interest in position	☐	☐	☐	☐
Team orientation	☐	☐	☐	☐
Technological literacy	☐	☐	☐	☐
Match between salary expectations and what PBS can offer	☐	☐	☐	☐

Comments and general impressions: _____

_____

_____

_____

Would you hire?   ☐ yes   ☐ no

Signed _____

figure **4-1** *continued*

Research the Company

Find out about the organization. Ask everyone you know about the organization. Prepare some intelligent questions before the interview. Be prepared to discuss personnel policies and future directions. Know the general trends in the industry. The knowledge you demonstrate will show your interest in the position.

As you do your research, ask questions about salary. You want to enter the interview with a salary range, a high and low figure. Make sure your low figure is one that you can live with: think about rent, food, car payments, entertainment, college loan repayment, and the other costs of living. Your high figure should be at least $3,000 more than your low; it may be even more.

---

locating information on an organization

- Go to the library and read:

  International Directory of Company Histories (St. James Press)

  Million Dollar Directory: America's Leading Public & Private Companies (Dun & Bradstreet, Inc.)

  Moody's Industrial Manual

  Who's Who in Business and Finance

  Thomas Register of American Manufacturers
  Hoover's Handbook

- Contact professional societies, trade associations, or labor unions.
- If the organization is a private company, call and ask for an annual report.

How can you find out about salary?

- Ask your classmates.
- Call former students who graduated in the last two years and ask them about starting salaries.
- Visit the college placement office.
- Contact your local office of the U.S. Department of Labor Statistics.
- Look in your library for current salary information in your field. Ask the reference librarian for assistance.

What to Wear

Now think about the clothes you intend to wear. As a very general rule, dress at least one level above what you would wear on the job. For men, a tie and jacket would be appropri-

---

business sites on the web

Entrepreneurs on the web
Business information and services for entrepreneurs
http://www.eotw.com/

Yahoo—Business and Economy
http://www.yahoo.com/Business_and_Economy/

Small Business Resource Guide
http://www.Lycos.com/small biz

---

dressing for the interview

Dress conservatively for your interview. Wear subdued colors. For a man, a suit with a collared shirt and a conservative tie is usually appropriate; for a woman, conservative dress would be a dark suit or a skirt and jacket, and shoes with relatively low heels. You will feel uncomfortable if your interviewer is significantly more formally dressed than you are, so always err on the side of formality.

Many college students find that they must change their appearance before attending interviews. Grooming does matter. You may need to shave your beard or change the way you style your hair. (Few organizations, for example, would tolerate spiked hair on an individual who represents the company image with clients.) This does not mean that you must alter your personality. Of course, in some industries, idiosyncratic dress and behavior are encouraged. If you view appearance as an unalterable expression of who you are, consider entering a field where you need not make such compromises.

In general, wear minimal jewelry and avoid flashy colors and suggestive or provocative clothing. Work on your posture; be reasonably relaxed, not stiff. A subdued self-confidence and a positive approach are an integral factor in appearance, contributing as much as the clothes you wear to the way people receive you.

ate if you expect to wear a shirt with collar and tie on the job; if you expect to wear a tie and jacket daily, consider wearing a suit to the interview. For women, a conservative dress and jacket combination may be the right blend.

Your interviewer will expect you to be somewhat nervous. After all, you are aware of being compared to other candidates. You know that you are being judged on how you present yourself. An interview is a stressful occasion. For a short time, you are required to perform at a very intense level. Be ready.

Your Portfolio

One way to control your nervousness is to bring along a portfolio of previous work you have done. If you do not have relevant experience, bring examples of work you have accomplished during your college career. (If you are still in college as you read this, now is the time to begin assembling your portfolio.) Tailor the portfolio to the specific business area of the organization. Place all the work into a folder or under a hard cover. Insert several copies of your résumé; a list of the names, addresses, phone numbers, and job titles of at least three references; all of the correspondence between you and the organization; and a list of questions you intend to ask. Bring your social security number, a notepad, and a pen.

When you arrive for your appointment, learn how to pronounce the name of the person conducting the interview. Ask the receptionist or secretary. (Be aware that your interview begins as soon as you walk in the door, so act appropriately. Don't smoke; some companies will reject a candidate because he or she smokes.) Now you are ready for the interview itself.

ATTENDING THE INTERVIEW

Greet the interviewer directly, being careful to let the interviewer control the situation. Make eye contact and search for any visual clues—the appearance and clothes of the interviewer, the size of the office, the seating arrangements—that will help you during the interview. Place yourself in a comfortable position relative to the interviewer.

You want to make a good impression. This means a firm handshake, a pleasant smile, and a confident attitude. If you have prepared well, relax. You are responsible for providing your interviewer with information about your skills and abilities that correspond to the organization's needs. Be energetic, friendly, self-confident. Above all, speak well: grammatically and clearly. Yes, there is a reason why you take so many communication courses in college. You need to present yourself, and in an interview that means speaking.

---

interview questions you may be asked

- Why do you want to work here?
- What do you expect to be doing five years from now?
- What was your previous salary?
- Have we covered everything?
- Are you a good student?

You should be prepared to answer these types of questions. The more you prepare yourself, the more confident and reassured you will be during the interview. Here are some more:

- What professional associations do you belong to?
- Would you rather work alone or in a team?
- Why should we hire you?
- What do you do in your spare time?
- What is your major weakness?

There are more questions in the exercises at the end of the chapter.

Answer the questions fully but concisely. Don't ramble.

Remember, when a company or organization is hiring a new employee it is making an investment in time and money. Naturally the people who do the hiring are going to be careful. They need to discover what sort of person they are hiring. Interviewers will want to know how your various experiences and achievements relate to their requirements and how you will perform in the job. They will expect you to provide the relationships between your abilities and their needs.

Think long-term—your interviewer will. Organizations will invest quite a lot of money in your training and progress, and they want their investment to pay off. They want a dependable employee who plans ahead and thinks about the best interests of the organization. In short, they want a caring attitude. Your task is to develop and then convey this attitude. If you do, you significantly improve your chances of getting the job. Ask questions about where and with whom you will be working, about what opportunities exist for advancement, about the long-range goals of the organization, about what products or services the organization will offer in the future.

What If the Interview Doesn't Go Well?   This happens. It may become clear that you are not qualified for the position, the salary is too low, or the fit between you and the organization is just not right. Don't panic, and don't lose heart. Every interview is a learning experience. Use the opportunity to practice your interviewing skills. You may even want to ask the interviewer what you can do to improve your presentation. Ask the interviewer to make suggestions on how you can improve your portfolio.

When Should You Mention Salary?   This is a very tricky problem. Ideally, your interviewer will bring up the question of money near the end of the interview and provide you with a salary range. Many negotiators believe that the person who mentions money first in a business transaction puts himself or herself at a disadvantage, so don't feel that you have to bring it up. You may not need to discuss it at all in an initial interview.

Your research should provide you with a salary range; by *range,* we mean at least $3,000 between the high and low figure. As we stated previously, you need to do this before the interview. You want the interviewer to give specific dollar figures first; you can respond much more easily, and interviewers have a clear sense of what the position is worth. (Most organizations have specific job categories with predetermined salary levels.) If you start too low, the interviewer may accept a figure substantially lower than what the organization was prepared to pay. If you start too high, you may price yourself out of the job.

---

legal considerations

State and federal laws provide strict guidelines to interviewers. You should not be questioned about spouses, children, age, or other personal information. Discriminatory questions are illegal.

There are no absolute rules governing how to respond if you are asked such illegal questions. Use your judgment. Determine the intent of the interviewer and consider some options:

- Answer the question.
- Respond with a question: "Will the answer to this question help you evaluate me?" or "How is the answer to that question relevant to my work experience?"
- Reply that you would prefer not to answer the question.

If the interviewer pushes you to state a figure first and you feel that you must begin the negotiation, start high. You can always come down. Watch the reaction of the interviewer carefully. Pay attention to body language and facial expressions as a way of gauging how your first offer is received.

Remember that salary is only one component of compensation. A company car, a lengthy paid vacation, full health coverage, profit sharing, a pension plan, reimbursement for further education, and other fringe benefits should be factored into the equation. Sometimes a low salary can be more than offset by such benefits. Make sure you know the full package before you accept or reject an offer.

What Should You Do If You Are Offered the Position During the Interview?
Pause. Don't accept the offer simply because you are thrilled to gain approval, particularly if you have other interviews lined up. No organization will think less of you or withdraw the offer if you don't respond with an immediate, resounding yes. A career move is a significant step, one that requires careful consideration. If you are at all unsure, tell the interviewer when you will call with your answer. You will think about the offer more rationally when you are away from the interview and have time to reflect.

If this is your first full-time position, accept the possibility that you will not be happy with every aspect of the job. However, you are gaining valuable experience that will help you find better positions down the road.

Let the interviewer decide when the interview is over. Conclude the interview on a positive note. Make sure you know when the final decision will be made before you leave the interview. Try to get a commitment on a specific date when you will be contacted, or when you may call. Shake hands firmly, thank the interviewer, and follow the lead of the interviewer as you exit the office.

FOLLOWING UP

What should you do after the interview? Write down what happened. Take ten minutes to record the most significant events that occurred, including any salary negotiations, and to record any information that you forgot to mention about your qualifications, or questions that you forgot to ask. You will be sending a follow-up letter to your interviewer and these details will help you.

Within a week after the interview but preferably within two days, send your follow-up letter, thanking the interviewer, and using the information in your notes. Do this even if you are no longer interested in the position. This letter should be printed on high-quality stationery, preferably using a laser printer.

If you have not heard from the organization within the time specified during the interview, call the organization. Don't feel as if you are intruding; your interviewer will understand. If the organization has not made a decision, get a specific time frame when you will call again.

What If You Have Two or More Job Offers and One Organization Is Looking for a Commitment? Congratulations! You're in an enviable position. You can let your contacts in the organizations know. They may be able to offer a more attractive package. In the end, weigh all of the alternatives and make your decision. There's no one magic formula (beyond hindsight) that determines what is the best job.

a sample follow-up letter

May 27, 1998

1510 Andrews Drive
Houston, TX 77002
(713) 555-5789

Ms. Sandy Pascal, CEO
Pascal Business Systems
Texas Commerce Tower, Suite 5A
600 Travis St.
Houston, Texas 77002

Dear Ms. Pascal:

I would like to emphasize my continued interest in the position of Sales Representative that we discussed yesterday afternoon.

I believe I could contribute the following to your organization:

-
-
-

Once you have met with the other candidates, I would like to meet with you to discuss how my background fits with the position you outlined during the interview. I will call you in two weeks to arrange a time that is convenient for you.

Sincerely,

Lourdes Santiago

Lourdes Santiago

MAINTAINING YOUR CREDENTIALS

Whether you are in school or happily employed in a job you enjoy, it is a good idea for you to stay in touch with the job application process. Scan the classified ads in the Sunday papers. Read the trade publications and journals in your field. Keep aware of employment trends, current salaries, and job descriptions.

Maintain your employment credentials by keeping them current and easily available. This means reviewing your résumé on a regular basis and adding accomplishments or changing the emphasis. Don't let your résumé get more than six months old and keep some fresh copies at home and work. Be sure that you have up-to-date references who can provide specifics about what you are currently doing.

Your ability to respond quickly to an immediate employment opportunity may be the difference in whether or not you get a special job. Even if you are satisfied with your present position, awareness of the current job market is a valuable tool.

INTERVIEWING: EXERCISES

1. In this exercise you will role-play a job interview. Two members of the class or group are needed: one to serve as the interviewer, a personnel manager for a large manufacturer of household products, and one to serve as the interviewee applying for a specific job. (The interviewee should be allowed some time to work out the details of the job.)

   When the interview begins, the personnel manager should explain that one of the members of the secretarial pool accidentally misplaced all of the paperwork. The personnel manager will need to find out what job the interviewee is applying for. The interviewee should make up a job based on his or her career goals. The six-minute interview will be held in the office of the personnel manager.

   After the interview, members of the class or group should discuss their observations with both of the participants. Remember, you may very well find yourself in each of these roles at some time during your career, so both are important to do well. You might consider having the participants reverse roles and try to see themselves in the other position.

2. Pascal Business Systems wants to hire a Project Team Member who will be able to work with a variety of temporary project teams. The firm is looking for an individual with a wide range of interests and abilities, someone who is flexible and can contribute to different types of projects.

   Look carefully at each of the résumés in Chapter 3 and decide which of these people you would recommend for the po-

sition. Write a memo to Herman Tannebaum in Human Resources in which you rank the candidates. Provide brief explanations for your decisions.

3. Using the interview questions that follow, role-play a job interview with someone else in the class. The interviewee needs to remember to bring a résumé to the interview. The interviewer should be sure to ask at least seven of these questions in some form during the course of the interview.

   Tell me about yourself.

   Why do you want to work here?

   What do you expect to be doing five years from now?

   What was your previous salary?

   Are you a good student?

   Which of your college courses was the most important? Why?

   What professional associations do you belong to?

   Would you rather work alone or in a team?

   Why should we hire you?

   What do you do in your spare time?

   What is your major weakness?

   If you have the opportunity, videotape the interview and play it back for discussion and analysis. How well did the interviewee handle the tough questions? What strategies can you suggest to make the interview go more smoothly?

4. One effective way to practice for something as stressful as a job interview is to

engage in a negative rehearsal. In other words, work up the worst possible interview you can imagine, one in which everything goes wrong. Both the interviewer and the interviewee should plan some strategies beforehand. Discuss with your partner the types of mistakes which create the worst impressions.

5. Interview three people who have had a variety of different positions with a number of organizations about the interviews they have had. What were the best interviews? What were the worst? Ask them to offer general guidelines about interviews. Write a summary for your instructor.

6. Practice with a partner to respond to the following interview questions:

I'm sorry. I haven't had time to look at your file. Could you tell me something about yourself?

What do you think determines a person's progress in a good company?

What types of books have you read?

Do you like to travel?

Are you willing to go where the company sends you?

How much money do you hope to earn at age 30? 35?

What qualifications do you have that make you feel you will be successful?

Why did you decide to attend this particular college?

Can you take instructions without becoming upset?

Are your feelings easily hurt?

Do you have any debts?

Which of your working experiences did you find the most rewarding? Why?

What can you contribute to an organization?

What is your major weakness?

7. Compose the body of a follow-up letter to send to the person who conducted your in-class interview in Exercise 6.

8. Prepare a list of ten additional questions to ask at an interview. Here are five to get you started:

What companies are your major competitors?

Why is this job now available?

Do you have a written job description for this position?

What is the company's current financial situation?

How would you categorize your management philosophy?

9. Below are nine interview "don'ts." Add three items to this list.

---

interview don'ts

- Don't be late.
- Don't complain; don't complain about your life, or your college, or the weather.
- Don't talk solely about yourself.
- Don't answer without thinking.
- Don't interrupt the interviewer.
- Don't act as if you know more than your interviewer.
- Don't drop names.
- Don't discuss salary until your interviewer opens the subject.
- Don't try to close the interview. Let your host end the interview.

section 2
DISCOVERING YOUR ROLE IN AN ORGANIZATION

● ●

In this section we look at what happens as you enter the world of work, the typical tasks you perform, and the skills you need to accomplish these tasks. Our focus is communication—the skills and the tools you will need—since communication will be a very important part of your experiences on the job. Studies have concluded that we spend the majority of our time, approximately 70 percent, in some form of verbal communication. (Sproule, 327) Note that the studies don't record the time spent in nonverbal communication. You will spend a great deal of your time on the job communicating: writing memos and business letters, talking with colleagues, attending meetings, discussing work assignments with your supervisor, speaking with clients, and attending to numerous other communication tasks with other employees. Your communication skills and your ability to adapt to the workplace will, to a large extent, determine how your career develops.

This section is designed to prepare you for the challenges of the workplace. In order to communicate successfully in the business world, you need to be familiar with the tools of the modern office—the electronic mail system, the fax machines, the telephones, the computers—and you need to be comfortable with these tools. In this section, we present a chapter about adjusting to the workplace, a chapter on improving your meetings and your telephone and fax skills, and a chapter on using electronic tools. You will also need to be able to gather information, so we devote a chapter to reading and research.

Chapter 5 *Learning About Your Organization*

Chapter 6 *Encountering People on the Job*

Chapter 7 *Using Electronic Tools*

Chapter 8 *Surveying Your Sources: Reading and Research*

LEARNING ABOUT YOUR ORGANIZATION

Discovering the Communication Styles of Your Organization
Gathering Information About the Organization
    The Grapevine
    Electronic Mail
Discovering Your Responsibilities
Developing Profiles
Improving Your Work Site

The interview process was a success. You're hired! The hard work has paid off with a job—actually, not a job but a first position. We want you to remember your time horizons, for this is but a step on your career road. Now begins the challenging and rewarding process of career development.

In this chapter we keep looking ahead. Once on the job you want to learn about your organization: how it functions, how to adjust to working conditions, who has power to make decisions. You need to develop a profile of the people you work with most closely. You need to be clear about your duties and responsibilities, and you need to understand the criteria by which your performance will be reviewed.

DISCOVERING THE COMMUNICATION STYLES OF YOUR ORGANIZATION

Every organization has its own unique communication patterns. Certain key words and phrases are essential to the way the organization functions. Certain forms of address are acceptable in meetings, conversations, and written documents. Certain ways of describing products and processes are used by all employees. Certain attitudes about how to behave, how to dress, and how to live your life exist within any social group, and businesses are no different.

All of these things can be lumped together under the heading *corporate cultural norms,* the particular ways an organization operates. Each organization has its own culture—a collection of behaviors, attitudes, and histories that define the organization. (Deal and Kennedy, 13) You need to be particularly sensitive to such norms, and, like it or not, adjust to the culture you find. This is not about hypocrisy, about ceasing to be an individual by changing your personality to the pressures of the workplace; it is about the cultural conformity we all must go through to be part of a society.

For example, let's say you are hired by a particular organization; during the interview, you were informed that every employee in your department receives an hour for lunch. Once you begin working, you discover that no one in the department takes longer than 30 minutes for lunch. The department head doesn't seem to monitor the individuals. You also discover that this practice is true in other departments. The practice of taking only 30 minutes for lunch seems to be an unstated corporate norm. What would you do in this situation? Would you demand that you get the full hour? Conforming to this particular corporate cultural norm seems to be a rational decision.

The important thing to remember is that every organization, across time, has developed a set of behaviors that help define the organization. Your task is to discover the corporate cultural norms of your organization.

Listen closely to the way people talk. You will hear them use words and phrases unique to the organization or the type of business. Such words and phrases are called *jargon.* In many ways, learning the language of the workplace—learning the meanings behind such jargon and, more important, learning to use the words and phrases fluently in conversation and in writing—is similar to learning a foreign language. You are learning the vocabulary of your particular workplace.

For example, you may find yourself in an office where employees routinely refer to value-added resellers, or to ergonomics, or to a midi interface. You may hear an employee say, "They run a big watercooled shop."* You need to learn this new language. Ask questions about the vocabulary. Be attentive to the phrases and terms you hear, and try to incorporate them into your vocabulary.

Here are some questions that will help you analyze the environment. What are the key terms and phrases used by the organization? How is information communicated? Are there standards for written messages? Some organizations have editors who check every piece of business correspondence that leaves the organization. The message must conform

---

*Translated, the sentence says the organization uses large mainframe computers, which are cooled by water.

to specific rules. Ask yourself, what kinds of messages am I responsible for? What rules exist within the organization that I need to observe?

Also watch the nonverbal communication cues of the organization. Learn when it is appropriate to speak freely and when it isn't. Watch how your colleagues behave, and be particularly attentive to how they interact in different settings. It may be acceptable, for example, to call supervisors by their first name in some informal situations, but in a formal meeting you must use a more formal address. Similarly, you may be encouraged to speak your mind freely in some settings, while in others—in front of certain clients, for example—you should not offer your comments. Every organization is different, and each has different corporate cultural norms; by paying careful attention to all of the information available to you, you can significantly improve your opportunities within the organization.

GATHERING INFORMATION ABOUT THE ORGANIZATION

Do research. Go to the library, get whatever literature exists about the organization, and read it. Then go to the organization's library. A rich history may exist in the organization's files. Learn about how the business was started, what products were originally sold, and how the organization evolved. You'll be able to use this knowledge again and again. Read the annual report for the most recent years, and study the vocabulary in the report. Write down any questions you have about the report, and get your colleagues and your supervisor to answer your questions.

Find a map of the physical location. What about other sites? Who are the principal customers? What products do you manufacture? If this is a for-profit business, what are the principal sources of revenue? If the organization is nonprofit, what services or information are you responsible for? Even if an organization's primary reason for being is not to make money, it still must pay attention to the bottom line: few organizations can afford to lose money.

Are there shareholders in the organization? How many? How has the stock performed in the last three years? The last ten years? Does management control a significant share of the stock?

In general terms, there is a difference between how large, medium, and small organizations function. There are no absolutes when looking at the vast array of organizations

---

learning about nonverbal communication

Posture, body position, movement, hand gestures, facial expressions, eye contact, attentiveness, distance between individuals: all are communication signals. Often we communicate more by such signals than by the words we use. When people listen to us, they judge our message by all of the cues available to them. Be aware of how you communicate.

learning about annual reports

Annual reports can be difficult to comprehend. They are long documents containing a profile of the company, a description of its products, and sheets of figures. They are written by the company, which is obviously trying to put a positive spin on everything. How do you make sense of them?

According to Robin Micheli of *Money* magazine, there are some ways of making it easier. (We aren't covering all of them here.) First, get at least four years' worth of annual reports so that you have a basis for comparison. (Call the company and ask for the last four years.) Now look for trends over these years in the *shareholders' letter* (the message from the CEO to the shareholders summarizing the performance of the company in the last year and its prospects), the *balance sheet* (divide the company's *current assets* by its *liabilities;* a 2-to-1 ratio means that a company has sufficient assets to meet debts), its *long-term debt* (divide long-term debt by long-term capital [long-term debt plus shareholders' equity]; you are looking for a result below 50 percent), *accounts receivable* in light of *sales* (It's good if they're growing at roughly the same pace, bad if receivables are outdistancing sales), and *current inventories* compared to sales (again, these should be growing at roughly the same pace; it's not good if the company is producing more than it can sell). Make sure you compare all of these items across a number of years. Finally, read the footnotes carefully. Watch for any changes in accounting procedures, lawsuits, or pending liabilities that could affect the company in the future. (Micheli, 181)

in the corporate world, but perhaps some loose generalizations may help you understand your particular environment.

Large organizations, because of their size, responsibilities, and tasks, tend to be fairly rigid. Lines of responsibility are not easily crossed; the hierarchical structure will be very important. You need to be aware of *protocol*—the approved procedures, frequently regarding rank, of an organization. In small organizations, you may perform many tasks and be responsible for a wide variety of operations. Larger organizations offer stability, a history of growth and success, and developed policies and practices. Forecasters believe that the size of most large companies will shrink in the future. (Kiechel, 39)

Small organizations offer risk—the company may not be around later if it's not able to compete—but they also offer the possibility of rapid growth, and thus rapid promotion for you. You will know almost everyone. You will have more responsibilities, a greater variety of tasks, and a better understanding of the whole system; since there are fewer people to do the work, everyone pitches in and relationships tend to be more informal. Tasks are not segmented.

Medium-sized companies tend to have a blend of the characteristics of the two extremes.

Whatever the size of your work environment, get the organizational chart and study it. Add names to the departments or groups within the chart; then try to add faces to the names. Read the company policy manual to find out about everything from employee safety standards to dress codes, overtime policies, performance reviews and evaluations, benefits, retirement plans, grievance procedures, and severance pay standards. Ask questions about your future. Walk around. Use your lunch time productively. Find out where things are. Notice who has the "real" power, the power to accomplish things.

The organizational chart will tell you about the formal structures of the organization. Organizations also have informal paths, less easily observed, but still very powerful in terms of how information is conveyed. You may have to work in the organization for many months before you become aware of these informal communication channels, but they are there; if you pay attention, you will learn quite a lot.

The Grapevine

The *grapevine* is an informal communication channel, transmitting unofficial news, rumors, bits of gossip, and other important information. While you cannot always trust the information you receive as truthful, it is important because it expresses the real concerns of the organization. Listen to the hints of a change in operations, rumors about the reorganization of departments, problems with a new product line, gripes about managers, and fears of layoffs, and learn which individuals you should trust, who has reliable information, and who is merely spreading malicious gossip.

You will find that upper management is well aware of what is circulating in the grapevine and, if the managers understand the organization, they are also capable of influencing the grapevine. Sometimes ideas are tested in the grapevine to study the reaction of the organization before they are implemented.

Electronic Mail

Many workers in the modern office have direct access to a computer networked through parts of the organization. Electronic mail, or *e-mail,* has become a primary communication link and thus an important communication channel for you. In some organizations, the grapevine runs through the e-mail system. If you work in an organization where electronic mail is a major conduit for information, you need to become competent at using the system as quickly as you can.

Many people assume that electronic mail is private; however, you should be aware that your correspondence may be monitored at various levels of the organization. Never send a message hastily or without careful consideration of the consequences. Someone could be eavesdropping, and this could have serious ramifications for you.

DISCOVERING YOUR RESPONSIBILITIES

As soon as you are hired, you will begin learning about your duties and responsibilities. You may attend formal training sessions either individually or in a group, and you may receive an informal walkthrough of your assigned tasks. Listen carefully, ask questions, and don't be frustrated if you are unable to do these tasks correctly the first time. Learn when important meetings occur, and schedule your time, attempting to budget your time

position description	
Job title:	Job code:
Department:	Date:
Written by:	Approved by:
Pay scale:	
Duties and responsibilities:	
Qualifications:	
Supervisor:	

appropriately. (Don't spend three hours on an unimportant memo and leave yourself no time to file an important report.)

You may receive a written list of your duties, such as the position description shown above. If you are unable to get one, write down what you believe to be your responsibilities and ask your supervisor to verify your list. It is possible, however, that your real duties may be very different. Make sure you know what is expected of you. How can you do a good job if you are unclear on what it means to do a good job? Find out the answers to questions such as these:

- When is your first review?
- Who will evaluate you?
- What will he or she be looking for?
- Will there be a salary increase?
- How will you be rated?
- Will you have the opportunity to provide input into your review?

If you can, obtain a copy of the particular form your organization uses. It may not look like the performance review we have included in this chapter, but it will probably use many of the same categories and criteria for evaluating you. Typically, you will be reviewed every six months. No matter what your job is, your employer will be concerned about your organizational skills, your knowledge of the field, your decision-making skills, your ability to communicate and work with a team, and your commitment to the organization.

Pascal Business Systems

Employee's name _____ Job title _____
Supervisor's name _____ Date of review _____

	Outstanding	Very Good	Satisfactory	Improvement needed
Job skills _____				
Knowledge of work _____				
Ability to organize _____				
Quality of work _____				
Communication _____				
Teamwork _____				
Judgment _____				
Dependability _____				
Attitude _____				
Problem solving _____				

Areas needing improvement _____
_____
_____

Areas where employee has improved _____
_____
_____

Summary of evaluation _____
_____
_____

_____ _____
Name of employee   Date

_____ _____
Name of supervisor   Date

performance review

DEVELOPING PROFILES

Your supervisor will become a very important person to you. Your supervisor will evaluate you, recommend you for pay raises and promotions, and determine what projects you work on and how you spend a great portion of your time within the workplace. You need to develop a profile of your supervisor.

As you work with your supervisor across time, you will build a storehouse of knowledge about who this person is and what he or she finds important. Since this individual plays such a significant role in your career, you need to pay careful attention to the messages you receive. Look at the style of writing of the memos you receive, observe group meetings carefully, and try to learn from one-on-one encounters. Soon you will develop a profile that you can utilize each time you communicate.

Let's use as an example a writing assignment you receive from an instructor at your school. Your teacher will give you guidelines and rules for completing the assignment. She may say, "Papers with more than seven spelling errors will be returned." Or your instructor may want you to observe a particular footnoting style. Or she may return a paper with a grade and an explanation of why you received this grade.

The instructor will also give you hints and clues as to what she expects. You may be able to tell from what she stresses in lectures and class discussions what she feels is important, both in terms of content and style. The more perceptive you are about the teacher and the teacher's expectations, the more successful you will be in the course. (Good students can frequently predict the questions that will appear on an exam simply by using their knowledge of the instructor.) The principle is the same in a work situation: *use what you know of your audience.* Keep building your profile with each communication situation.

Wherever you work, you have a variety of relationships, formal and informal, with your co-workers, your clients, and associates in other organizations. Before you address any of these people, you should review your most recent contacts and your general perception of your relationship with your audience. Be aware that there is more than one component to a working relationship; you may regard an individual as both a friend and a colleague, for example. Pay careful attention to the cues, both verbal and nonverbal, that people send.

IMPROVING YOUR WORK SITE

As soon as you are hired, you will receive some work space to inhabit during working hours. Even if you are a field representative who will spend most of your time on the road, you will still require some space within the home office. It's up to you to make this work space as pleasant and functional an environment as you can.

If you are assigned a desk, try to use the desktop to your advantage. Create spaces to file the documents you read and write. Create an organizational structure that will enable you to locate and file the documents quickly and easily. If you are given a computer, take the time to learn the software programs you will be responsible for. You may receive training sessions for some of the more sophisticated or specialized programs, but you need to familiarize yourself with the general operating system that will let you move around on your computer. (See Chapter 7, "Using Electronic Tools," for more information.) Learn about the photocopier, the fax machine, the telephone system, and whatever else you may need to do your job.

Since at least part of your job will involve writing, we recommend that you assemble a small resource library in a convenient location, preferably right on your desk. No individual can write without occasionally stopping to check on a detail: the spelling of a word, a rule of grammar, a fact, a date, an interpretation of material, or any of a hundred other possible items. When we check our work, we are ensuring that the things we say and the way we say these things are precise and accurate. Whenever possible, you should verify your statements.

When we fail to check our work, we open ourselves to error. One major cause of writers failing to check their work is distance from reference materials. When the materials that would help us are far away, we are reluctant to use the time away from our writing. Sometimes we convince ourselves that we will check the material later, but we never do. Therefore, we recommend that you use the following list as a foundation for your resource library:

- General dictionary
- Grammar handbook (your word processing program may have one)*
- Thesaurus (your word processing program may have one)
- Current almanac
- Current atlas
- Manuals for the computer software you regularly use
- Company policy manuals

We hope that you will find this book valuable enough to include on your shelf. You may also want to include one or two reference works from your special field.

If your organization has research librarians on staff, take the time to visit them. This will help you when you have to call quickly for information. There may be a central location for the company files; learn how they are organized and what the policy is on taking files back to your work area. Learn how and when in-house mail is distributed; if the entire organization employs electronic mail, learn how to send and receive messages.

Learning About Your Organization: Exercises

1. Locate the annual reports of two companies in a field you would like to enter after you graduate. (If the company is publicly held—if its stock is traded—it has to file an annual report to stockholders. You can call the company and request a copy.) Analyze the companies and write a brief summary of what you discovered.

2. Complete a position description (see p. 66) for a job you have held. If you have never held a job, write down your duties and responsibilities as someone who attends school. Treat your school career as a job.

3. Develop a profile of an instructor you had in a previous course. Write a description of the individual, explain his or her expectations for the class assignments—tests, papers, lab reports, research assignments—and offer specific examples of how you used your understanding of the instructor to help you do well in the course.

4. Make a list of the resources available to you in your current educational or work situation. This list should include all of the books, people, and computer software you can access if you need help. (Your list may be quite a bit longer than you think.)

---

*Be careful; the rules of grammar are very complicated, and the most sophisticated grammar checker is not currently prepared to check all of the nuances of a complex language system.

position description	
Job title:	Job code:
Department:	Date:
Written by:	Approved by:
Pay scale:	
Duties and responsibilities:	
Qualifications:	
Supervisor:	

5. If you have ever had to write within a work setting, write a memo informing your instructor about one particular task and what was involved. Describe the task, the length of the document, the audience, the research you performed, and the time restrictions placed on you by this writing situation. What resources did you utilize? What problems did you encounter? Is there anything you would have done differently?

6. Working within a group of four people, brainstorm a list of ten ways of improving a work site. How much would each item on the list cost?

7. Read the description of Pascal Business Systems in Appendix A. Then research Houston, Texas. Look for information about population, lifestyle, climate, cost of living, education, and housing. Now imagine that you have been hired by Pascal Business Systems; you may determine the details of the job. Your annual salary is $37,500. Write a one-page memo (see Chapter 9) to your instructor explaining why you would or would not take a job with Pascal Business Systems.

ENCOUNTERING PEOPLE ON THE JOB

6

Being a successful employee requires more than simply staying out of trouble. In a fast-changing marketplace, your ability to learn new information and to navigate successfully through the complex world you will confront can make all the difference in your career. In this chapter, we will examine some of the more significant skills you will need to succeed: participating in meetings, using the telephone, and sending and receiving messages via different technologies. These common tasks may not appear on your job description, but they are crucial to the successful performance of your job.

PARTICIPATING IN MEETINGS

Meetings are a crucial part of any career in business, and for that reason it is particularly surprising that so little time is spent in classrooms or in boardrooms discussing ways to make meetings more productive. As your career takes you into a variety of levels and functions within a company, you will participate in daily, weekly, monthly, and impromptu meetings, interviews, and briefings. In certain careers, as much as 50 percent of your time can be spent in meetings.

A *meeting* can be defined as any event where two or more people get together to discuss a subject or group of subjects. There is no one standard for a meeting. A meeting may be held to assign projects and tasks, present timetables, summarize completed work, provide briefings on new products, brainstorm solutions to a problem, or inform a group about advances in a specific field, among other purposes. Whether a meeting is a daily ritual that begins the activities of the day or is a rare event within your organization, you should remember four essential elements about meetings:

- Leader
- Agenda
- Minutes
- Closure

After we look at each of these items, we will discuss your role as a member of a meeting when you are not the leader, which will be the case more often than not in the formative stages of your career.

The Leader

Every meeting requires a leader, even if that leader has little power or authority. The leader's task is to facilitate discussion and decision making. If you will be the leader, you need to prepare. The leader needs to do homework, as follows:

- Locate all the necessary background information.
- List objectives: what should the meeting accomplish?
- Decide beforehand what course of action should follow the meeting. This may change during the meeting, but it is important to know what you want the next step to be.
- Select an appropriate site.
- Prepare the site.

The leader must decide whether a meeting is the best way to use the time. Sometimes, a memo is far more efficient. The memo, or a series of memos, may detail six or seven key points that need very little elaboration or discussion. The leader must ask the question: Do we really need to meet to discuss this? Should *x* number of people sit in this room for two hours? Or is their time more valuably used in some other capacity? (The cost of placing ten highly paid executives in a room for two hours can be enormous.)

Too often, meetings become lectures. One key to a successful meeting is interaction. People like to feel that they have some input into a decision, particularly one that may have a significant impact on their lives. It is the leader's responsibility to get every-

A meeting expands to fill the available time. If you allow 30 minutes for a meeting, the meeting will take 30 minutes. If you allow two hours for the same meeting, the meeting will take two hours. Always err on the side of a shorter meeting.

one involved, to make sure that all of the participants know how decisions will be made, to monitor the progress of the meeting, and to cut off inappropriate behavior.

Meetings reflect the values of a company or organization. The leader needs to resolve conflicts and ensure that everyone has an opportunity to participate. Every employee, regardless of rank, needs to be treated fairly.

As a meeting leader, you should be aware of how you are perceived by the other members of the meeting. We frequently communicate more by our nonverbal behavior than by the words that come out of our mouths. Posture, movement around the room, hand gestures, facial expressions, and the way we look at other people may mean much more to people than a promise we make or a compromise we suggest. When people hear what we have to say, they evaluate our words by all of the signals we transmit as we say the words. They trust us more for the way we speak than for what we say.

We may believe that our nonverbal methods of communication are seen in a positive light, but sometimes we are fooled by our desire to be liked by our audience. The best way to learn about this is to videotape yourself speaking in front of a group. You may be surprised by what you discover.

The Agenda

For a meeting to be successful, the participants have to know what it will be about beforehand. The agenda, usually distributed in a memo, provides appropriate advance notice of the topics that will be covered. Frequently, having the agenda beforehand gives participants a chance to prepare and thus saves time. Without an agenda, those in attendance at a meeting can legitimately feel that something has been sprung upon them unfairly. People are much more receptive to new ideas when they have had time to organize their thoughts.

The agenda should be relatively simple. Two or three key items are all that can reasonably be covered in a meeting. An agenda containing a list of ten items is overwhelming, and no progress may be made at the meeting.

Finally, and obviously, the agenda provides structure to the meeting.

The Minutes

The human mind is prone to forget. What can seem to be the most important business decision you have ever made can quickly fade from your memory. We all need to be reminded of what we have said and done, and we need to keep a record for other people. It's

---

memo

May 20, 1998

To: All staff
From: Stan Cohen, Project Coordinator
Re: Meeting on Friday

There will be a meeting of the staff this Friday at 12:00 in Room C-23. Please bring your files concerning the Gruber account. We need to discuss:

1. The revised timetable for production.
2. The design changes recommended by Engineering.

cc: Bart Jones, Vice-President
        Ann Smith, Area Manager

---

possible that of five people in a room making a key decision, not one will be with the organization in five years.

The leader needs to assign some competent individual the task of recording the minutes of a meeting. The recorder need not write down every word that is said, but should offer a summary of the key ideas and decisions made during the meeting. The leader must make sure that everyone receives a readable copy of the minutes.

The tasks of the leader do not end here, because the minutes need to be filed into some logical and accessible storage system—whether in a filing cabinet or on a computer disk—for future reference. A similar situation may arise five years down the road, or you may need to answer a question about company policy six months after the meeting. Having the written record provides you with a hard copy of what happened, not just some hazy memories. You may need the minutes of the meeting as a legal document, or someone else may need to know information long after you have left the company. Minutes are legal documents only if they are approved by a quorum of those in attendance at the next meeting.

Closure

All of us know the value of completing tasks, of getting things done. We all need to see where we've been and the value of the time we have spent. Meetings, particularly those that are scheduled on a regular basis, can become frustrating experiences when participants begin to feel that nothing gets done. The leader is responsible for *closure,* so that the participants know that the meeting has ended successfully.

The leader should summarize what has been discussed, paying careful attention to the variety of viewpoints that have been expressed and to the conflicts that these viewpoints have generated. Whenever possible, the leader should blend viewpoints to attempt to generate compromise. The leader should also finalize plans for future action.

At the very least, the leader should reserve the final five minutes of the meeting to answer the following two questions:

- What have we done?
- What happens next?

The best time to schedule a follow-up meeting or to assign an individual a specific task to accomplish is right now, at the end of the meeting. What is said at the end tends to stay with us the longest, and it is what we, the participants, will take back to our offices.

The Role of the Audience

Most of the time you spend in meetings will be spent as a member of the audience, not as the group leader. Your listening skills will be critical. Far too many people assume that if they are in attendance they do not need to listen actively, that somehow the message will enter their ears and stay. But to retain information, we need to listen with a focus on the issues: not just hearing the words, but interpreting their intent and their consequences.

Attention at a meeting is more than a professional courtesy; it is a way of improving job performance. Be aware of your nonverbal communication with the leader and with other group members.

When the leader distributes the agenda before the meeting, he or she may ask you to add items. Here is your opportunity to participate in the decision-making process of the meeting, and hence the future course of your department or organization. You need to give careful thought to your contribution, keeping in mind your audience and its history.

During the meeting, whether you have supplied an agenda item or not, the leader may ask you to speak or you may have an idea to volunteer. Remember to speak clearly and direct your comments to all of the audience, not just the leader. Try to gauge how specific and technical you need to be by paying close attention to nonverbal cues. If you are paying attention, you will know just when to stop.

Finally, those in attendance should come prepared to take notes at meetings. Your notes, even if they are brief jottings made at the conclusion of the meeting, can provide

---

suggestions for your notes

- List the key items of the discussion.
- List any decisions that have been made.
- List important dates, especially any deadlines that pertain to you.

you with an invaluable written record of the major items of importance. So take notes. It takes discipline, but it is worthwhile.

Some consulting companies require all their employees to sit down for five minutes after a meeting and write up their notes. The practice supplies the employees with a record of what was accomplished at the meeting and a reminder of what tasks they need to complete.

USING THE TELEPHONE

In the last few years, the telephone and switchboard have evolved into a complex electronic messaging center. The copper lines that used to carry only human words and voices are crowded with bits and bytes, data, information, and machine talk—machines talking to each other. Even the copper wires are being replaced—by fibers!

Defining telephone communication in the 1990s is a matter of choosing among telephone devices. Alexander Graham Bell's "electrographic voice transmitter" has become a telecommunications system. The telephone outlet is a terminal through which you can send and receive information to and from different people in many different ways. You can use a telephone line to send your voice, numbers, drawings, and data to almost anywhere in the world. Your information, whether it is audio or visual, is modulated, demodulated, microwaved, and bounced off satellites orbiting the earth. So much for the simple telephone! But while new devices are changing the ways we communicate by phone, most business telephone calls are still voice-to-voice communications between individuals.

The telephone system provides an immediate form of communication necessary to most businesses. What you need to remember is that all of these telephone calls are made for the same purpose: to pass information between people. The secret for successful communication remains courtesy. Whether you are using a fax, modem, or telephone handset, your object is the same: to communicate your information. Consideration for other people requires accuracy, clarity, and politeness.

---

a glossary of telecommunications terms

The communication of voice, data, and images over telephone circuits and systems involves a variety of equipment and transmission facilities from the telephone itself to the computer and fax machine. Here is a partial list:

Answering machines   A device that answers your telephone. The caller hears your recorded message and is able to leave a message for you.

Cellular phone   A portable phone that sends and receives signals on a cellular network instead of telephone lines. These are generally found in vehicles such as cars and planes. They can be used with modems and fax machines to send text and images as well as voice.

Centrex Local phone companies are providing centralized services as an option to hardware solutions. Some of these services include selective call forwarding, priority ringing, call return, and calling-party identification.

Electronic mail Computer utilities that allow text messages to be sent from one terminal or computer system to another. The message is stored until the recipient retrieves the mail by logging on to the system.

Facsimile/Fax A device that sends and receives copies of documents over regular telephone lines. Any image which is on paper—sketches, handwritten notes, drawings, text, photos—can be sent and received with facsimile machines. *Fax modems* can be installed in personal computers, allowing users to send and receive whatever they can place on their screens.

Modem Short for *modulator/demodulator.* This device changes digital signals to analog and vice versa so that computers can exchange information, text, and graphics across telephone networks.

Pager/alpha pager A device that signals a person that he or she has messages or is needed. *Alpha pagers* can transmit brief text messages as well as numbers and signals.

PDAs *Personal desk assistants* are computerized scheduling and planning helpers that have a number of special features, such as the ability to recognize handwriting and to send faxes and other transmissions.

Satellite communication Several companies, including NASA, provide satellite-based, high-capacity digital services for voice, image, and data communications. Satellite link-ups allow for direct communications with remote projects and locations.

Videoconferencing An online meeting between two locations linked with video and sound. Facilities available in many large cities eliminate the need for direct travel.

Voice mail A voice mailbox using a computer phone system that allows you to pick up and leave voice messages using a touch-tone phone. This same technology can provide information and data by providing telephone access to text files and databases. This is what happens when you combine the computer with the answering machine.

A telephone conversation requires the same type of planning that goes into a written document. You will need to consider your audience—the person who will be listening to what you say. You will need to know what you want to learn or what you want to be done. Your listener will be wondering too, and it is up to you to provide the answers.

Whenever you are on the telephone, you need to remember that you are in direct and immediate contact with someone who cannot see your expressions or the chart you are pointing to. You need to be prepared to give your listener the verbal assistance which will help him or her to meet your needs.

The telephone sometimes gives us the sense that we are face-to-face with a person. Instead, we are voice-to-voice, and neither one can see the other. When we are explaining technical details, we need to be particularly careful that the information is passed on accurately.

a few simple telephone rules

Identify yourself. You should always start out a phone conversation by telling the listener who you are and why you are calling. Not many people can be helpful while they are wondering who you are.

Identification can be many different things. Some computer systems require elaborate passwords when calling by modem. For most person-to-person conversations, however, simply stating your name and organization is enough. Then say what you want.

Answering the phone requires the same type of directness. Unless your organization has a particular phone protocol, you should answer by stating the organization's name and your project group, if necessary. Your name is optional. You do not have to give an elaborate response that includes your employment qualifications.

Tell the person what you want. Your listener needs to know this. Before engaging in any telephone communication, you should always be prepared to respond to the direct question, "What do you want?" Very few people will ask this, but if you do not make it clear, all of them will be wondering.

Keep it brief. The phone is most effective for short communications. For one thing, busy people don't have a lot of time for conversations, particularly ones they didn't schedule. Technical information may not be available to them when you call, and complex technical details are easily confused on the telephone.

Write it down. Don't rely on memory. If it is important enough to remember, then it is important enough to write down. We are trying to shout this rule. So listen: *Write it down!*

A telephone call may often seem to be the easiest way to deal with a situation. You should remember, however, that telephone calls have advantages and disadvantages.

The phone is immediate. You don't have to wait for a decision or agreement. You can get the information you want when you need it. On the other hand, there will be no written record of that information or agreement. Complex technical details can easily get confused. Busy people do not like to be interrupted. Some material is too sensitive to be discussed on the phone. You want to be sure the message is appropriate for the telephone. In general, phone conversations are useful for transmitting small amounts of information that is relatively simple.

One reason many people dislike the telephone is that they consider it an interruption, an unplanned interference with their schedule. When you initiate a call, you are responsible for seeing that things get done, that the purpose of the call is accomplished, and that you do not waste your listener's time.

- *If the person you call is reluctant to talk to you,* ask for a convenient time to call back.

- *Take control of the discussion.* You can do this with your voice, tone, and confident delivery. This means preparation: knowing what you want and what you are prepared to do. When you have planned your call, you will sound prepared and confident.
- *Outline your call.* Before you make an important call, take the time to fill out a call focus sheet. This will keep your conversation focused and you will not forget important matters.

Call Focus Sheet	*Pascal Business Systems*
1. This call is important because: 2. At the end of this call I want to accomplish:	
Promises I agree to: They agree to:	Key Phrases

- *Be prepared with transition phrases.* You should have a few phrases ready to help keep the conversation on track. Simple expressions such as "I understand, but . . . " or "That's interesting; however, . . ." can keep the discussion focused on what you want to talk about.
- *Have an excuse ready.* Be ready to get out of a conversation if you want to. "I have a call on the other line. Let me get back to you," is a polite way for you to get further information or check with others in your organization. If you have to leave the phone to get information, offer to call back.

You can help others listen to you by using a pleasant voice and a lively tone. Organize what you have to say ahead of time and let your listener know how you have organized your message. For instance, you might describe the steps needed to do something in sequence, or the parts of a device from back to front. Let your listener know so he or she can follow along. Even more important, follow through. If you agree to return a call or to provide further information, make sure that you do so.

Many business calls do not reach their intended audience. The person you should be most prepared to speak to when you make a call is a person who is not there. Be ready, at least, to do your best in reaching this person. Be prepared. Tell the person you *do* reach the name of the individual you want to talk to, the time and date of your call, and why you are calling: *who, when,* and *why.* Ask the person who answers to record this information.

Then be prepared to receive a return call. There is little sense in asking a person to call back if he or she will not be able to reach you. If you are going to be away from your phone, leave instructions concerning how to reach you. It takes two sides to play a really good game of telephone tag.

If you do not receive an answer within a reasonable time—two days, for instance—then send your message in writing. Don't forget to keep a copy for yourself.

These suggestions, of course, apply in reverse. You should return calls as quickly as possible—certainly within two days if you are going to return them at all. You should also be prepared to collect full information (*who, when,* and *why*) for fellow workers who cannot take a call.

SENDING AND RECEIVING MESSAGES

"Put it in writing" is still the first rule of business and industry. If you need to remember something, put it in writing. If you want someone else to remember, put it in writing too. Written words reduce the possibility of garbled and confused messages. Today the telephone system can be used to communicate in writing.

The *facsimile machine* (fax) is a wonderful piece of phone equipment that can be used to send and receive documents—sketches, text, or any kind of visual information. A fax unit combines the benefits of the telephone and the copy machine.

Fax output should consist of documents that are virtually error-free. There can be no misunderstanding about what was said or suggested. You can fax drawings, charts, maps, blueprints, and photographs. Fax machines have followed the computer into offices and businesses everywhere, putting people into written contact with each other. Public machines are now available in many U.S. Post Offices, stationery stores, and copy centers.

Electronic mail is another technology that is increasingly available and generally much cheaper than faxing, particularly when sending messages overseas. Regional, national, and international networks are being created that will let industry, schools, and government rapidly communicate with each other by electronic mail and file transfer. *Computer networking* allows people to exchange ideas and information quickly and effectively. The "information superhighway" is a reality; instantaneous information transmission is in the process of changing all our lives.

---

some e-mail symbols

:-)	I'm happy.		=:-)	I'm a punk rocker.
:-(	I'm very sad.		'-)	I'm winking.
:'(	I'm crying.		:-J	I'm being tongue in cheek.

Look at the symbols sideways to see the faces.

Networking has changed the ways in which people work together. Collaboration is no longer limited by physical locations. Through computer and telephone networks, people have immediate access to distributed resources from distributed locations. Technical projects can involve people, instruments, and software located in many different places, even continents apart.

The speed with which messages are transmitted by telephone, fax, and electronic mail has been blamed for an increase in poor manners. Rehearsal time is eroded and replies are requested without sufficient time for reflection and thought. Even so, courtesy remains a key component in any successful communication.

If you are using a fax or a modem to send images or text, there are some simple rules of etiquette to follow. These are very similar to those for telephoning by voice. You need to say who is sending the message, to whom it is addressed, and how many pages or bytes of information will follow. A cover sheet is often the most important consideration in whether your message reaches its intended audience.

The *teleconference* represents another instance where special courtesy is required. When multiple parties are attempting to talk by phone from various locations, a moderator is necessary. People need to be invited into the discussion and encouraged to participate by the moderator, who clearly sets up and maintains the format of the conversation since the visual signals to do so are absent. Most of the suggestions regarding meetings presented at the beginning of this chapter apply here as well.

Whatever telephone device you use to communicate, your purpose is the same. The common denominator to all of these choices is that you are sending a message. For the past ten years, new products and innovations have been coming into the telecommunications marketplace at a rate that exceeds many people's ability to use them. What this means is that some equipment is not being used because people don't know how to use it.

You can improve your abilities as an effective communicator by learning as much as you can about the telecommunications system used by your school or business.

---

fax etiquette

Simplify your messages.

Use legible typefaces and big font sizes. Some typefaces recommended for fax documents are Lucida, Bitstream Charter, Officina Serif, and Swift. Typefaces not recommended for fax documents are Aurial, Bodoni, Garamond, and Futura. The minimum type size for faxing is 12-point.

Keep your faxes short.

Don't send a fax if the recipient can't respond by fax.

Provide your fax and voice numbers in the heading. For overseas faxes, provide your dialing sequence.

(Kawasaki, 306)

Whether you send your message as voice, image, or text, you are still trying to deliver a message to another person accurately and clearly. You can also improve your abilities as an effective communicator by paying close attention to the meetings you attend, by copying the styles and strategies of those you find particularly effective at leading meetings, and by carefully judging when it is appropriate for you to participate.

ENCOUNTERING PEOPLE ON THE JOB: EXERCISES

1. The various parts of this exercise are interconnected and require the participation of the entire class. The entire process may require about two hours of class time.

   (a) Divide the class into groups of five. The class as a whole should decide how to divide into these smaller groups. (You may want to use an arbitrary distinction—for example, the color of the shoes that people are wearing.)

   (b) Each group should elect a spokesperson. Write down the process used to decide upon the spokesperson.

   (c) Each group should decide on three low-cost ways of improving the student experience at your school. Make sure you discuss the rationale behind each of your concepts.

   (d) Each group will contribute three ideas to a meeting of the spokespeople. The agenda for the meeting will have only one item: to decide to implement *one and only one* low-cost way of improving the student experience at your school. Only the spokespeople will be allowed to talk at the meeting. The other members of the class will watch, but will not contribute at this point. (They will contribute in part (e), so note-taking should be considered.)

   (e) Once the spokespeople have come to a final agreement on the one way of improving the experience of students, each member of the audience will write down his or her analysis of

   how the decision was made. You may want to look at the process of the negotiation, the steps that led to a compromise, and the force of individual personalities in determining the final decision. Be particularly aware of nonverbal cues. Discuss two nonverbal communications you witnessed.

   (f) Discuss the written analyses as a group. The spokespeople may have been so involved in trying to influence the decision that they were unaware of many of the subtleties of the process.

2. Choose either a hardware or software product you are familiar with—for example, you might select an answering machine or a word-processing program. Assume that it is not working properly and you are planning to call a toll-free technical support number. List the preparations you would make before placing your call.

3. One way to improve your telephone skills is to practice them. Sit back to back with another person and conduct a simulated telephone conversation. One advantage of role-playing is that you can reverse roles with the other person and experience both sides of the conversation.

   You might want a third person to observe, take notes, and provide feedback to you both. Try role-playing some of the following conversations:

   (a) You are very upset with Ken Bolton, an electronics supplier whose delivery did not arrive by overnight delivery as he promised it would. The result is that your project is on hold with the deadline fast approaching. You absolutely need these parts by tomorrow and it is too late to look elsewhere for the parts.

(b) A Mr. Yelpir Noj calls from the Maldives, where he represents the Maldivian Research Collective. At least you think so. Mr. Noj's accent makes his strained English difficult to follow. You are not sure what he wants. Arrange for a return call with Mr. Noj and then describe how you would make this call.

(c) Choose a device with which you are familiar. Give it to another person. Sitting back to back with that person, try to answer the person's questions without looking at the device he or she is holding. Describe the results.

4. Make a list of twelve common American English idioms. *Idioms* are phrases and combinations of words that have a unique or unusual meaning. For example, *take a break* has a meaning different from the literal meaning of the three words that make up the idiom; *break a leg* means "good luck" when used before a performance; and *went broke* also suggests something quite different from the usual meaning of *to break*.

Now imagine receiving a phone call from someone who has learned English from textbooks. Will this person know the idioms on your list? What strategies would you employ to make sure that you could communicate clearly and accurately with this person?

5. Exchange an e-mail message with a friend of yours who attends a different school. Print out both your message and the returned message. Analyze the effect that such ease of communication will have on your life.

6. If anyone in the class is connected to the Internet, ask him or her to discuss the following questions:

- For what do you use the Internet?
- How did you find a service provider?
- On average, how much time do you spend per week connected to the Internet?

USING ELECTRONIC TOOLS

7

In recent years the microcomputer has become a powerful and flexible device for business communication. Improvements in the technology of writing, drawing, and publishing have reduced the expense and production time of creating documents and presentations. New products are changing deadlines, costs, and expectations. You must keep up with the business standards of your field.

Writing, particularly business writing, has changed dramatically because of the personal computer. Today many writers use new methods, new skills, and new computer-aided writing resources. Effective business communicators make full use of current electronic writing tools.

Even a few years ago most business documents were drafted in longhand before they were typed. Rough-draft versions of the illustrations were sketched by hand. Clerical tasks were often tedious and time-consuming. Today you can use a microcomputer to carry out a marketing projection; then write, edit, and illustrate a report on the results of that analysis; and then send the final document to a co-worker hundreds of miles away.

Documents created with electronic tools can read better and look neater. Readability and appearance can improve because you have the opportunity to write and rewrite, to organize and reorganize. You have the chance to polish your text. Electronic writing tools won't *make* you write better, but they will *allow* you to write better.

Facility with these developments is a highly valued skill in the workplace. You should plan to learn how to apply the personal computer to your many business communication tasks. By becoming familiar with the main features of the most popular commercial software products, you increase your value to employers and your own ability to perform your job well.

DISTINGUISHING HARDWARE AND SOFTWARE

Some of the advantages of microcomputers include their portability and versatility. They can be used to collect, analyze, and report data from a variety of locations. Data and results can be transferred electronically to wherever there is a telephone and modem. The personal computer is a multipurpose machine. You can use the same computer to accomplish hundreds of different tasks by using different programs.

---

some electronic abbreviations

CD-ROM	compact disk read-only memory
DTP	desktop publishing
GB	gigabyte (1,000 megabytes; a memory measure)
GUI	graphical user interface (icons and visual images a person uses to manipulate a computer; an operating system design), pronounced *gooey*
K or **KB**	kilobyte (1,000 bytes; a memory measure)

(continued)

LAN	local-area network (for connecting computers)
MB	megabyte (1,000 kilobytes; a memory measure)
MHz	megahertz (a speed measure)
OCR	optical character recognition (for scanners)
RAM	random-access memory (the computer's work area)
ROM	read-only memory (can't be revised)
VGA	video graphics array (describes screen capabilities)

A microcomputer system consists of two mutually dependent parts: hardware and software. *Hardware* is the physical equipment that makes up the computer. Generally this includes a keyboard, a central processing unit (CPU), a monitor, storage and input devices, and a printer. These are the basic physical components of every computer system, from mainframe to laptop.

This hardware will not do anything until you furnish it with data and instructions. These instructions are called programs or *software*. The term *software* refers to the fact that these programs are stored electronically and cannot be physically manipulated and touched, as the hardware can.

There are two general types of software. *System software* refers to programs that control the various computer components, including input/output devices. *Application software* is a set of programs that instruct the computer to carry out particular tasks and operations.

ethical considerations: software and intellectual rights

Respect for intellectual labor and creativity is vital to academic discourse and enterprise. This principle applies to works of all authors and publishers in all media. It encompasses respect for the right to acknowledgment, the right to privacy, and the right to determine the form, manner, and terms of publication and distribution. Because electronic information is volatile and easily reproduced, respect for the work and personal expression of others is especially critical in computer environments. Violations of authorial integrity including plagiarism, invasion of privacy, unauthorized access, and trade secret and copyright violations may be grounds for sanctions against members of the academic community.

Source: EDUCOM and ADAPSO (now The Computer Software and Services Industry). Reprinted with permission.

DISCOVERING SOFTWARE PRODUCTS AND PROGRAMS

In the following sections, we describe a variety of electronic writing tools—software applications designed to improve personal and group communications. We hope you will make the effort to investigate some of these and try them as ways to improve your own writing and presentations.

Word Processors

During the past ten years, personal computers have replaced dedicated word processors, using many different software packages with an astonishing array of features. Word-processing software is the most common application used on microcomputers. While each of these packages has its own advocates, most of them offer similar features and advantages. What you should expect is the ability to display, store, retrieve, and manipulate your text in ways that are not possible with typewriters.

Word processors are particularly useful for any writing task that involves repetition. Writing tasks with repetitive elements—names, addresses, phrases, or summaries—can be automated to save time and effort. Use the computer to free yourself from tedious and time-consuming retyping tasks.

Whether you are updating a proposal, making major revisions on a long report, changing a few words in a memo, or correcting typographical errors, editing is quick and easy with word-processing programs. Correcting spelling, grammar, and sentence structure is fast and simple because you can accomplish it electronically. You can move, delete, and insert text wherever you choose. You can see your changes on the screen as you make them. *Revising* includes operations such as deleting and inserting words, moving paragraphs, and correcting misspellings. *Formatting* includes such operations as changing margins and line spacing, boldfacing, centering, and underlining. Both can be accomplished with just a few keystrokes.

Another advantage to word processing is appearance. You can complete your document before you produce the paper copy. New printers provide crisp, sharp output. You can achieve professional appearance without correction-fluid marks, erasures, or penciled-in changes. Remember, expectations have been elevated because of these new technologies.

Special features included in many word processors can save you time and effort while you polish your finished work. For example, full-featured word processors can automatically number footnotes and make certain that they appear properly formatted on the correct page. Other features allow you to generate an index or table of contents quickly by marking the text to be included from a document. Most of these programs allow you to bring graphic images into your document.

Other features common to word processors can save you an appreciable amount of time. The most fundamental time-saving technique is *boilerplating*—recycling information by using small and large blocks of text over and over again. Text that you have reason to use more than once can be saved in a file and reloaded when necessary. *Merge* capabilities allow you to combine a single form document with a list of names, addresses, and personalized salutations or phrases. You can even record the format and print settings of documents for use again in similar documents.

Word processing is probably the most important application software for you to master. Many business professionals are expected to prepare their own short reports, memos, and letters. Using a word processor can make these tasks simple and routine.

Spell Checkers

New applications of computerized dictionary technology can change the way you write. For example, you can leave your concern for correct spelling aside until you are done creating your text. Then you can run the document through the spell checker and quickly repair your errors. Electronic proofers and computerized dictionary software allow you to find your mistakes and correct them. Most spell checkers offer alternate spellings and display misspelled words in context. Standard options allow you to accept a suggested spelling, type in another spelling, add the flagged word to a personal user dictionary, or continue on.

The quality-control benefits of this tool are considerable, and it is widely available. Spell checkers have gone from add-on, expensive, stand-alone programs to standard features in most word-processing packages. Your own spelling will improve from seeing the corrections on the screen. Even if you are an excellent speller, there is an insurance factor in having your work double-checked by the computer. Spelling mistakes will cost you credibility and may interfere with your message.

What you need to remember is that spell checkers will not recognize correctly spelled but incorrectly used words. Any spell checker is only as good as the contents of the dictionary on which it is based. Words such as *dear* and *deer* can be spelled correctly but used incorrectly. For example, the word *from* is one of the most commonly mistyped

figure **7-1** An example of a spell checker.

words in the English language, but since the usual mistake, *form,* is correctly spelled, this mistake will be overlooked. The spell checker will not help you in such cases. Some programs have *homonym* (sound-alike words) checkers and allow you to suggest alternatives. Regardless, you should plan to proofread your writing even if you use the spell checker. Spelling mistakes will damage your writing and your presentations. Checking your work is a minimal, and required, step for any business document or graphic display.

Online Thesauruses

Keeping a dictionary and a thesaurus on your desk is one way to improve your spelling and vocabulary. Many word-processing packages put both of these tools at your disposal. By providing you with a variety of alternative words, a computerized synonym finder can help you become more clear and precise. Some users find this an excellent way to avoid repetitious word use; others find that it helps them choose the exact word they are looking for. Most of these programs allow you to substitute your synonym for the word you select to replace.

The biggest problem with this tool is that misuse of language can be as damaging to your writing as misspellings. Using a synonym incorrectly can confuse your readers. Some words are trite and overused. Other choices may be old-fashioned, likely to be misused, or inappropriate in a particular context. Language is tricky stuff, particularly when you are translating from one term you are not sure of to another you aren't sure of. Pragmatic word choice requires that you be familiar with the words you choose. Know what your words mean and what they suggest.

Grammar and Style Checkers

Automatic writing analyzers provide immediate, on-screen feedback about possible grammar and style errors. These programs use lists and algorithms to search for mistakes in usage, punctuation, grammar, and style. Some of these programs also provide a summary of your document, offering statistics about word, sentence, and paragraph length, and generating readability levels. Advanced grammar checkers use expert systems to parse the text and discover mistakes in agreement and usage.

One of the difficulties with these programs is their lack of flexibility in applying grammatical and stylistic rules. This software routinely rewards short words, short sentences, and short paragraphs, even when they are inappropriate. Some of the suggestions these programs offer are wrong and misleading. Some grammatical conventions, such as split infinitives, are really questions of style and author's approach. Good writing involves questions of organization, structure, audience, and intent, questions that cause problems for rule-based systems.

In general, we believe that grammar and style checkers will not make significant differences in your writing. They may help you discover crude errors, but careful proofreading will do the same. If you need a computer program to tell you that you are using too many long sentences, then we think you should spend more time looking at what you write.

Outliners

An outliner is a drafting tool to help you organize your document. Your outline can help you decide whether your material is connected, appropriate, and correctly located. Outlines can be sorted, shuffled, and shifted around before the first draft is even created. Stored outlines called *templates* can be used over and over for standardized tasks such as laboratory or progress reports.

Some word processors, and many writing strategies, are designed to use an outline approach. When you are working on multipage documents, it is probably a good idea to begin with a simple outline, even if you use it only as a source for your headings and sub-headings. Outlines are easy to create with computer software.

The biggest advantage of an outline is that it allows you to shuffle information from place to place while you determine your final document design. Most presentation software includes outline utilities. An outline helps you rearrange a random series of notes or slide ideas into an ordered set of ideas grouped by topic and importance. As your ideas develop into a longer outline with more intricate headings and subheadings, you can test your alterations by viewing them immediately.

Current software allows you to cut and paste between different levels of headings. The outline can provide you with a detailed blueprint of your document plan. Many outliners allow you to collapse levels of headings and focus on the overall design. Even if you don't have a software outliner, you can use almost any word processor for this function. The ability to delete and insert allows for easy changes.

Spreadsheets

Spreadsheets are electronic versions of an accountant's ledger. A grid of rows and columns allows you to arrange data in ways that provide a wide variety of business uses. You can enter numbers, labels, and calculations that are mutually connected. Changing a part of the system sends a ripple of fast and accurate recalculations through the entire worksheet. This linkage permits you to test out a variety of business assumptions. For example, you can project sales, costs, and profits over a three-year horizon and then calculate the effects of varying interest rates on your projection. You can get answers to your "What if?" questions, enabling you to compare and contrast different assumptions.

Graphics and data management have been integrated with the basic spreadsheet to provide attractive, easy-to-understand outputs. Graphic presentation programs enable you to represent your information visually, converting your data into a remarkable variety of two- and three-dimensional charts and graphs. Database-management programs store your data as fields and records similarly to a card file, assisting you in creating reports for specific purposes. You can sort and select your data. For instance, you could print out a list of customer names and addresses for people who have spent more than $500 with your business in the last month, converting data into useful marketing information.

It is widely believed that the invention of the spreadsheet led to the widespread adoption of the microcomputer by business and industry. Because spreadsheets are such versatile tools, hundreds of thousands of custom applications have been created by individual users. Many organizations and small businesses have designed models or templates

AutoCorrect

☒ Change 'Straight Quotes' to 'Smart Quotes'
☒ Correct TWo INitial CApitals
☐ Capitalize First Letter of Sentences
☒ Capitalize Names of Days

☒ Replace Text as You Type

Replace: With: ● Plain Text   ○ Formatted Text

	projection

(r)	©
adn	and
don;t	don't
i	I
incl	include
occurence	occurrence

OK
Cancel
Help
Add
Delete

figure 7–2 Some word processors can be set to correct common errors automatically.

into which they plug data. Some common business uses include income and sales analysis, price lists, inventory control, financial projections, and sales databases.

Whatever type of business and commerce interests you, we believe you will discover spreadsheets to be an indispensable tool in your work. As these programs have added features and capabilities, they have become easier to use. You need to become familiar with how they perform. Courses, tutorials, workshops, and videotapes all provide ways for you to learn how to use this powerful tool. The time you put into this effort will be returned to you many times in your future career.

Databases

Databases are collections of records that contain similar types of data. A telephone book is a database. Names of people and organizations are accompanied by addresses and phone numbers. This data can be viewed, sorted, selected, and reported, turning it into information. For example, a customer record is a collection of all the data about that customer, broken into fields: name, account number, address, contact name, and so forth. Records and fields need to be comparable if useful business information is to be obtained.

A database is particularly useful for keeping track of people and things. As with spreadsheets, a list of custom applications would be endless. Some typical business uses include records on employee hiring, salaries, and training; inventories of supplies and equipment; mailing lists; and building and vehicle maintenance lists. Electronic databases are available for everything from mailing lists of magazine subscribers to online product catalogs.

Graphics Software

Graphic images are showing up more frequently in commercial offices, on factory floors, and in business training. Personal computers make it possible and affordable for you to provide illustrations to accompany your documents and presentations. Desktop scanners, symbol libraries, and clip-art disks are easy to use and increasingly inexpensive. Output devices such as laser printers, color plotters, and slide makers are widely available in many companies and through service bureaus.

In the last few years, the quality of graphics generated on personal computers has moved from being merely functional to having boardroom appeal. More and more frequently, the responsibility for producing text charts and simple data charts falls directly on the person who will be using them. It is likely that you will be involved in creating at least some of the illustrations you will use.

Remember, it takes time to turn your ideas into symbols that work. Creating text charts and other simple graphics can help you think your ideas through, but careful consideration is essential. Restraint is the secret of good graphics. Don't get carried away with all the options in the program. Mechanical ability needs to be supported with design and layout skills. Keep your graphics simple and easy to understand. One advantage to doing it yourself is that you can make changes up to the last minute.

Another thing to remember is that good graphics can't save a poorly thought-out and badly organized presentation or document. Instead, the graphics will display the flaws in a way that draws full attention. Your images should support what you say, not compete with your message.

Text charts can reinforce your key points. They also double as a script for your presentation, keeping you relaxed, focused, and comfortable. Keep your charts consistent. Stay with the same facts and the same style throughout. Keep data-driven charts simple, or comparisons and significance will be lost. Don't clutter your images with unnecessary information.

Desktop Publishing Software

Desktop publishing software provides page design applications that can turn reports and memos into professional-looking documents that include graphics, captions, type in various fonts and sizes, and flowing columns of neatly proportioned text. This software is useful for flyers, newsletters, proposals, brochures, and other types of professional publications.

Desktop publishing software is part of a spectrum that extends from powerful graphics-capable word processors to extremely sophisticated page composition systems. There are entry-level products that can be used by beginners and full-fledged electronic publishing systems. These advanced systems allow you to design and produce complex, graphically rich documents in an interactive mode; you can see exactly what you are doing as you make changes in your document. These programs can provide input to a high-resolution imagesetter, allowing for professional quality.

Don't begin with a package that is too sophisticated for what you need. A good word-processing package with font and graphics support will allow you to merge text and graphics on the same page. This is enough for most simple documents.

Presentation Software

With currently available software you can use a personal computer to design and produce all four important presentation formats: paper, overheads, slides, and video. A polished presentation will generate interest and create understanding. Pictures provide a quick translation from numbers and ideas, and they help to focus your audience's attention on important information.

You can use *paper* images to create interesting handouts with a crisp, professional appearance. One advantage to paper presentations is that they can be delivered to people who were unable to attend the meeting. They also make an effective supplement to your slides or overheads. Unlike projected images, a paper graph can be accompanied with as much explanation as you want to include. Use handouts to emphasize key points and serve as reminders to your audience.

You can include the output from graphics software in paper presentations or photocopy it onto transparent sheets for use with overhead projectors. *Overheads* are a convenient and inexpensive presentation tool, with projectors available in most companies and business locations. Some software provides predesigned templates for bulleted charts, title charts and other common chart types discussed more fully in Chapter 13. You enter your data and the program supplies large-scale lettering and punctuation symbols. Color overheads are more and more common as software capabilities improve and color printers and photocopiers become available.

Remember, the quality of your presentations will reflect the quality of your product or service. Hand-sketched graphs or dirty overheads will not help your credibility. Keep your overheads simple and to the point. They are used to amplify and echo your spoken words, not to replace them. Make sure that the text is big enough for everyone in the room to read. Overheads work best with fewer than 50 people. With a larger audience, you should use slides.

Color slides are a versatile and portable presentation format, suitable for large and small meetings. Slide projectors are standard equipment in many business organizations. Graphics that you have created on your personal computer can be captured on film and developed into color slides. Major graphics software packages usually offer service bureaus to provide slides. Since you design the visuals, the cost is lower than that of commercial preparation.

Some graphics packages allow you to simulate a slide show on the computer screen. Special projectors allow these images to be shown on a large screen. This software typically lets you use special effects as you move from one image to another. Again, restraint will have a positive effect. Some features can distract your audience and cause them to wonder what your next effect will be instead of concentrating on your message. Keep it simple. You don't want your visual supports to compete with you.

Finally, you have the option of using one of the new animated *video* presentation packages where you can create the illusion of motion within and between your graphic images. Animation offers an exciting visual element. Some people make video copies of their computer-generated graphics to show with a VCR. Digitized video is developing quite rapidly and will become common in the next few years.

Whether you choose paper overheads, slides, or video, the personal computer can help you maintain an image of quality and professionalism. Remember, though, that a poorly prepared, inadequate presentation will not be saved by flashy graphics. Instead, you will call attention to the flaws.

Other Business Software

A whole variety of computer-aided communication tools have elevated standards for everything from the appearance of correspondence to the visual quality of business reports and presentations. We encourage you to learn to take advantage of the full range of these technologies. At the same time, we want you to realize that many of these programs have very steep learning curves. This means you will have to expend a good deal of time and effort before you become productive with them. Begin with applications that you can use in your current situation, whether you are going to school or working or both. Software that can help you do your job is easier to practice and learn on a daily basis. As a general rule, it is easier to learn the features of any software product when you have a specific task to accomplish.

Some people will tell you that writing with a computer will save time. We don't claim this. Certainly you can accomplish some tasks more quickly and easily with a computer, but your capacity to do more may make your task more complex. Your increased ability to accomplish high-level tasks such as editing, reorganizing, and illustrating may lead to more work as you push for perfection.

What we *can* assure you is that the professional appearance of your work will be noticed. Appearance communicates design, organization, care, importance, and credibility to your audience. You can make your documents look as good as your ideas by learning to use electronic tools.

what is the internet?

The Internet is a global network of computer networks.

What uses can you make of the Internet? One of the first and most practical uses is information. The Net functions as a round-the-clock library system for globally distributed information. It also serves as a government information service for national governments, as well as local. Almost every city and town has some sort of presence on the Internet where you can obtain information on everything from taxes to population statistics and census data.

A second practical use is communication. The Internet functions as a continuous communications system you can use to transmit all kinds of messages ranging from simple text to graphics to sound to video, to animations and interactive multimedia displays. You can communicate with people throughout the planet by connecting to the Internet and using its common communications technologies.

The Internet has many business uses. Increasingly, it is being used for commercial transactions. In the future, the Internet will be a global marketplace

(Continued)

where commercial transactions are commonplace. It is also being used more and more as a business and corporate communications medium. There are few businesses which do not have some sort of presence on the Internet. Using the Internet requires that you have the following:

- Your computer network or computer itself must have the necessary electronic linkage to the Internet. Most schools and colleges provide access to the Internet. You can use a commercial service or a local access provider to link you by modem from your home or office. Most public libraries provide Internet gateways and there are even cyber-cafes where you can log on from your table.
- Your computer must use software (browsers) which will link you to various sites on the Net. These browsers are available free from Internet access providers and you can download future upgrades as they occur.

The World Wide Web provides powerful search capabilities which make it a popular research site. You can retrieve photographs, maps, and illustrations. Whether you are looking for information on automobile prices, weather reports from South Africa, or the latest pictures from Mars, the Web is the place to begin. A color monitor, graphics capability, and a mouse are required, but these are standard items in all new computers.

Whatever your field of interest, the Internet will have something for you. While you are in school, it is a good idea to explore the Net. What you learn will make you more valuable to employers in the future.

LEARNING ABOUT NEW INFORMATION TECHNOLOGIES

A host of new products and services are now available as a result of the development of ways to link computers together. The organization you work for may be connected through an in-house network or may be connected outside of the organization to a wide variety of general and specialized information sources. We cover a number of the more popular new information technologies in the following sections.

Online Information Services

Online databases are one of the new information technologies that make it possible for you to access technical and business data electronically. For example, you can search the *Readers' Guide to Periodical Literature,* check for recent stock market quotations, or make airline and hotel reservations.

Information-retrieval services such as BRS (www.BRS.com), Dialog (www.dialog.com), and Internet (www.Internet.com) provide commercial access to hundreds of databases. These encyclopedic enterprises attempt to provide a gateway to a comprehensive collection of information files, with an emphasis on business, technical, and professional interests. Narrowly focused databases can provide information on such specialized subjects as health service plans or insurance providers.

You should prepare before you use these services. Practice with local bulletin board systems to master the basics of logging on, downloading and uploading, and moving around the system before you experience the connect-time charges of commercial online services. Become familiar with the commands and overall structure of the service before you log on. Online systems will become familiar and routine if you use them regularly.

Groupware

Groupware is computer software designed to support task-oriented project teams in business and technical activities. Users located in different parts of a building or different parts of the world can work together almost as closely as if they were sitting at the same desk. There are new group writing, group communications, and group productivity tools. Electronic meeting rooms use same-time/same-place groupware designed to improve face-to-face meetings. All of these programs are designed to help people work together in more productive and effective ways.

Portable computers and laptops allow for *telecommuters,* persons who work from a distance, to participate in file sharing from many different locations. Workgroup software makes the editing process easier because only a single document is accessed by the group. This software allows you to keep track of changes made and also numbers the revision cycles for easy reference.

Bulletin Board Systems

Bulletin board systems (BBSs) allow users to call a central *file server* where they can leave messages, transfer files, and carry on real-time conversations. You need a personal computer and a modem to access these systems. These boards offer electronic mail, interactive forums, public-domain and shareware programs, and other services.

Some companies have found electronic bulletin boards to be a practical and inexpensive way to provide up-to-date product information. Customers can leave questions and problems in the mail system and expect to receive an expert answer within a day or two. Technical forums allow customers to make suggestions for future product upgrades and to share problems and solutions they have encountered. Remote field-site employees can send a message or leave a request at any time convenient to them.

USING ELECTRONIC TOOLS: EXERCISES

1. The following data show the increase in online databases available for electronic distribution of information:

Year	Number of Databases
1980	400
1986	2901
1987	3369
1988	3699
1989	4062
1990	4465

Source: Directory of Online Databases.

What conclusions can you draw from the data? With a personal computer, design a sample graph that illustrates your results. If your library has the *Directory of Online Databases,* find more up-to-date statistics. Will online databases continue to be popular as more and more people use the Internet?

2. Small groups of students or participants should work together on this exercise. Each group should create lists of ten words you think will stump the electronic thesaurus. What generalizations can you draw after testing your lists? What kinds of failures did you find? Were there any surprises? Compare your lists with the lists produced by other groups.

3. Create a three-level outline for a long report on the topic of computer access for the disabled. Show your outline to other people in your group and ask for suggestions. Revise your first outline by cutting and pasting. Then compare the two outlines.

4. If you have access to a personal computer with a modem, try logging on to a BBS (bulletin board system) in your local area. Bring some screen dumps (printouts of the contents of the screen) to class to show others what the system offers.

5. Sandy Pascal called Loretta Cedrone this morning and asked her whether Pascal Business Systems was using shareware programs. A friend of Ms. Pascal's showed her some very useful software which was available at very low cost. Ms. Pascal wants a short report from your Special Projects group in response to this question: What shareware programs are available that could benefit Pascal Business Systems? (Try www.shareware.com for information.)

6. See Exercise 5 before completing this exercise.

   Ms. Pascal called back this morning. She was impressed with your short report. She wants to make a decision today, and would like a memo from you describing your sources of information for the report. She wants to be sure that it is reliable information.

7. Pascal Business Systems has been invited to make a presentation to the Ministry of Development in Cozumel, Mexico. What computer equipment will we be able to use in the hotels there? What is the availability of audiovisual equipment? Will we encounter compatibility problems? Check all of this out. Report by memo to Michael Benevento as soon as possible.

8. Choose a document that you have designed and print it out in three different fonts. How does the communication change with the change in type style?

9. Choose three different short documents and put them through a grammar or style checker. Write a short report to your instructor summarizing the response of the software program. Add a discussion section to your report: Do you think it is worth the time and expense to use this program? Do you think this software would be useful to you or to your organization?

SURVEYING YOUR SOURCES: READING AND RESEARCH

8

Reading on the Job

Improving Your Reading Skills
Prereading
Formulating Questions
Clumping
Taking Notes
Seeing Patterns
Looking for Specifics
Considering Context
Reading Illustrations
Skimming

Finding Time to Read

Conducting Research

Why We Need to Do Research

Utilizing the Library
Books
Periodicals
Reference Works
Online Databases
The Internet

Searching Company Records

Using Nonprint Media

Gaining Perspective on Reading and Research

Some people, even successful businesspeople, view reading and research as an unproductive use of time. They think that while they are reading, they are not producing anything. They also think that research is simply a means to an end; the document they will create when they have completed the research is the only important thing, the tangible end product of their labor. We would, however, encourage you to think of reading and research as something different: as a particularly productive use of your time, as a time when you develop the ideas that will drive your career, as end products in themselves.

Reading and research are inextricably linked. We have divided them in this chapter purely for organizational reasons. While you certainly acquire information in ways other than reading, such as listening and viewing, reading may be now—and may become—the primary way you receive and retain information in your career. Reading requires an active mind; while there may be "nothing new under the sun," insights, inventions, and solutions to problems result from new ways of envisioning information. This chapter attempts to give you an overview of some of the resources at your disposal.

READING ON THE JOB

If you are serious about developing a career as a business professional, reading will be a regular part of your job. People in professional positions depend on reading as a way of keeping up with key developments and trends in their fields. They also rely on reading to keep them in touch with the activities of their project team and the rest of their organization.

Reading business documents can be difficult work. You have to extract information and organize it so it will be useful. You need to use different strategies for different reading tasks. You have to shift your attention between numbers and words. Sometimes you will have to puzzle your way through a poorly written document, trying to figure out what the writer intended. What makes this even more difficult is that you will need to get through lots of business reading but you will never have enough time.

Reading business materials effectively, with speed and comprehension, requires a wide range of skills and techniques that can be mastered only by practice and use. The further you progress in your business profession, the more you will be asked to read and evaluate recommendations, reports, and marketing and sales proposals.

The activity of reading business materials means taking in the sense of the words and illustrations you are looking at and understanding what these documents mean, not simply looking at them. Reading is one of the most common and frequent tasks performed by business professionals, yet it is seldom considered in employment interviews or referred to in job descriptions. It is assumed, often without justification, that business professionals will know how to read efficiently.

It is highly likely that you will be involved in communicating information: collecting, storing, retrieving, handling, and distributing written material. What you need to remember is that people have to read most of this information, extract the data they need, and organize it in some useful fashion. Different people will read the same document in different ways, because they have different needs, different levels of expertise, and different responsibilities. Some of these people will be reading for overall meaning, while others will be searching for specific information. All of these people will need to grasp, understand, and remember what they are reading.

IMPROVING YOUR READING SKILLS

Reading for work is different than reading for pleasure, diversion, or entertainment. The suggestions we make in this chapter are not designed for reading the sports or hobby pages of your favorite newspaper or magazine. They are designed to help you approach business reading with systematic, logical techniques that will increase your ability to grasp and use what you read.

Prereading

Prereading is a technique in which you use every resource of the text to help you efficiently process the information it contains. By becoming familiar with the organization, key words, and general plan of the document, you increase your chances of understanding and retaining what you read. Prereading involves a general review of the text before you read from beginning to end.

Read the table of contents and any other introductory material, and then scan the index looking for familiar terms, distribution of topics, and key terms. Headings and subheadings indicate relationships among different topics. Flip through the text and quickly look at the illustrations, reading the captions. What you are trying to do is to build a mental map of the text, so as you read specifics you will have a place to locate them.

Formulating Questions

Avoid mechanical, monotonous reading by focusing your attention with questions. If you are looking for specific answers, you will find it easier to maintain your interest in what you are reading. If you know what you are trying to find, it will be more recognizable when you encounter it.

Begin the reading task by defining your purpose. It helps to know why you are reading something. What do you want to know or do after reading the material? Secondly, consider the sender: Who wrote the message or sent it? Is he or she looking for a particular response from you?

Clumping

A very important skill you should work to acquire is the ability to grasp information from groups of words rather than from one word at a time. Two suggestions:

- Train yourself to look at more than one or two words at a glance. Look for chunks of words, or blocks of text.
- Practice reading for sense rather than sound. Grasp for the idea, not the details. Go back for the details later.

Taking Notes

Make notes as you read. Your notes can include key words and phrases, headings and subheadings, concise summaries, simple diagrams or sketches—whatever will help you organize and use the information. Many people make the notes on the document itself, marking it up and highlighting key information.

The effort of making the notes will reinforce your memory of what you are reading, and it will help you to make discriminations between what is important and what is not. The notes will help you review and refresh your knowledge of the material later.

Seeing Patterns

Another useful technique is to read for patterns. Try to remember this number quickly:

1491625364964

This is a lot easier to do when you recognize the series as the squares of one through eight ($1^2 - 8^2$). Information is easier to remember and understand when you know how it is organized. Frequently a complex business document can be broken down into a list of details and subcategories, but only when you realize how the material is classified and organized. Use chapter titles, headers and footers, headings, and highlights to look for patterns in the information.

Looking for Specifics

It is important to consider how much of the information you actually need. If you are looking for specific information, can you go directly to it? The index and table of contents may be able to guide you directly to what you want to find. Ask yourself if you can get what you need from reading selections instead of the whole text. By confining your search to the specific information you need, you can save time and effort.

Considering Context

If you want to keep current with business developments in your own and related areas, find out what new products and services are offered, and get an overview or context for your work, developing a reading list of the important magazines, newsletters, and journals in your field. Regular reading is an important way for business professionals to keep up with current developments in their fields. Many professional organizations provide periodicals and journals of special interest to their members. These magazines keep you informed about people, products, services, and trends in the industry in which you are employed.

We strongly recommend that you subscribe to several professional journals, even if you are still in school. You will get the opportunity to read the words of your fellow busi-

ness professionals. You will be developing a sense of context, building your sense of standards and what is appropriate, and responding to the written voices of your peers. If you
actively read and pursue the ideas and suggestions in what you read, you will become a
better employee and your job will stay a challenge instead of a chore.

Reading Illustrations

Some people are quite comfortable reading text, but they avoid illustrations because they
find them confusing and frustrating to decipher and interpret. This is unfortunate, because
if they are used correctly, graphics can add a great deal to the understanding of a written
explanation.

   One of the chief difficulties of reading illustrations is the effort of switching between reading numbers and reading text. Read the text first, including all labels and captions. This will help you to make sense of the graphics and numerical information. A systematic, problem-solving approach will enable you to figure out what each illustration
means.

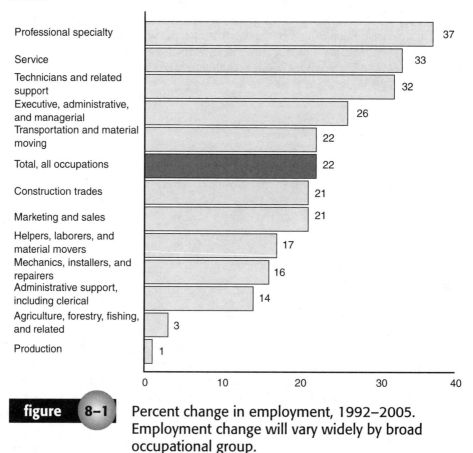

figure **8-1**   Percent change in employment, 1992–2005.
Employment change will vary widely by broad
occupational group.

Reprinted with the permission of the Bureau of Labor Statistics.

Skimming

Frequently you will be called on to read reports, journal articles, technical directions, and other short documents. Begin by skimming the text. Read the first and last paragraphs. The introduction and conclusion provide valuable summaries. Then quickly read the first sentence of every paragraph. This will help you get oriented to the material and provide a framework for the information you are reading.

FINDING TIME TO READ

Don't let your reading tasks become a gray blur of rushed responsibilities. Set aside a regular and sufficient time to accomplish your reading, time where you will not be interrupted. Reading is as much a part of your work as anything else you are required to do. Treat this task as important and plan to do it right.

Prioritize your reading. Make a list of the reading tasks you do on a regular basis. Don't forget to include mail, company memos, professional journals, and trade publications. Decide when you will do this work, and in what order. Reading is a task that must be managed carefully, just as any other business activity needs to be managed. You may discover that you will have to read at home as your responsibilities become more time-consuming and complex.

---

learning about speed-reading

If you want to read more quickly, you have to read more quickly. This sentence isn't a mistake. It represents the simple truth about speed-reading. You are the one who is doing the reading. Only you can speed up your reading.

In order to read more quickly, you have to read faster. The first and most important step is to begin to make the effort to read faster. Try to read faster, and you will read faster.

You need to remember that different materials are read at different rates of speed. A long-term lease deserves more careful examination than the instructions for installing the paper cups in the distribution device. You don't want to speed-read when you are reviewing the applicant qualifications for a major contract. On the other hand, you don't want to dawdle over routine, repetitious information.

The more familiar you are with a topic, the more quickly you will be able to read information about that topic. Familiarity supplies the context that we need for the easy acquisition of business information. When you are reading business material, you want to discover the essential message, the main idea. You also want to judge, reliably and quickly, whether this idea is supported sufficiently to be credible. The more familiar you are with the topics discussed, the more easily you will accomplish this task.

Can ignoring your reading be dangerous? Yes. Consider the fate of John LaPlante, acting transportation commissioner of Chicago, who was fired by Mayor Richard M. Daley in April of 1992 because he ignored a memo from the city's chief bridge engineer that warned him that a 6-by-20-foot crack in a wall of a tunnel under the Chicago River should be repaired immediately; the memo noted the potential danger of flooding the entire tunnel system. The tunnel wall did fail and millions of gallons of water flooded the Loop district and paralyzed the business operations of Chicago for a number of days. (Nordgren, 3)

CONDUCTING RESEARCH

When you approach any communication task, you either know all you intend to communicate, or need to find out something to include. Many times you will conduct research to find out information.

Research does not necessarily mean going to the library to search through books and magazines. It can also mean picking up the phone to call a colleague to get the exact date, time, and location for a meeting. It can mean walking down the corridor and asking someone for the exact amount paid for a shipment of replacement parts. It can mean accessing a computer file for the specifications of a product your company manufactures. In this sense, we are conducting research every day of our lives. When we need to know something, we find it out.

If you are like many people, the word *research* may cause you to feel anxiety or boredom. You perceive research to be a turn-off, a long and tedious process that should be avoided whenever possible. Research can be time-consuming and it can be tedious, but it can also be exciting and rewarding. Research is discovery. The process of writing down our ideas forces us to check our statements, and by so doing sharpens our thinking. There are magical moments when you can lose your sense of time in the quest for information. And, the more research you do and the more familiar you become with your sources of information, the more exciting the search becomes.

WHY WE NEED TO DO RESEARCH

Writing must be clear and accurate. We must ensure that our writing is accurate by verifying our information. Doing research to obtain expert opinion is crucial to the process of writing or speaking about technical matters.

We live in a time when we have more research options than ever before. The following are some of the ways we conduct research to get the information we need:

- conducting experiments
- interviewing people with information (using the telephone, speaking face to face, sending letters of inquiry, and so forth)
- gathering information from surveys and polls

- using college and local libraries (asking the reference librarians; employing the card catalog; finding periodicals, including journals, magazines, and newspapers; consulting reference books; conducting online searches of databases)
- searching the Internet
- using company libraries and reference librarians
- searching company records (checking file cabinets and computer files; examining other internal records in reports, memos, and letters)
- viewing screen images and hearing recorded sounds, including visuals, videotapes, movies, radio, taped messages, television, computers, and newer media.

With such a vast range of information sources, it is no wonder that this period is being referred to as the Information Age. The better you are at gaining access to this wealth of information, the more success you will achieve. While this text cannot possibly discuss all of the different information sources at your disposal, we do present some of the more common ones.

UTILIZING THE LIBRARY

Business professionals need the ability to enter a library and quickly locate specific material. However, it can be somewhat intimidating to walk into a library for the first time. You may feel out of place in unfamiliar surroundings. In time, however, as you begin to know the physical layout of the library and how to access information, you will become more comfortable, and you will make discoveries about what materials can be found there. For this reason, you may want to visit your reference library on a regular basis.

What can you find there? First, you can find reference librarians who know the library facilities and are very willing to help you. They will take the time to work with you in your investigation. You will find books, magazines, journals, newspapers, and general and specialized reference material. You may also find videotapes and audiotapes. And you may be able to access information that exists in other libraries through computerized databases.

Books

A collection of books on a vast array of subjects is the foundation of a library. Information on the book collection is stored in a *card catalog,* which can be organized in one of two ways: the Library of Congress system and the Dewey Decimal system. College and university libraries use the Library of Congress system, while public libraries use the Dewey Decimal system. The Library of Congress system divides books into 20 categories identified by a letter followed by specific numbers; the Dewey Decimal system divides books into 10 categories identified by numbers. Under both systems, each book has an individual call number to help you locate it on the shelves.

While some libraries still have actual cards with the data on the book collection, most libraries have gone to computerized card catalogs. You conduct a search by entering certain key words, and the computer will search its memory and locate the material for

The Dewey Decimal System		*The Library of Congress System*	
000–099	General works	A	General works
100–199	Philosophy	B	Philosophy, religion
200–299	Religion	C	History, auxiliary sciences
300–399	Social sciences	D	Foreign history, topography
400–499	Philology	E–F	American history
500–599	Pure science	G	Geography
600–699	Useful arts	H	Social sciences
700–799	Fine arts	J	Political sciences
800–899	Literature	K	Law
900–999	History	M	Music
		P	Language and literature
Each of these divisions is further divided into ten parts. Each division is further divided, and so on to form the specific call number of a book.		Q	Science
		R	Medicine
		S	Agriculture
		T	Technology
		U	Military science
		V	Naval science
		Z	Bibliography
		Each of these sections is divided by letter and numbers to form the specific call number of a book.	

you. With either a computerized or a card system, you can locate books by title, subject, and author. Many libraries now utilize interlibrary loans so that you can have books located at other libraries delivered to your library.

Periodicals

The term *periodicals* refers to any publication that is published in intervals, or in periods, such as monthly or quarterly. (The intervals need not be evenly spaced.) Therefore, magazines, journals, bulletins, newsletters, fact sheets, and newspapers qualify as periodicals.

Three Examples of Searches Conducted with a Computerized Card Catalog	
T=The soul of a new machine	(T=Title)
S=computer engineering	(S=Subject)
A=Kidder, Tracy	(A=Author)
Note: The card catalog is frequently where audiovisual material is filed.	

The main advantage of periodicals is that they are current. While a book takes time to get published, a recent periodical will likely contain up-to-date information. In many specialized fields, staying current is a priority. If you fall behind, you lose your competitive edge. If, for example, your company depends on government funding for which you submit bids and proposals, you need to be informed as soon as possible after a project is announced.

Most libraries have a current periodicals section, where you can locate very recent issues of the periodicals to which the library subscribes. Back issues (usually twelve months old or more) are stored on shelves or transferred to film where they are substantially reduced in size. Most college libraries have specialized periodicals in the fields where students have degree programs.

If you are researching a specific subject and you would like current material, a productive approach is to check general and specialized periodical indexes. The indexes organize articles from a variety of periodicals according to subject. A list of the periodicals compiled by an index and the abbreviations for each periodical can usually be found in the front of the index. Here are the names of some of the many indexes you may find helpful.

General indexes:
  Readers' Guide to Periodical Literature (H. W. Wilson)
  Humanities Index (H. W. Wilson)
  General Science Index (H. W. Wilson)

More specialized indexes:
  Business Periodicals Index (H. W. Wilson)
  Wall Street Journal Index (University Microfilms)
  Canadian Business Index (Micromedia Ltd.)
  Harvard Business Review (John Wiley & Sons)
  Applied Science and Technology Index (H. W. Wilson)

---

ethical considerations

It is ethically and often legally wrong to include someone else's words, ideas, or data as your own work without credit to your source. You need to acknowledge your sources through appropriate references, including parentheses, endnotes, and footnotes. You must let your audience know when you are directly quoting material by using quotation marks for shorter quotes and indentation for longer quotes (more than 50 words). Even when you paraphrase a person's idea, opinion, or theory in your own words, you should indicate the original source of the material.

A *bibliography* is a separate alphabetized list of all of the sources you consulted in assembling the document. A *"Works Cited"* list details the sources actually referenced in the document.

>   *Engineering Index Monthly* (Engineering Information, Inc.)
>   *Social Sciences Index* (H. W. Wilson)

Abstract indexes can help you save time because they provide you with a summary of each article along with the title, author, and details about the article.

Some indexes are accessed through a computer terminal. For example, ABI/INFORM is a computerized database that covers approximately 800 journals—all English-language—stored on a CD-ROM. You can conduct a search for material organized by subject by entering key words and phrases and receive information about articles, including a significant number with the full text. Many of the general and specialized indexes listed here are also available in CD-ROM and on the Internet.

Reference Works

Most libraries have reference sections where you can find a wide range of general and specialized sources: everything from telephone books, business guides, general encyclopedias, and atlases to specialized handbooks, encyclopedias, and dictionaries. The material in this section cannot be taken from the library. Since the material in your library will be varied, you should walk the aisles to get a sense of what is available. You will find most reference sections organized from general to specific.

Here are some specialized sources that you may find valuable:

The Thomas Register of American Manufacturers (Thomas Publishing Company, New York; published annually) contains alphabetical listings of products and services, and company profiles with addresses and telephone numbers. A product index and a brand names index are included.

U.S. Industrial Outlook (U.S. Department of Commerce, International Trade Administration) has business forecasts for 350 industries.

U.S. Industrial Directory (Reed International, Stamford, Connecticut) compiles product directories and company directories for industrial companies.

The Directory of Federal Laboratory & Technology Resources: Guide to Expertise, Facilities and Services (National Technical Information Services, Springfield, Virginia) lists federal laboratories that will share expertise and equipment. The directory includes subject, state, resource name, and agency indexes.

The Monthly Catalog of U.S. Government Publications (U.S. Government Printing Office) lists federal publications, which are indexed by author, title, subject, series, and classification number.

The Macmillan Visual Dictionary (Macmillan Publishing Company, New York) uses graphic representations, many in color, instead of written definitions of words and terms.

As you become more experienced in a particular field, you will want to progress from general reference works to more specialized texts. Most business fields have specialized handbooks, encyclopedias, and dictionaries, such as the *McGraw-Hill Encyclopedia of Economics* (McGraw-Hill) and *The Source Book of Franchise Opportunities* (Dow Jones–Irwin).

Online Databases

Most libraries now have substantial online database facilities. The databases allow users to tap into computerized networks and retrieve information from sources that would far exceed the physical capabilities of most libraries. While database searches can be very helpful, they are also very costly, so consider them only for large and significant research projects.

You will need to work closely with a librarian to prepare for your search. You will use key words and terms to begin your search, so spend time carefully deciding which key words to choose. You will receive a printout of the findings of the search.

The Internet

The Internet is clearly the information resource of the future. It allows quick and easy access to a host of options. Connect to the World Wide Web and you are in a virtual library stocked with up-to-the-minute information from anywhere in the world.

SEARCHING COMPANY RECORDS

Virtually all companies keep files. These files form a history of the business matters of the company: records of business transactions and decisions, the minutes of meetings, company policies and rules, annual and quarterly reports, descriptions of projects, and so forth. Important documents may be centrally located in a company library staffed by professional librarians, or they may be spread throughout the organization in file cabinets and on computer disks.

---

research sites on the web

U.S. Library of Congress
http://lcweb.loc.gov/homepage/lchp.html

Free On-Line Dictionary of Computing
http://wombat.doc.ic.ac.uk/

Reference Shelf
http://www.nova.edu/Inter-Links/reference.html

U.S. Census Bureau
http://www.census.gov

Wherever you work, you should have an understanding of the filing system, and you should know how to access the information you need. Knowing what was done and how it was done can save you time and help you avoid errors.

USING NONPRINT MEDIA

Many individuals limit themselves to the printed word when they are gathering information, perhaps because of a bias against nonprint resources. This bias is gradually being erased as more options become available to us, and as we realize that nonprint media can inform us and entertain us. We can gain important information from a television program, for example, as long as we proceed carefully and do not trust our memories to capture each fact. (Transcripts of many television shows are available for purchase.)

We recommend that you take accurate notes as you watch or listen. You may want to contact the station or company responsible for the program to verify key information. Playback features on videocassette recorders allow you to view important or complex material on a videotape many times. Accuracy and precision are crucial when we use nonprint media.

GAINING PERSPECTIVE ON READING AND RESEARCH

The world is much too complex for any one individual to know everything; in fact, no one can know all there is to know about any one field. Since we are unable to know all, we should know how to access information when we need it. We learn about the world by doing research, whether it involves asking a friend for advice on how to repair a part in your car's engine or traveling to a library to consult a specialized reference work. Much of the research you will do will entail reading and processing what you have found. The more you can build your ability to draw accurate, appropriate conclusions from what you read, the more valuable you will be to an organization.

READING AND RESEARCH: EXERCISES

1. Bring three magazine articles to class. Choose one that is below your reading level, one that is above, and one that you find appropriate. Examine the three articles and explain what criteria you used to place them at a particular level of difficulty.

2. Figure out how much reading you need to do on a weekly basis. Write down a brief description of the strategies you use—or intend to use—on a regular basis.

3. Choose an article from a professional journal and read only the first and last paragraphs, and then the first sentence of every paragraph. Did you get a good sense of what the article had to say? Experiment with this technique on different types of reading material.

4. Examine the following illustration carefully. Given the general nature of the graph, who is the intended audience? What organization conducted the survey? What questions did they ask? What were they trying to discover? What is the main idea of the illustration? What are some other implications that you can draw from the information presented in the graphic? Send your answers to these questions in a memo to your instructor.

The Perceived Value of Vacations

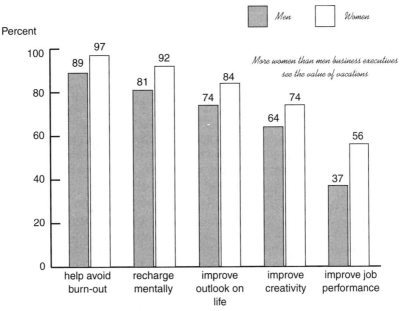

Source: Hyatt Hotels and Resorts

5. Find out how electrical units are measured in Europe. Write a memo explaining how conversions are done.

6. Write a one-page summary of the life and accomplishments of Thomas J. Watson, Sr.

7. Make a list of reference works in your area of study contained in the library most available to you. Group the list into a general category and a specialized category.

8. The following is a list of short-answer questions that will test your ability to utilize the resources available in a library.

(a) Who was Antoine Lavoisier?

(b) How often is the *Readers' Guide to Periodical Literature* published?

(c) What is the address of the U.S. Patent Office? What does the office do?

(d) Who are the two U.S. senators from New Mexico?

(e) What is the definition of *parallax view?*

(f) Where can you find a topographical map of California? Be specific; include the name of the reference and the page number.

(g) What was on the cover of *Time* magazine in the issue dated in the first week of June in the most recent year?

(h) What was the temperature range in Paris, France, last Thursday? _____high _____low

(i) Where was Buckminster Fuller born? Who, briefly, was he?

(j) Explain the significance of the *Enola Gay.*

(k) What is haggis?

(l) What is the official language of Kenya?

(m) What is the population of Sweden?

(n) What nation currently has the highest per-capita income? What is the income? (Make sure you record the year and the source of the statistics you are using.)

(o) What is the world's busiest airport?

section 3
COMMUNICATING IN YOUR ORGANIZATION

In this section we offer practical advice on producing the documents and presentations you will be responsible for on the job: memos, business letters, short reports, presentations, and graphics. You may at some time in your career have a week where you need to do all five different tasks. (Graphics could be designed to stand alone or to be inserted within documents and presentations.)

In most organizations, you will be evaluated on what you produce: business communications that you design and distribute within and outside your organization to inform, persuade, and perhaps motivate co-workers, current and prospective clients, government agencies, and sometimes rival organizations. The business tasks discussed in this section may represent the bulk of the work you will do during your career. Your career will be greatly helped by your ability to complete these tasks accurately, on time, and well.

COMMUNICATING WITH MEMOS

9

Many memos are written to make clear what was already written in a previous memo. Poorly designed memos create increased document costs and a less productive workforce. This chapter will provide you with techniques to reduce the time you spend writing memos and increase their effectiveness. You will learn strategies and techniques that can be applied to a variety of memo tasks, including requests for information, short reports, reminders, and statements of company policy.

DESIGNING EFFECTIVE MEMOS

A *memo* is a document designed to pass information between people and departments within an organization. Memos are used to make readers aware of something, to offer instruction, to prompt action, and to serve as reminders. They are vital to the smooth operation of a business organization.

It is important for you to remember that memos are designed as in-house documents. They are written for and to people *within* a company or organization. They provide a written record and history of company decisions, of alternatives considered, and of responsibility for actions. More frequently they are used to tell people in the company about a new policy or product or even a new place for the company picnic.

Within organizations that have more than just a few employees, it is impossible for all information to be shared in face-to-face meetings. Even if it were possible, some information is too important to be trusted to memory. It makes more sense to send one written memo to 20 employees than to spend an entire day going to see 20 people.

In business and industry, "put it in writing" is common practice. The memo is second only to the telephone in terms of modern business communication and the sharing of information.

Here, for example, is a typical memo:

To: June Joseph
From: Mike Benevento
Subject: October Catalog Storyboard
Date: June 17, 1998

The October Catalog Group will meet in my office on Friday morning at 10. We will do a walkthrough of the storyboard with Sandy, so bring any thumbnails you have on file.

I told Sandy that you would bring copies of the layouts and draft copy for the magazine ads. Please review this material with me before Thursday noon.

This document, like any other, tells a lot about itself. For instance, you notice that the style is less elaborate than a letter. There is no Dear Ms. Joseph, just a simple *To:*. Because this document is intended to communicate within an organization, there is no need for formality. Workplace terms (*storyboard, walkthrough*) can be used without explanation. Communication is very direct.

Notice how Mike uses his nickname, something he ordinarily would not use in documents intended for people outside of the company. We also notice that Mike is giving June the instructions as to what he wants done and the time by which he expects it completed. This says something about Mike and June and their positions within the company hierarchy.

When to Write a Memo

A good time to write a memo is when you want to do one of the things in the following list and you need to have a written record of your having done so.

- *Confirm*—You can use a memo to confirm the details of a meeting, conversation, or telephone call. Your purpose is to have a written record of decisions that were made or promises that were given.
- *Suggest*—You can use a memo to recommend solutions to business problems, to offer your services or those of your department, or to bring up new ideas or ways of doing things.
- *Request*—Use a memo to ask for action or information. This way you have a written record of what you have asked. It is more difficult for your audience to forget or ignore a written request.
- *Explain*—You can use a memo to define clearly for the reader something that is not understood. Your purpose in this case is to make something clear for your reader.
- *Announce*—Memos are useful for giving formal notice to readers, publicly informing them about new procedures, new products, or anything that you want to be publicly known.
- *Report*—Memos are often used informally to give an account of a project at regular intervals as a way of helping the organization keep track of progress and problems.

Whichever of these purposes you have, it is important for you to document your activities and decisions in writing. Having a good idea doesn't matter if you are unable to communicate it to others within the company. No matter what business activity you are engaged in, your work and ideas exist as information for other people working with you. If they do not have this information, they cannot use it in their own work. Much of this necessary information is shared through memos.

---

when *not* to write a memo

- When you are in a hurry. If time is very important, use the telephone.
- When the subject is very sensitive or confidential. Many writers have been embarrassed when their memos turned up in unexpected places.

How to Write a Memo

Begin with a brief summary. The best way to start is to set down in a sentence exactly the point you want to make to your reader or readers. This helps you to be sure of what you are doing. Are you going to explain to your reader how to build a better mousetrap or tell him you need a key for your office? If you are not clear about what it is you want, then how can you expect your reader to be clear about what to do?

One good way to summarize is to complete this sentence: The purpose of this memo is _____. If you have difficulties in completing this sentence, you have a problem that must be resolved. Do not try to skip over this step. Keep working at it. Until you know exactly what point you are trying to make, you are not ready to communicate. It's amazing how often ideas that sound good while you are thinking about them lose all of their clarity when you set them down in words. However, you cannot send ideas. You must use words to document what you mean.

When you write, your point is most important. Begin your memo with your point. Say what you want to say. Stick to your point. All of these are ways of expressing what ought to be obvious. Your readers expect you to say something, clearly and directly, and they should not have to wonder what it is. A memo is not a mystery story in which the readers search for the writer's clues.

- Start by saying something. Beginnings are strategic. They determine whether memos are read or filed away without any further consideration.
- After making your purpose known, give your audience any background information that they will need to understand your point.

For example, suppose you write a memo explaining how greater reliability can be achieved in a balance beam without linking this to the company testing lab where this process occurs. Why would anyone be interested in this information? You must make it clear to the audience how what you are saying affects them and the organization. No one reads memos for entertainment; the usefulness of what you are saying in your memo is the key to its value. Make it clear what difference your memo will make.

FORMATTING YOUR MEMOS

Many people will judge you on the basis of the memos you send them; it is important to be correct as well as clear and accurate. The first thing you need to be sure about is your format. A typical memo format is shown in Fig. 9–1.

What distinguishes a memo from a letter, other than its internal audience, is the format. Many companies have preprinted forms for the sending of memos. Sometimes these forms include a space for the reader's response; these are known as *turnaround memos.*

Electronic mail refers to the distribution of messages by computers. Many large organizations have computer systems that allow everyone with access to terminals to communicate directly with each other and with individuals outside the organization by leaving computer messages.

Most electronic mail systems automatically format your document as a memo, as shown in Fig. 9–2.

All of these formats are simple and direct. Since memos are designed to communicate within a company, they can be less formal than a business letter. Memos can leave

Pascal Business Systems

Date:

To:
From:
Re:

figure **9–1** A typical memo format.

out greetings and salutations, and get right to the subject. Clearness and accuracy are expected, not elaborate politeness.

If you look at each of the parts of the memo in Fig. 9–3, you will be familiar with the format that is standard in most organizations.

To:

Frequently this is obvious. You know to whom you are writing and you know how this person will respond to what you are saying.

Sometimes, though, your memo will have a multiple audience. A number of different people may end up reading what you write. For example, suppose you send a routine memo reporting your weekly progress on a chemical sorting process. This week you write about a possible method of recycling one of the more expensive chemicals used in the process. Your idea could save the company a good deal of money. It is quite reasonable

From: ERNIE:RIPLEY   18-AUG-1998 11:56:47:71
To: GREENEM
CC: SMTP%"Beuttner@BBN.COM"
Subj: E-mail

Electronic mail is a computer utility that allows you to send digital information (text, graphics, sound, video, and animations) from your computer, local-area network, or computer system to another. Your message is stored until the recipient retrieves it. You can send your message to one person or a list of people.

figure **9–2** An electronic mail message.

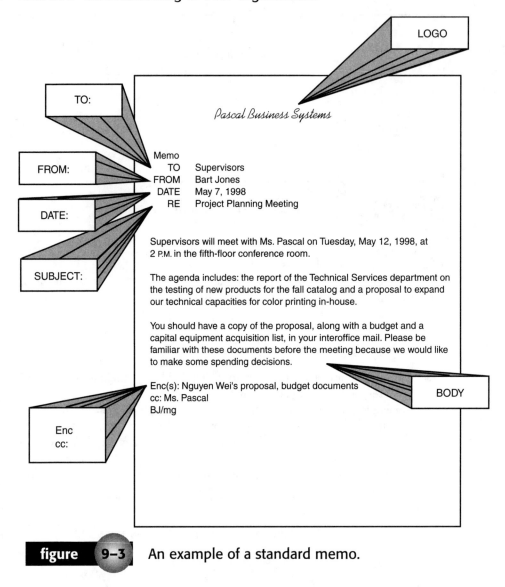

figure 9-3 An example of a standard memo.

for you to expect that this memo will be read by people other than your usual supervisor. He is going to pass this memo up through the hierarchy, and it will be read by people even further away from the process. Will these people have the technical expertise and background data necessary to understand what you are saying?

In a situation like this, where a number of people will be reading what you write, it is a good idea to give extra consideration to audience and style.

Something else often overlooked in both the writing and proofreading processes is the pleasure people take in seeing their names spelled correctly. It is worth the trouble to check, if you are not sure. The smartest spelling checker in the personal computer world will not notice if you spell the name of your supervisor incorrectly, but her misspelled name will help your supervisor form an opinion of you.

To: Marty Weiss   Date: June 6, 1999
From: Frank Topler
Subject: Installation of Temporary Outlet Board

Please check the power available at our booth site for the Jacksonville Electronics Exhibit. Sales will need a temporary outlet board installed at the Fredericks Armory for the Robotics display on the first three days of next month.

Because we will be demonstrating the Zona 3 model Industrial Welder we will need a minimum of 15 amps and a maximum capability of 600 volts.

We are located in the same spot as last year (AA12), but the new power requirements may force us to change location.

Let me know by Thursday noon if we have to move to another floor location.

cc: Lois Greer

You also need to consider whether to include the person's title or job responsibility when you are addressing your memo. Generally you will use titles (Dr., Ms., Division Director, and so forth) when your memo is intended to be somewhat formal. In informal situations, titles are often left out, as in the memo above.

From:

When you are sending a memo, the same question applies about whether or not to include your title or department. Again, this is a decision based on the degree of formality you want to achieve. Generally, the more important the message, the more formal the style. For example, if you are writing about a dangerous safety hazard, give your message all the weight you can. If you are inviting people to join a bowling league, you don't need titles.

Subject:

This one is important. Remember, the subject line is the only way people will know what the memo is about when they find it in their files seven months after you first wrote it.

Mysterious subject lines like "Important Matter" make your memos difficult to file. If they are meant as a record for future action, they are quite useless since they are unlikely to be looked at again.

Some people are very busy. They spend more than half of their work time attending to documents. They want to know what they are looking at immediately. You need to be specific. The subject line is what will draw the attention of your reader to what you are saying. Generally your memos should contain only one idea, particularly if they are short documents. Try to restate the whole idea of the memo in the subject line.

Subject: Pat Bowen's Promotion to Sales

This subject line makes it clear what the memo is about and makes the memo easy to find in the files. *Note:* Some memo formats use "Re" (*regarding*) instead of "Subject."

Date:

Putting the date on your memos can be very important. Some people file memos by date rather than by subject. Sometimes the date of a memo determines its meaning. A memo that is written about safety procedures the day after a fire is less useful than one written the day before. Electronic mail often has features which provide automatic date stamping.

cc:

This stands for *courtesy copy.* It means that a copy of the memo has been sent to the person or people listed after the colon. It is an expected courtesy to let your readers know who else has a copy of the document they are reading.

Enc

Letting your readers know when they should expect to find something else included is always a good idea. An enclosure line alerts the audience to look for what you placed with your message.

STRENGTHENING YOUR MEMOS

The only reasons you should have for writing a memo are to share information and to get something done. This means that you have to be clear and accurate. In order for you to be clear and accurate, you must know what you want. Ask yourself what you want to accomplish before you write a memo. Remember, what you write will be used to make judgments about you. Good design and courtesy will always communicate value.

The A, B, C, and D of Memo Design

*A*nnounce your purpose immediately.
*B*e sure that you have a point to make.
*C*onclude by telling readers what to do.
*D*on't ramble. Stick to your point.

A **Announce your purpose immediately.** It is very important that you state your purpose right away. This is true even if you are conveying bad news. Nothing annoys memo readers more than having to search for the reason the memo was sent.

If you think about this from the viewpoint of the readers, you'll see that this makes sense. At a minimum, the readers have a right to know why you have sent this memo. And if they don't know that, what makes you think they'll be able to figure out the rest of your message?

B **Be sure you have a point to make.** The first rule of style is to have something to say. It is no courtesy to send a memo that says little or nothing in several paragraphs to a busy person. If your reader needs to contact you to find out what point you were making, you have not written your memo properly.

Stick to making one point in a short memo. If you have to talk about more than one subject in a memo, keep the subjects separate. First say one thing and then the other.

C **Conclude by telling your readers what to do.** Unless you are simply sharing information, you should design your memos to call for action. The best way to do this is to end your memos by setting some sort of deadline for what you want accomplished. If you want your readers to do something, then you need to tell them what, where, and when.

D **Don't ramble.** This rule is a good one to follow. Far too many memos are too long. Unless your organization uses the memo format for lengthy reports, then it is a good idea to keep your memos to a single page. Think about what it is that you want to make happen. Say it and leave out irrelevant detail.

LEARNING MEMO MANNERS

Whatever suggestions we give you here, it is still important for you to remember that memos are for use within an organization. Each organization sets its own rules and standards for how, when, and why memos are to be used; sometimes these are printed in a formal set of guidelines. You have to pay close attention to the environment in which you are working.

For instance, one company might encourage frequent memos to its top management, keeping them up to date on a variety of projects, while another company may discourage written communication to anyone but immediate supervisors. Some bosses hate to send or receive memos. Whatever the situation in your company, it is up to you to discover what is expected and to follow those corporate cultural norms.

COMMUNICATING WITH MEMOS: EXERCISES

1. Over the weekend you have read about a business writing seminar offered by a nearby college. This seminar, which focuses on the skills necessary to write clear and accurate reports, takes place on a Thursday and Friday three weeks from this week, and is scheduled from nine A.M. to five P.M. You believe that taking this course would improve your prospects within your company. In order to take this

seminar, however, you will need to be absent from work for those two days and you will need to have the tuition paid for by the company.

Write a memo to your supervisor, Ann Smith, asking if this can be arranged. Be sure to include enough specific information so that Ann can make a decision without writing back to you. (Be sure to include the cost of the seminar.) You want to avoid the circular response, which just wastes time.

2. Sandy Pascal has asked that any time one of her employees sees an article containing information that might be useful to the company, the employee summarize the information in memo form and forward it to her. Find a recent article in your area of technical expertise that might be of interest to Ms. Pascal and send this idea to her in memo form. Keep your report to one page and remember to send a copy (cc:) to Ann Smith, your immediate supervisor, to keep her informed.

3. You have arrived at your office and the window has leaked again, this time staining the plaster, soaking the carpet, and destroying some computer diskettes with important information on them. You have asked Frank Topler, the building superintendent, to fix this problem before, but he has not done anything. You have heard stories in the cafeteria that he does not have enough helpers and you think that he should hire a temporary worker from an agency. You also think that the whole window frame will need to be replaced and recaulked. It would be nice to have a thermal window with triple glazing because the office gets drafty in the winter months. You have also heard rumors that Frank is looking for another job because he is unhappy with the condition of the building. Jorge told you that Frank is having problems at home with his teenage son. Write a memo to Frank Topler to address this situation. Delete any unnecessary information.

4. Several times in the past month you have mentioned to Sandy Pascal your idea that Pascal Business Systems should put together an employee manual. This manual would be a complete record of company policies and procedures for everything from vacation schedules to sick leave to reporting formats. Finally Sandy says to you, "It's a good idea, but put it in writing so that I can bring it to the managers' meeting on Friday and get a decision."

Write a memo in which you put your suggestion forward. Address it to Sandy, but remember that it will be read and discussed by all of the department heads within the company.

5. The idea you put forward in Exercise 4 has been approved. Write a memo to the members of your team asking that your idea be placed on the agenda for the next meeting. Give them sufficient information so that they will be prepared to discuss your topic.

6. If you have access to electronic mail, print an e-mail message and bring it to class with you. Discuss with your group how easy or difficult it was to communicate via electronic mail.

7. In some organizations, a good memo is hard to find. Careless writing, inattention to detail, and poor organization all combine to produce confused communications. If you have the opportunity, collect several bad memos. Show them to the others in your group and discuss what makes these memos negative examples.

8. You recently worked on a very important file for Artistic Designs Limited, a client of Pascal Business Systems. All of your information was in a manila folder that you placed on Chris Foley's desk after staying at the office late last night. When you came in this morning, Chris reported that the file was not on her desk when she arrived. You have looked everywhere in your office. Write a memo to the members of your department (Sales) to inquire whether anyone has seen the folder.

CORRESPONDING WITH BASIC BUSINESS LETTERS

Defining Business Letters

Formatting Letters
> Letter Formats
> Parts of the Business Letter

Writing Letters
> When to Write a Letter
> What Patterns to Use
> How to Write a Business Letter

Strengthening Your Letters
> You Comes Before I
> Building Credibility

Every day millions of people send and receive business letters. These letters are designed to get things done: claims adjusted, bills paid, products ordered, machinery repaired, proposals accepted. Letters are the written record of commerce between people and organizations. People expect them to be well prepared.

Your letters will represent you and your organization when you are not present to explain what you really intended to say. You need to carefully prepare letters that get things accomplished. Your ability to write these kinds of letters will be an important and valuable tool for business success.

DEFINING BUSINESS LETTERS

A *letter* is a written message sent to an individual or a group of people. Generally, it is contained in an envelope and sent through the mail, public or private. Business letters are most frequently addressed to people outside the organization. Sometimes, for formal occasions, they are used within the company. Accepting and resigning a position, for example, are situations in which you should use a letter.

What is most important to remember is that letters are always sent, not to a company, but to a person or a group of people. Business correspondence consists of written messages between human beings. It needs to be both professional and friendly at the same time.

FORMATTING LETTERS

Format includes the arrangement, shape, size, and general design of your document. You can use these elements to improve both the readability and impact of your letters. Wide margins, short paragraphs, and appropriate emphasis using headings, boldface, and italics can help you get your message through to your readers.

Letter Formats

Several formats can be used for business letters. All of these formats, you will notice, provide key information which allows for accurate delivery, storage, and retrieval.

The date, address, and signature are often used for filing and referencing. Attention and subject lines are sometimes used to assist the recipients. Like most business documents, business letters are meant to be used and your format should be chosen to help your readers.

The most common letter formats are *full block, modified block,* and *modified block with indented paragraphs* (see Figs. 10–1, 10–2, and 10–3). If your company has a uniform design for its letters, then obviously you should use that one. If your business does not have a preferred format, you can use any of these.

What is most important to remember here is that your readers will be influenced by the design and appearance of your letters and business documents. You are trying to communicate balance, pride, and careful attention to detail. The way your document looks will convey all of these things.

Parts of the Business Letter

Letterhead Stationery Most companies use stationery that has their business name, address, telephone and fax numbers, and e-mail or Internet addresses printed on it. If you use letterhead stationery, only the date must be added. The block form is preferable

Pascal Business Systems

Texas Commerce Tower
Suite 5A
600 Travis St.
Houston, Texas 77002

June 17, 1998

Mr. Thomas Burke
Communication Consultants Center
534 Drysdale Avenue
Jamestown, ND 58401

Subject: Graphic Tablets Pen Upgrade

Dear Mr. Burke:

The fourteen graphic tablets (Artpad 6X8) that we shipped to you on June 6 (Invoice #2862-R) were equipped with the wrong pens. The DuoSwitch pens are being shipped to you by Delivery Express today.

I am sorry that this problem occurred. The difficulty was a small change in our subcontractor's packaging schedule. Unfortunately, several dozen tablets were shipped before the problem was discovered. You will be pleased to find that the new pens offer double functionality with a two-way switch assembly.

Again, I want to apologize for any inconvenience and thank you for your kind understanding. We will keep you informed about future product releases.

Sincerely yours,

Gary Delabotti

Gary Delabotti
Quality Assurance Director

cc: Sandy Pascal

Phone (713) 555-4321   Fax (713) 555-6745

figure 10-1 An example of the full-block letter format.

Pascal Business Systems

Texas Commerce Tower
Suite 5A
600 Travis St.
Houston, Texas 77002

June 1, 1998

Wentworth Institute of Technology
Office of Continuing and Professional Education
550 Huntington Avenue
Boston, MA 02115

Dear Wentworth Institute of Technology:

I would like to obtain some information about your five-day Professional Writing Institute.

Pascal Business Systems, where I work in the Quality Control Department, frequently produces reports and proposals for government agencies and other contractors. I am looking for a short-term course that will improve my ability to write quickly and with more confidence.

Please let me know whether your program has any special prerequisites and whether accommodations are available on campus.

Sincerely yours,

Ai-Li Chin

Ai-Li Chin
Marketing Department

Phone (713) 555-4321   Fax (713) 555-6745

figure **10–2** An example of the modified-block letter format.

Pascal Business Systems

Texas Commerce Tower
Suite 5A
600 Travis St.
Houston, Texas 77002

August 27, 1998

Dr. Carol Resnick
Educational Resources, Inc.
P.O. Box 456
Albany, NY 12201

Dear Dr. Resnick:

Thank you for your kind assistance at the recent Education Resources Conference. Your quick loan of a video board saved my presentation.

As I told you, this was my first time through a public demonstration of our Internet service sites. The difficulties I was experiencing with my video board would have forced me to cancel the session.

Again, I want to thank you very much. Your help was invaluable and your subsequent interest in the presentation made me feel more confident.

Thank you,

Loretta Cedrone

Loretta Cedrone
Technical Services

Phone (713) 555-4321   Fax (713) 555-6745

figure **10–3** An example of the modified-block letter format with indented paragraphs.

with a left-side letterhead. Use the letterhead for the first page alone. Additional pages are on plain paper.

Heading If you do not have a letterhead, then you need to use a heading. This includes the date and your complete address. You do not include your name in the heading. The heading is located at the top of the page, placed according to the format you select.

Inside Address The inside address is placed even with the left margin, at least two spaces below the heading. You should include the full name of the person or company and the complete mailing address:

Dr. Edith Twining	Nevil, Miller & Rose
Communications Learning Systems	Marketing Department
16 Bay Road	435 Kern Avenue
Wellesley, MA 02181	Portland, OR 97202

You should always try to address your letter to a particular person rather than to a company or an address. You may need to call the company and ask to whom your letter should be directed, but this is worth doing. Don't forget to ask for the person's title.

Salutation The salutation is a greeting, located two spaces under the inside address, flush with the left margin. Most often, the greeting begins with the word *Dear* followed by a title and last name. If you are unable to direct your letter to a particular person, you can address a company with "Dear Pascal Business Systems" or simply "Pascal Business Systems." The salutation is followed by a colon (:).

The Body of the Letter The body of the letter, containing your message, should begin two spaces below the greeting. As with other documents, it is structured in paragraphs. Even if your message is complex, you can make it more readable by making your words, sentences, and paragraphs short. Usually your letter should be single-spaced within paragraphs and double-spaced between paragraphs.

The Complimentary Close and the Signature The complimentary close is a conventional expression, indicating the end of the letter. "Yours truly," "Sincerely," and "Sincerely yours" are frequently used. Notice that only the first word is capitalized.

Now include your handwritten signature in ink. Do not forget to sign your letter; a legible signature is considered necessary and courteous. Type your name and title underneath the signature. Placement of this part of the letter depends on the format you have chosen.

Optional Parts Sometimes attention and subject lines, placed between the address and the salutation, are used to direct your letter to a particular department or person, or to save time and space.

Attention: Legal Dept.	Subject: Rocky Point Lease
Attn: Joan Fontanella	Re: Cash Receipts Batch

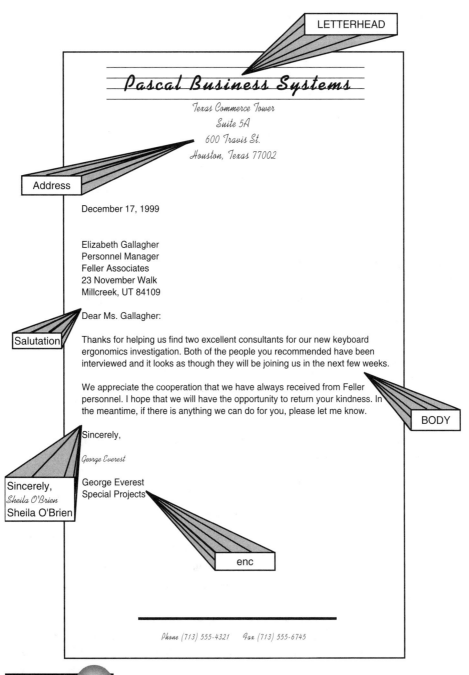

LETTERHEAD

Pascal Business Systems

Texas Commerce Tower
Suite 5A
600 Travis St.
Houston, Texas 77002

Address

December 17, 1999

Elizabeth Gallagher
Personnel Manager
Feller Associates
23 November Walk
Millcreek, UT 84109

Dear Ms. Gallagher:

Salutation

Thanks for helping us find two excellent consultants for our new keyboard ergonomics investigation. Both of the people you recommended have been interviewed and it looks as though they will be joining us in the next few weeks.

We appreciate the cooperation that we have always received from Feller personnel. I hope that we will have the opportunity to return your kindness. In the meantime, if there is anything we can do for you, please let me know.

BODY

Sincerely,

George Everest

George Everest
Special Projects

Sincerely,
Sheila O'Brien
Sheila O'Brien

enc

Phone (713) 555-4321   Fax (713) 555-6745

figure 10–4   Parts of a business letter.

As in a memo, enclosure lines are used to let your reader know what you have included with your letter. For example, if you include a brochure or a check, you may want to indicate this:

Enclosure: Pascal License Agreement

When you send a copy of your letter to another person, generally you indicate this with a copy notation:

cc: Ms. Ruth Hibbard

Envelope   The envelope has two regular parts: the outside address and the return address. Needless to say, both need to be correct. The outside address should be exactly the same as the inside address. Usually business stationery includes preprinted envelopes. According to the U.S. Postal Service, single spacing allows for electronic sorting, providing you with quicker and more reliable deliveries.

WRITING LETTERS

Organizations send millions of letters every day, each with a purpose. Written communication drives the business world.

When to Write a Letter

People write letters to do all sorts of things: send greetings and news, exchange information, collect money, and solicit new contracts. Business letters are written to get something done.

If you need to write a business letter, you need to begin with your purpose. Here are some common reasons for writing business letters.

- *Adjustments*—Letters are frequently used to deal with customer problems. Acknowledge the difficulty and describe clearly what steps you will take to resolve it. If you do not intend to do what your customer requests, explain why not in detail.
- *Reports*—Letters are sometimes used for short reports that do not include illustrations or extensive graphics. Headings can be used to improve readability. A subject line should be used to indicate that your letter is a report.
- *Claims*—When you have a complaint or a problem, you need to explain exactly what is wrong and then state clearly and definitely what action you think should be taken. Be polite. You need to decide between anger and action.
- *Requests and Inquiries*—You need to be precise and specific in saying what you want. If you are requesting more than one thing, you should place the items in a list. Remember to say thanks.
- *Transmittals*—These are cover letters that accompany reports and proposals. They allow you to make necessary comments that do not belong in the body of your main document. Your letter can identify problem areas or emphasize key points.

What Patterns to Use

For all of the variety in types of letters, most letters come down to a simple pattern: open, body, close. This is a three-stage process in which you state, elaborate, and summarize your message. A good formula for letter-writing is: "Say what you are going to say, say it, and then say what you have just said."

Begin by telling your reader why you are writing, your purpose, and what you want to happen. A good way to open is to say, "The purpose of this letter is to . . . " Then tell the reader whether you are writing to inform, request, complain, adjust, support a particular decision, or something else. What do you want? Why did you write the letter and why should someone finish reading it?

In the body of your letter, exercise judgment. You have to decide how much detail is sufficient, what to include, and what to leave out. In general, if you are conveying bad news—a refusal, for instance—then it is courteous to explain in detail. Good news requires less supporting information.

Explanations should be handled in as simple and clear a manner as you can devise. Consider what your audience already knows while you are deciding on the level of detail. Try to include enough information so that a second letter or explanation will not be necessary.

Something that few letter writers consider is the value of an enclosure. If you have brochures or samples, something that can be seen and examined physically, send this with your letter. Always include a letter with an enclosure. The letter is evidence of your interest and attention.

Your close has to tell your reader exactly what you want. You should summarize and restate your purpose. Everything in the letter has led up to the conclusion. You need to be direct at this point. You cannot always rely on your reader to understand you. What you want from your audience needs to be clear, definite, and specific.

A good letter is like a boomerang. It returns to its starting point. Like a circle, your letter should finish by returning to its beginning. Summarize your purpose and directly state what you want to happen.

How to Write a Business Letter

Imagine   The first step in writing a business letter is to try to imagine your reader. Start by studying your audience. This is what a coach does when analyzing the opposing team, or what a businessperson does when evaluating the competition.

Begin with the Ending   When faced with difficult subjects, begin at the end. If you write endings to your letters first, the beginnings will come much easier. In a letter, everything leads up to the conclusion. The best way to think about how to begin your letter is to think about the ending. What do you want to happen? Business letters are written to get something done.

Make It Readable   The best way to make your letters readable is to keep your words, sentences, and paragraphs short, even if the letter is long. Be sure to repeat your major ideas.

Include "Keep on Reading" Signs   Your letters should provide reasons to keep on reading. Most people will be interested if you are writing about their problems, their benefits, or their questions. These topics will sharpen your readers' focus. The more you remind your readers of the benefits to them, the closer their attention to your message.

Stay on the Trail   When you are writing a letter for business purposes, stick to your subject. Don't mix things together. Separate matters should be taken up in separate letters. The sudden introduction of new subjects will confuse your readers, slow their response, and perhaps cause them to stop reading. Don't let every thought that occurs to you become a detour from your path. Stay on the trail.

Stick to the Facts   Writing is a way of conversing with someone who is not there with you. Your written words cannot respond to your reader's confusion or disbelief. You need to anticipate and answer objections before they actually occur. You are better off to write only what you can support with evidence. If you can demonstrate something, it is a fair and factual claim.

STRENGTHENING YOUR LETTERS

No matter how much practice you have had writing business letters, you should review, with each letter you write, how well you have met the needs of your audience.

You Comes Before I

When you spell the word *business, u* comes before *i.* When you are writing letters that are meant to do business, *you* comes before *I.* This is an important point to remember when you are writing letters that are intended to get something done.

If you need to refer to yourself, of course you may. Feel free to use the word *I,* but use it no more than once in a sentence, and not in every sentence. The pronouns you use in your business letters signal your attitude to the people who read them. Don't fill the message with references to yourself and your problems.

Instead, keep your focus on the reader and try to write letters from the other person's perspective. This means understanding and responding to problems from your reader's point of view. Leave yourself out and put the reader in when you are writing a business letter. Make an effort to imagine why someone is upset or angry about something. When people take the trouble to write a letter of complaint, they are convinced that they are correct. You should show attention and concern.

Whether you convey concern or interest, you need to understand if you want to be understood. Try to imagine your audience and put yourself in the place of the reader. That person may have different problems, needs, and responsibilities than you have. You need to recognize these differences in order to communicate effectively.

Building Credibility

Building credibility with your readers is a step-by-step process. Each step has to be correct. Perception is everything here. Many readers see a grammar mistake, a misspelled word, or even a typographical error as evidence that your whole document is careless and wrong. Even if their perception is unfair, it is a fact of life.

Letters need to be prepared very carefully because they are read very carefully, sometimes again and again. They have to withstand this kind of scrutiny. If your readers distrust what you write, your letter cannot respond to their disbelief. It cannot explain names that are misspelled, statements that are exaggerated, or factual errors. Mistakes cost credibility.

Your goal should be to create letters that build confidence in your ability to get a job done. Here are some effective techniques that will work to create confidence in your readers:

- *Fast answer.* A quick response is one of the most effective techniques a writer can use. The faster you respond to a letter, request, or telephone call, the closer you respond to what motivated the person who tried to reach you. Even if your message is negative, a rapid response will be appreciated as an indication that you are trying hard.
- *Good paper.* It is difficult to overestimate the importance of a good letterhead and good-quality, high-rag-content bond paper. The letter represents you. Envelopes and stationery should match. Your letter should have a professional appearance.
- *Direct language.* You want to use a low-key, reasonable approach to the reader's interests. Be straightforward. Tell facts simply and directly. This will build credibility with your readers.
- *Formal style.* In business, written communications are more formal than when we are talking. "No problem!" is an acceptable response when you are speaking on the phone, but in a letter may be inappropriate and even upsetting. A respectful professional style is the correct style for business letters to people, especially when you are not friendly with them already.
- *Friendly.* Remembering that you are a person and that you are talking to people may be the most effective technique for building trust. Writing is a way of talking to someone who isn't present. If you are friendly when you write to people, even when you have to convey bad news, they will recognize your attitude and credit you for it. If you want people to feel friendly toward you, then you need to feel friendly toward them.
- *Brevity.* "I've made this letter longer than usual," French mathematician Blaise Pascal once apologized, "because I lacked the time to make it shorter." It takes work and effort to design a letter that is brief and to the point. It is easier to put extra information in than to write a short letter.

Two things you should remember: busy people get lots of letters, and busy people are very busy. They expect you to be direct and to the point.

learning about a professional style

A professional style is more elaborate than the informal style we use in relaxed and social occasions. Greater care is taken to explain things fully. This style is cautious and deliberate and marked by strong concern for the audience. In business and industry it is essential that we are understood when we speak and write to each other.

Often this means preparation and rehearsal. A professional style is not spontaneous and immediate. Rather, it is expected to be careful and deliberate. Sales proposals, system procedures, business letters, and presentations are just some of the business tasks that require a professional style. Such documents and presentations are designed ahead of time, reviewed, and then revised to be precise and exact.

This does not mean that your professional writing and speaking styles cannot be conversational and easy to understand. However, even if your writing resembles conversation, you need to take extra care to explain things completely to avoid the chances of misunderstanding.

Using a professional style means taking responsibility for the successful transfer of the message. This means clarifying, explaining, defining, demonstrating, illustrating, making things clear, and spelling them out.

CORRESPONDING WITH BASIC BUSINESS LETTERS: EXERCISES

1. You receive a letter from Pascal Business Systems that says they have narrowed down their candidate search to three people. They are impressed with your résumé and your performance during the two interviews you had.

   The hiring process has reached a snag, however, because Sandy Pascal has raised a question about communication skills. She wants to see a letter from each candidate briefly describing their job goals and where they want to be in five years.

   Obviously, this is more than a simple task. You need to choose a style and a strategy. You want to sound energetic, lively, practical, and competent. The head of the company will be reviewing your work and you will be creating a long-term impression.

2. Find the name of a professional society or trade association in your area. Choose a letter format and write an inquiry letter asking about the requirements and costs for membership. Ask whether there are special rates for students or new members.

3. A friend of yours who works at another company tells you about a U.S. Postal Service program to update company mailing lists and avoid delivery problems. Contact your local post office, find out about this program, and write a memo to Sandy Pascal suggesting that we use this free postal service to improve the efficiency of our mailings.

4. You have been offered a very attractive position in a company in your spouse's hometown. Although you are regretful,

you decide this is too good an opportunity to let pass. Both you and your spouse would like to live near your relatives and you prefer country life to living in Houston.

Write a letter to Sandy Pascal resigning your position. Try to make sure that your tone expresses your sincere regret, along with your determination to do what you think is right for your family and yourself. Leave a good impression behind your exit.

5. Choosing your words carefully is very important to both style and strategy. One way to learn about correct language is by playing with your word processor's thesaurus or synonym finder. Choose a short article from *Time* or *Newsweek* and type it into your word processor. Now use the thesaurus to replace every adjective with a synonym that is not quite correct. (You can also try this technique with song lyrics or a poem.)

6. Design a letter to acknowledge Mr. Peter Broom's request for the Fall Pascal Business Systems catalog. Mr. Broom's address is 111 Medway Avenue, Houston, TX 77002. This letter will be stored as a template so that it can become the standard response to catalog requests.

7. Write a letter of reply/adjustment to an order for an AV400 16-bit TV card with multiple input reception. This order cannot be filled because this product is out of stock and its manufacture has been discontinued. Be sure to explain fully and offer some attractive alternative.

CORRESPONDING WITH FUNCTIONAL BUSINESS LETTERS

11

Business letters are so important to the success of businesses that we have included two chapters on the subject. View this chapter as a continuation of Chapter 10, "Corresponding with Basic Business Letters." In this chapter, we discuss some of the more difficult letters to write. These include refusal, collection, and adjustment letters.

CHOOSING AN ATTITUDE

Think before and while you are writing a letter. The best way to write a good letter is to know what you want. You need to decide between feelings and actions. If you are writing a letter to show that you are upset, there is little reason to expect it will get the job done.

You can't be angry with people whom you want to cooperate with you. Instead, you need to give your readers the opportunity to respond in a positive way. As we said in the previous chapter, if you want people to feel friendly toward you, then you have to feel friendly toward them.

Be definite. Say what you want done. When you are writing a letter, discuss *when* your reader will do something rather than *if* your reader will do something. You want to focus your reader's attention on what you want done in a pleasant and positive way. Whenever you write a business letter, strive for an active conclusion. End by telling your reader what you want him or her to do.

One thing to remember is that the same message can be presented in a positive or negative way. Readers will sense your attitude by the way you write to them. Even routine correspondence can build a good impression. Here is an example of the central messages conveyed by two ordinary confirmation letters:

Thank you for your telephone order of October 4. Your software will be shipped on Tuesday.

Thank you for your telephone order of October 4. Your software will not be ready until Tuesday.

It is not difficult to distinguish the positive attitude.

Saying No and Saying Yes

One of the most difficult letter-writing tasks is having to say no. Whether you are refusing to honor a warranty claim or rejecting a proposal, you want to make particular efforts to avoid offending your audience. You don't want to blame or embarrass the person who writes to complain or ask for something you will not do.

People who take the trouble to write are sure that they are correct. If you have to disagree with them, your letter should convey your sympathetic and helpful attitude. You want to explain your refusal from your reader's viewpoint. The best way to convey bad news is with this simple formula: *Thanks, Sorry, Because, Thanks.* Surround your negative message with courtesy and polite attention.

- *Thanks:* "Thank you for the opportunity to explain this situation." This is the type of positive attitude you want to display. If you are responding to an angry complaint, an effective technique is to restate the complaint and then offer a complete explanation. By repeating the complaint accurately, you demonstrate that you understand the situation and are giving it your full attention, not just sending a form letter back to an address.
- *Sorry:* There is nothing wrong with sending an apology. You can simply say you are sorry and move directly to the bad news. If you need to apologize, do so.
- *Because:* You should always explain a refusal in detail. Your effort to explain gives evidence of your sympathy and concern. A brief refusal is seen as abrupt and dismissive. A "no" letter requires explanation. Give reasons, details, specifics, and support for your decisions. The more trouble you take to explain, the more your reader will appreciate your attitude.

• *Thanks:* You should end your letter with courtesy and appreciation. Say again that you are sorry for the circumstances and offer to do whatever you can. This will be remembered along with your negative message.

Then there is the business of saying yes. When you are agreeing to a customer's request, say so politely. Many people think that if they are saying yes, they can be as curt and abrupt as possible. Instead, think of this as an opportunity to gather points with your readers.

---

politeness quiz: should A or B go before C?

A: "You claim your air conditioner failed."

or

B: "I understand that your air conditioner overheats."

before

C: "I agree to repair it under the warranty."

In other words, don't be afraid to be a pleasant human being just because you have to write a letter. A negative attitude can destroy the effect of the kindest agreement. Remember, the tone you use for letters should represent your company's attitude toward its clients, not your mood while writing. Every letter is a public-relations effort.

Refusal Letters

Two of the most delicate matters that can be discussed in business letters are credit and debt. Money matters; when you write about money, you have to be concerned with tone. People identify your words about their finances with your personal judgments about them. You need to be particularly sensitive to the ways that you phrase refusals.

Usually it is an easy task to write a letter granting credit. Begin your document with a welcoming statement, provide details of the company's credit terms, and close with a re-selling of your company's product or service.

In the United States, 5/7/98 will be read as May 7, 1998; in Europe and Latin America, it will be understood as July 5, 1998. For international mail, write the date out. Be aware that different localities use different dating conventions.

Pascal Business Systems

Texas Commerce Tower
Suite 5A
600 Travis St.
Houston, Texas 77002

March 6, 1998

Mr. John Buettner
Buettner Brothers, Inc.
465 Madison Lane
Huron, SD 57350

Dear Mr. Buettner:

Thank you for your recent request for an account with Pascal Business Systems. We communicated with the references you provided as well as the Talbot Credit Information Agency.

At this time we would suggest that it is in your best interest to establish a cash account with our company. This would entitle you to an automatic 5 percent discount on all purchases. Your recent problems with first-of-the-month payments would be avoided. Further, this account would help your firm build a relationship with Pascal Business Systems that would benefit both companies in the future.

We look forward to hearing from you and have enclosed a catalog of monthly special orders which may interest your company. Thank you for your continued business.

Sincerely yours,

Michael Benevento

Michael Benevento
Account Representative

Phone (713) 555-4321   Fax (713) 555-6745

figure **11-1**   A refusal letter.

fair credit reporting act

If you've ever applied for a charge account, a personal loan, insurance, or a job, someone is probably keeping a file on you. This file might contain information on how you pay your bills, whether you've been sued or arrested, or whether you have filed for bankruptcy. The companies that gather and sell this information are called *credit reporting agencies,* or CRAs. The most common type of CRA is the credit bureau. The information sold by CRAs to creditors, employers, insurers, and other businesses is called a *consumer credit report.* This report generally contains information about where you work and live and about your bill-paying habits.

In 1970, Congress passed the Fair Credit Reporting Act to give consumers specific rights in dealing with CRAs. The act protects you by requiring credit bureaus to furnish correct and complete information to businesses to use in evaluating your application for credit, insurance, or a job.

Refusing credit is a more difficult task. First, you must be very careful to stay within the boundaries of the laws that govern the credit process. A business or an individual who provides credit information or subjective evaluations is considered a credit reporting agency under the law. You cannot state your opinion that someone is financially irresponsible and a bad credit risk, but you can describe someone's payment history. Stick with descriptive statements which can be measured and avoid making evaluative judgments.

Sometimes you will have to deny credit to people or companies who have the potential of becoming future good customers. You want to avoid the appearance of being condescending or judgmental. You may want to provide alternative suggestions such as a period of cash payments to provide the basis for a future credit relationship, as Mike Benevento did in Fig. 11–1.

Again, it is important to treat credit requests with care and sensitivity. Express appreciation for the request. Explain clearly why you cannot grant the request and end by suggesting alternatives. Your positive tone will be appreciated even by disappointed readers.

SELECTING TYPES OF LETTERS

While there are many different reasons to write a business letter, we can make some classifications concerning the most common types of functional business letters.

Form Letters

Occasionally you will see advertising for prewritten business letters. These ads suggest that you will never have to write another business letter. You can just copy your letters from a diskette or a book. You simply make minor changes, such as names and addresses.

If you consider this product seriously, you can see how unlikely a solution it is to your need for effective correspondence. Real business letters have to be designed for particular situations and people.

Yet some people treat letters as if they were simple commodities, to be taken from the shelf, dusted off, stuffed in an envelope, and sent out on their way. You do not want to be represented by the equivalent of a photocopied letter. Writing letters to people is not a recitation where you repeat rote phrases. Every letter is an opportunity to make a favorable impression. People who receive your letters will make judgments about you and your abilities.

This does not mean that you should never use form letters. Sometimes you need to communicate the same message to many different people, or you may find yourself writing the same letter on a frequent basis. The merge and file functions of most word processors allow you to save and reuse effective letters.

You need to remember, though, that you are writing to people. You should sound like a human being, not a phrase-making computer program. A personal letter is more effective than a form letter, but a form letter can be personalized.

Reference Letters

At some point in your career you will be asked to provide a letter of reference for someone. Whether this person is someone you work with, an employee, or an acquaintance, this task is the same. You are being asked to provide an evaluation of that person's abilities and performance to the extent that you are familiar with these items. You are expected to be honest and truthful.

Begin your letter by identifying yourself. Give your name, title or position, employer, and address. Describe how long you have known the person and in what capacity. Stick to factual details, material which can be verified. Instead of saying, "Joshua always did a good job," give specifics of his performance: "Joshua worked with the marketing team to produce the fall advertising special in *MacWorld*."

End your letter with a specific recommendation and summarize your specific impressions and judgments.

Collection Letters

The collection process is an expandable series of steps that involves communication all of the way. It begins with sending the bill. This document generally includes an itemized list of charges and a payment due date. You may be required to inform your customers of their legal rights if you extend installment credit or charge interest on the balance. This notification is commonly printed on the bill.

If your customer returns payment within the specified time, the process is over. If your customer does not respond, then the collection process continues. This type of business communication requires that you think carefully about style, strategy, and tone. Why are you writing this letter? What is your purpose? Your primary purpose is to secure payment; an important secondary purpose is to keep the customer.

learning about tone

Tone is a manner of speaking or writing that reveals a certain attitude on the part of the speaker or writer. Tone is disclosed in the ways you choose to express yourself. Your style and strategy combine to let your readers and listeners know how you feel about them and your subject.

Enthusiasm, for example, is communicated in the ways we say or write things. So are reluctance and dislike. Your attitude toward your audience and your topic is easily recognized by most people. So it makes sense to choose an attitude while you are choosing your words.

Style and strategy consist of doing the best you can to communicate information to a *person*—not a business or an address, but a person who, like you, will appreciate the effort to communicate clearly and accurately.

When you are communicating face to face with people, you can adjust your message as you view their response. When you are writing to people outside your organization, you need to adopt an attitude that is positive and cheerful. Your words, phrasing, and approach to the reader will signal how you are feeling and affect the response of your audience.

Who is your audience? It is easy, but not necessarily productive, to speculate about the motives of your customer. This person or business may be careless and procrastinating when it comes to paying bills. Your customer may be unhappy with the goods or services you provided. Financial inability—a lack or resources or a sudden emergency—may be preventing your customer from paying. The least likely possibility is that your customer is dishonest and has no intention of paying you.

If you know the motive, it is easy to design effective communication. Most often, however, you will not, and the task requires care. Imagine for a moment that you neglected a bill for several weeks and then received a letter accusing you of attempted theft. You would feel angry and upset. You would be thinking of taking your business elsewhere. A friendly reminder would be a more effective way to communicate.

What should you include in your collection letters? At a minimum you need to request payment, stating the date(s) and exact goods or services provided. Remind the customer of the credit terms and refer to previous correspondence on this matter. The need to include this information does not mean that you cannot take a positive attitude. Refer to the benefits for the customer.

When should you write? A prompt request for payment is important. Often, a simple reminder will do. You can follow this with a second reminder, referring to the first. If this doesn't work, write and ask why the bill has not been paid. Is there some reason for dissatisfaction? Are there financial circumstances which are causing difficulty? All of these steps are reasonable before you write with threats of a legal collection. It is appropriate to request payment firmly as long as you are courteous; however, it is illegal to harass creditors by mail. You want to remain within the bounds of courtesy.

Pascal Business Systems

Texas Commerce Tower
Suite 5A
600 Travis St.
Houston, Texas 77002

September 27, 1999

Ms. Kristin Dailey
16 Bay Road
Wellesley, MA 02181

Dear Ms. Dailey:

Just a friendly reminder that the September payment of fifty-seven dollars ($57.00) on your Adapta external hard drive is past due.

Your payment in the enclosed envelope will be received with our appreciation.

Thank you in advance.

Melinda Quan

Melinda Quan
Credit Manager

Phone (713) 555-4321   Fax (713) 555-6745

figure 11-2 A friendly collection letter.

Pascal Business Systems

Texas Commerce Tower
Suite 5A
600 Travis St.
Houston, Texas 77002

October 15, 1998

Dr. Roberta Bramhall
611 Lawson Drive
Revere, MN 56166

Dear Dr. Bramhall:

As we reminded you on September 11, your payment for the Apple Quicktake 150 purchased on July 7 is now past due. The total amount now outstanding is $710.68, including the 1.5% interest charge for two months.

You received our special discount on office furniture purchases offered with 30-day settlement terms. Therefore, we ask that you send your payment of $710.68 as soon as possible.

A stamped, addressed envelope is enclosed for your convenience.

Sincerely,

Patti Cross

Patti Cross
Administrative Assistant

Enclosure

Phone (713) 555-4321   Fax (713) 555-6745

figure 11-3 A firm collection letter.

Pascal Business Systems

Texas Commerce Tower
Suite 5A
600 Travis St.
Houston, Texas 77002

December 14, 1998

Mr. Russell Webster
32 Oaksleeve Road
Houston, TX 77002

Dear Mr. Karanian:

Thank you for writing us about your difficulties with the 4 GB Internal Hard
Drive which we shipped to you on December 6.

We are unable to send you a duplicate drive for at least two weeks because we
have run out of stock and the manufacturer is back-ordered. We will, however,
provide you with a 5 gigabyte drive from the same manufacturer with the same
access speed for the price you have already paid.

If this is acceptable to you, please call our toll-free number (1-800-555-5432)
and ask for Ann Smith, our telephone representative. She will arrange for return
of the faulty drive and shipment of the replacement.

We are sorry for any inconvenience this may have caused you and we look
forward to your business in the future.

Sincerely,

Michael Benevento,

Michael Benevento
Account Representative

Phone (713) 555-4321   Fax (713) 555-6745

figure 11-4 An adjustment letter.

Adjustment Letters

Another very common type of business correspondence is the adjustment letter. Whether you are writing to request an adjustment or replying to a customer's request, there are some basic rules to follow.

First, you must be courteous and complete. If you leave out essential information or fail to provide sufficient details, then you will not achieve a positive result. All you will generate is a request for more facts. If you are requesting an adjustment, you must describe your problem, provide details, explain the inconvenience the problem has caused, and, most important, suggest a solution that would satisfy you.

If you are responding to a customer's request for an adjustment, you must either state that you agree with the customer's suggested solution or present your alternative. If you must refuse the request, then provide reasons for your refusal. Soften your negative message by placing polite and pleasant statements before and after the bad news. Every letter you write offers the opportunity to create goodwill.

Appreciation Letters

One type of letter that is not mentioned or written as frequently as it should be is the letter of appreciation. You can write a letter to thank people, to praise them for something well done, or to show your interest in what they are doing. People will appreciate and remember you.

Businesses that receive a high volume of mail tend to value positive letters more highly than negative ones. It takes a high degree of motivation to sit down and write a letter to praise excellent service, quality, or attention to detail.

Too often we write more complaints than compliments. It is worth considering the pleasure we get from other people recognizing that we are doing a good job. Honest praise and sincere compliments will be valued.

CORRESPONDING WITH FUNCTIONAL BUSINESS LETTERS: EXERCISES

1. Pascal Business Systems receives a letter from a client who has been wavering and indecisive about signing an office computer purchase order that you have written with her. Write a letter of reassurance that responds to the tone in the close of her most recent letter to you: "I need more time to make my decision."

2. Bertrand Russell, the British philosopher, devised a parlor game with language based on physical proximity and social distance. Imagine yourself talking to a friend and referring to a third person who is not present. Your task is to choose a series of adjectives, each increasingly less flattering. These adjectives will describe you, your friend who is present, and the person who is not. For example,

I am heavy.	I am thin.
You are fat.	You are skinny.
She (not present) is obese.	He (not present) is emaciated.

As distance increases we are less socially sensitive to the words and phrasings we choose. Find three examples of this to

discuss in class. How does this affect the ways we deal with people we perceive to be very far away from us?

3. Many different dimensions affect the ways we choose our words, our attitudes, and our approach to delivering a message. These dimensions include age, gender, and race, all sensitive subjects in the workplace. Geography, education, and experience also affect the way messages are sent and received. A professional style requires you to avoid expressions and manners of address that offend people. This means observing and anticipating the reactions to communications you design, and being aware of your audience and the responsibilities you have to them.

Discuss the ethical responsibilities involved in designing business letters for the general public. Break up into small groups of four or five individuals. Can everyone agree on three responsibilities you have to your audience that apply to every communication?

4. The most common strategy for delivering bad news in a letter is this simple formula: *Thanks, Sorry, Because, Thanks.* Can you suggest strategies for communicating in the following situations?

   (a) You are designing a fax message for a Mr. Lin Eng, who works in Kuala Lumpur, Malaysia. From his message to you, it is apparent that his English skills are fairly limited. Make a list of strategies to help get your technical message across to him.

   (b) You are designing a weekly progress report for Mr. Charles Auburn, president of a financial management firm. Mr. Auburn is 60 years old, a self-made man who has a temper and low tolerance for frustration. You know from past experience that Mr. Auburn has no patience with technical details. Unfortunately, your original estimates for the installation of an electronic mail network have been thrown off because of compatibility problems among his varied microcomputers. Describe your style and strategy for this important client.

5. On page 146 is a letter written by Samuel Clemens (Mark Twain) to his local gas company. Can you suggest some ways in which Mr. Twain could have made the same points with more tact?

6. A number of companies offer software that contains prewritten business letters for all sorts of occasions. You just bring the letter into your word processor and add the name and address. In groups of four or five, discuss whether these letters would prove useful. If you can, arrange to try one of these programs and report the results to the others in the group.

7. You work as an account representative for Pascal Business Systems. A small office has failed to respond to your requests for payment for the last four months. Five months ago Pascal Business Systems shipped $36,000 of computer equipment. No payment has been forthcoming.

To the gas company

Hartford, February 1, 1891

Dear Sirs:

Some day you will move me almost to the verge of irritation by your chuckle-headed Goddamned fashion of shutting your Goddamned gas off without giving any notice to your Goddamned parishioners. Several times you have come within an ace of smothering half of this household in their beds and blowing up the other half by this idiotic, not to say criminal, custom of yours. And it has happened again to-day.

Haven't you a telephone?

Ys
S L Clemens

Write a letter to Dr. Edith Twining, Communications Learning Systems, 16 Bay Road, Wellesley, MA 02181, as a first step toward collecting payment.

8. See Exercise 7. Three more months have gone by and no payment has been received from Communications Learning Systems. Write a second collection letter, more forceful than the first.

PREPARING SHORT REPORTS

Defining the Short Report
Types of Short Reports
Parts of the Short Report
Designing the Short Report
Considering Your Audience
Responding to Forms
Developing Perspective

We have designed this chapter to help you write short reports: organized, concise documents that circulate factual information through organizations. Organizations rely on short written communications to keep projects coordinated, supplied, and on schedule. Businesses rely on short reports to pass the information needed to conduct commerce in today's high-paced world. Timely, accurate, and clear reports are the foundation for success.

Important messages are communicated in writing so that there will be a record of them. Electronic mail, fax machines, and express mail have increased the pace of this activity while still providing documentation for future use. Today, employees traveling thousands of miles from an organization's headquarters can stay in close written touch.

Producing short reports involves collecting, organizing, and distributing written information. As an entry-level professional, you will be expected to provide technical and support information, sales and accounts records, activity reports, and other types of written documentation. Your ability to do this will have a direct impact on how your performance is evaluated.

DEFINING THE SHORT REPORT

Short reports are written documents organized to supply the results of some activity; a purely informational report that requires its author to research a topic is an example of a short report, as is a trip report or a progress report. Short reports can be defined by length, level of formality, or specific function. Generally, the shorter the report, the less formal it will be. Short, informal reports are located somewhere between memos and long reports on the spectrum of written communications. A short report will vary in length from several paragraphs to several pages. Actually, since some reports will be faxed or networked electronically and thus never printed on paper, it may be more accurate to say "from several paragraphs to several computer screens." Some high-tech offices may be completely paperless in the near future. Yet these documents will be stored to provide a record of activity.

Only the basic elements of a long report are included: the *introduction,* the *body,* and *conclusions and recommendations.* This simple arrangement is useful for a variety of different reporting situations. Generally, short reports contain more information than a brief memo, and the layout clearly reveals how the material is organized. They are usually arranged more carefully than memos, and their style is more elaborate and less personal.

Short reports have a very practical purpose. People use them to make decisions. This goes on all the way up through the hierarchy. The information in these reports is accumulated, refined, summarized, and rewritten as it moves through the communication channels of your organization. When your name is on a document that is being circulated, the document represents you and stands in for you when you are not present. Sloppy, careless writing does not make a good impression. Everything you write should be correct and understandable.

One of the most important things that you should remember is that your short reports can circulate more widely than you expect. Reports sent to your immediate supervisors and co-workers can end up on the desks of people throughout the hierarchy.

Writing a short report requires the kind of care and thought you would devote to writing an effective letter. As with other business writing, these reports follow rules of style and format that are familiar to your audience. Writing good short reports is hard work, but this type of communication can be an important part of your job responsibilities.

Types of Short Reports

Generally, short reports are intended to inform or persuade your audience. Apart from these two general functions, short reports are used for a variety of reporting purposes. There are as many types of short reports as there are uses for them. They provide a reliable and verifiable method of circulating information. Common types of short reports are discussed in this section.

Informational reports communicate information obtained through research. For example, you may be asked to find out about a problem with the delivery of a product to a customer, or to research and report on the inventory for a particular product. Be sure to check any statistics or numbers twice to ensure that the information is accurate.

Progress reports, also called *status reports,* are used to keep supervisors and management informed about a project or activity. They want to know five things: the current status of the project, problems you have encountered, and changes in the activity, the schedule, or the costs. The purpose of these reports is to make sure that managers will know whether they need to alter their budgets, provide new resources to meet deadlines, or make adjustments in the project plans. The information you provide will be crucial to their decisions.

A series of progress reports should stick with the same format. Each report should summarize the progress since the previous report, including any recommended changes in technical approach, schedule, or cost. Describe what you are doing to deal with problems and provide a realistic estimate of what you expect to accomplish in the next reporting period.

Progress reports are similar to the *activity reports* that some organizations require from field-site employees. Generally you report what has been accomplished, what will be done next, problems you have encountered, requests for support and equipment, and a brief overview. Again, since these documents are part of a regular series, there is little need for introductory material.

Pascal Business Systems

1. What work was in progress today? Give the location and a brief description of the work.

2. Provide the same for work of subcontractors.

3. What items of work were started today?

4. What work was completed today?

5. What is delaying progress?

6. Did any accidents occur? If so, describe what happened.

7. Were there any visitors to the site? Who? Why?

8. Were there any variations from the original plans?

9. Did anything else occur that should be reported?

10. What materials and equipment were received? Did they meet specifications? Describe in detail.

Progress Report

---

figure 12–1   An example of a progress report form.

As part of your job, you may be required to attend conferences and travel to various field sites. If your job involves sales, you may find yourself on the road for long periods, communicating with the main office through a series of trip reports documenting your activities, expenses, and progress. *Trip reports* provide your company with a written discussion of your activities. You want to provide specific information about your experiences and you also need to show the significance of your information to the company.

Short reports are frequently used to alert management to accidents, equipment failures, and property damage. *Trouble reports* or *accident reports* are important because they may be used as evidence in insurance liability and compensation judgments. You need to include detailed information about what happened, when and where it happened, who witnessed the problem, and why the problem occurred. Your analysis of the cause of the trouble must be detailed and supported by evidence. Don't forget to include steps you

Pascal Business Systems

memo

date   June 10, 1998
to   Supervisors
from   Joan Fontanella
re   Trip Report: Global Marketing Strategies

The purpose of this report is to describe my participation in a recent conference on ways in which U.S. firms can market themselves to other cultures.

Last Thursday and Friday I was in Mexico City, where I represented Pascal Business Systems at the 17th Annual Conference on World Business and Technology. Along with Juan Aguilera of the Mexican Ministry of Development and Patricia Becker from the U.S. Department of Commerce, I participated in a panel discussion titled "Doing Business in Central and South America."

The panel sessions went well. More than 30 companies were represented. (See attachment.) Dr. Aguilera used the Pascal Business Systems trade agreement with Mexico as a model of how private industry and government could create a mutually beneficial working environment. Representatives of several companies and the Brazilian Trade Council spoke with me after the session about possible participation in a joint venture in South America.

My attendance at the conference has convinced me that our attention to expanding our consulting to the world market makes excellent sense and that we should continue in this direction.

On Friday I plan to present a briefing on my trip at the weekly meeting of the International Sales Division.

figure **12-2** An example of a trip report.

have taken to avoid a similar problem or accident in the future. Keep an objective and factual tone and be as thorough and complete a reporter as you can be.

These are only some of the types of short reports that you might need to write; others include feasibility reports and proposals. The types of short reports are as varied as the situations and circumstances that require them. All types share similarities of purpose and design. When you write a short report, you are trying to communicate factual information quickly and accurately. Your organization, style, and strategy reflect your ability to do this effectively.

Parts of the Short Report

Your reports must first be accurate and correct. If they are to remain correct over time, while they are used by many different people, the reports must be clear and carefully designed. A well-constructed report consists of three fundamental parts:

1. The introduction, in which you tell the reader what is about to appear;
2. The body, in which you present a detailed report of the activity; and
3. The conclusions and recommendations, in which you elaborate on what needs to be done next.

Introduction   Your *introduction* should accomplish several things. It names the subject and tells the purpose of the report. Sometimes it gives the reader necessary background or context. Let the readers know with a glance what the report is about so they can focus on that message; state the objective; and summarize your findings, conclusions, or recommendations.

The top of your report helps readers get their bearings and fit your report into a larger context. Help the reader get started. Use a title line to identify key information. State the purpose of the report. Map the report by describing where to find specific facts. Use headings so that your readers can access information quickly.

Reference your document to further sources of information. By the time your readers leave the introduction, they should have a good idea of how the report fits into their activities and where to go in the report for detail.

Body   The *body* will contain the more detailed, complete information of the report. How much detail you will use depends on how much your audience knows and needs to know. Your report discussion needs to be complete, containing enough information for your readers to understand and judge your conclusions and recommendations. The text of your report needs to fully describe the technical details.

Effective short reports provide a clearly organized account of their message. A *problem* → *solution* structure works well for informational reports and feasibility studies. Accident and trip reports are often presented chronologically. Begin by describing the problem and lead to your solution. Use headings so your readers cannot miss your organization or your main points. Support your text with illustrations, even in informal short reports. Frequent illustrations can make your meaning clear and shorten your explanations.

Conclusions and Recommendations What goes into the *conclusions and recommendations* section depends on your purpose and what you were asked to do. If the purpose of your report is to provide information, then a simple summary will be sufficient. However, if your purpose is to convince the readers that your solution is correct, then include your recommendations. Obviously, documents such as a feasibility report or short proposal require that you make your judgments clear. Be sure to make the evidence that supports your recommendations clear and convincing.

Remember, key conclusions and recommendations should also be included in your introduction. The end section of the short report provides this information in full detail. By stating your key points at the beginning and end, you improve your chances of getting your message through.

DESIGNING THE SHORT REPORT

The format for short reports is fairly flexible. Generally these reports will use a memo format. A direct, informal-to-professional style works well for most internal communications. For external reporting or formal situations, use a letter format and a professional style. Include a subject line if you report by letter and include headings for easy reference. All reports in a series should use the same format, whether you choose memo or letter.

Short reports are supposed to provide easy access to information. The entire design—layout, headings, illustrations, and text—is intended to convey data to the readers as efficiently as possible. You can help your readers by making the report structure visible and easy to grasp. This means arranging your document into primary and secondary sections. Use distinctive headings and subheadings to label significant material and to indicate the relative importance of the report information.

Keep your reports short by using attachments. Your readers can decide for themselves if they want to read this supplemental information. Some people will be impressed by this data; others will ignore it. Be sure to separate your appendix material in an obvious way so you do not discourage readers who want the brief version. Package reference materials and detailed technical specifications differently.

CONSIDERING YOUR AUDIENCE

Few people would take the trouble to write or read short reports unless they were required to. This gives you a good starting place. Some person wants this report, plans to receive it, and probably has use for the information it contains. You are writing the report for this audience. Begin the document design process by discovering your purpose—*Why?*—from three *whats:*

WHAT do your readers expect to find out? If people are reading a report to extract information, they probably have a pretty good idea of what kind of information they are looking for. Progress, problems, scheduling, costs, and requests are just a few of the common categories of information transferred by short reports. You need to discover exactly what your readers require from the document.

WHAT do your readers already know? You have to include enough background information so that even an uninformed reader will follow what he or she is reading. If you assume that your readers are familiar with the report topic, then you should

The U.S. Advanced Battery Consortium–Automakers and DOE team up to establish American leadership in new automotive technology

The environmental benefits of zero-emitting electric vehicles (EVs) are substantial, but the lack of a battery capable of providing the range and performance that would be acceptable to the consumer has proven to be a major drawback in their development. American, Japanese, and European companies and consortia are actively working on producing advanced batteries that can help make EVs practical for everyday use. If American industry can take the lead now, it could herald an era of American dominance in a new automotive arena, as well as significantly further our nation's energy security goals.

The Big Three team up with DOE and others to lead the way

The level of R&D effort required to adequately explore all the promising battery technologies would be expensive and time consuming. It would not be practical for any one company to perform this level of activity while still meeting its responsibilities to its employees, customers, and other stakeholders. On January 31, 1991, Chrysler, Ford, and General Motors, the Big Three American automakers, entered an agreement to pool their technical knowledge and funding, looking to accelerate progress by collectively combining expertise and reducing individual risk. Their partnership is called the United States Advanced Battery Consortium, or USABC.

The U.S. Department of Energy (DOE), which has long had extensive battery-related R&D activities underway, joined the partnership later in the year, providing expertise and funding. DOE also acts in an advisory and oversight role for various USABC committees and projects.

To make EVs practical in the shortest possible time frame, many battery-related issues—such as standardization of charging systems—must be settled early on. As part of the partnership, the Electric Power Research Institute (EPRI), the technical research arm of the electric utility industry, and several individual utilities are providing vital input, as well as funding and staff.

The partnership among the Big Three is slated to run twelve years. The cooperative agreement between the Big Three and DOE covers a period of four years and establishes funding of $260 million, cost-shared equally between government and industry.

figure 12–3 An example of a short report.

The focus is on batteries

The key to making EVs practical is the development of batteries that can provide performance comparable with conventional vehicles, and at comparable cost. Today's lead-acid batteries have limited range, allowing drivers to travel only relatively short distances before they must recharge. Sustainable speeds are also not in line with those demanded by today's consumers. Current technology provides batteries with an energy-to-weight ratio of 30–40 watt hours per kilogram, at a cost of up to $150 per kilowatt-hour.

USABC has set a midterm goal to have in prototype production by 1995 batteries with energy-to-weight ratios of 80–100 watt-hours per kilogram, at a cost of less than $150 per kilowatt-hour. Other goals include power-to-weight ratios of 150–200 watts per kilogram and a five-year useful life. Nickel-metal hybrid, as well as sodium-sulfur and other sodium-beta batteries, are the likely technologies to meet these goals.

The consortium has also set longer-term goals, looking by late in the decade to have batteries in prototype production that can provide an energy-to-weight ratio of 200 watt-hours per kilogram at a cost of less than $100 per kilowatt-hour, as well as a power-to-weight ratio of 400 watts per kilogram and a 10-year useful life. Lithium-iron disulfide and lithium-polymer batteries are the most promising technologies to meet these goals, and other technologies are also being investigated.

USABC's midterm goals are consistent with the need to introduce EVs that meet California automotive emissions regulations by 1998. The longer-term goals are designed to produce zero-emitting EVs that are competitive in every way with conventional gasoline automobiles.

Diverse projects underway

Working toward both mid- and longer-term goals, USABC has awarded a number of research contracts to outside groups for work on specific battery technologies. These include Ovonic Battery Corporation (nickel-metal hybrid), Silent Power (sodium-sulfur), Saft American (nickel-metal hybrid, lithium-iron disulfide), and two multicompany efforts led by W. R. Grace and 3M (lithium-polymer). Where foreign-owned companies are involved, at least 50 percent of the batteries produced for the U.S. auto industry must be manufactured in the United States.

USABC is also sponsoring technical projects at several DOE National Laboratories by way of Cooperative Research and Development Agreements (CRADAs), which make it easier to partner government and private-sector resources. DOE laboratories involved include Lawrence Berkeley National Laboratory, National Renewable Energy Laboratory, Argonne National

figure 12–3 *continued*

Laboratory, Sandia National Laboratory, and Idaho National Engineering
Laboratory.

A model for intercompany and government/industry partnerships

USABC is actually only one of many partnerships among otherwise
competitive American automakers. Chrysler, Ford, and General Motors have
joined forces under the U.S. Council for Automotive Research (USCAR) to
tackle many crucial automotive technology challenges and help boost the
competitiveness of American industry. USABC is one of the largest ventures
under the USCAR agreement.

In addition, the automakers and DOE have, through USABC, developed and
pioneered several new procedures that could maximize the success of
government/industry partnerships, and could lead the way toward more such
partnerships in the future.

For further information, please contact:

Office of Transportation Technologies
U.S. Department of Energy
1000 Independence Ave. SW
Washington, DC 20585
(202) 586-2198

figure 12–3 *continued*

make this assumption explicit. Write it out! Let the readers know what you assume
they bring to the report.

WHAT do you want your readers to do? This question does not always apply. If
you are writing to inform, you do not particularly care what readers do with the
information. If you are writing to persuade, however, you need to be clear about
what you want the readers to do. This means directly stating what you want to happen.

RESPONDING TO FORMS

When the reporting schedule becomes routine, it may be a good idea to develop a
preprinted form to collect and assemble data. Many organizations use forms for informal
reporting. Using preprinted forms allows you to control the information that is gathered
and allows for easy reporting and quick tabulation. A simple instance is the accident report form shown in Fig. 12–4.

Effective forms make it easy to supply and retrieve information. This means they
must be carefully planned. You need to give a good deal of thought to the design of the
form, the kinds of information you request, and the ways it will be supplied. A well-

Pascal Business Systems

Your name _____   Telephone # _____

Employee # _____   Date of birth _____

Department _____

Date of accident: _____

Time of accident: _____

Location of accident: _____

Describe how the accident occurred: _____

_____

_____

_____

Describe injuries: _____

_____

_____

List Witnesses: _____

_____

_____

By signing below, you consent to the release of medical charts, reports, X-rays, diagnoses, and any other medical information to Pascal Business Systems or its authorized representatives from any health care provider rendering treatment or providing consulting or other services in conjunction with the diagnosis and treatment of the injuries described above.

_____   _____

Your signature   Date

accident report form

figure 12–4 An example of an accident report form.

designed form can provide a consistent method to report routine data that needs to be collected in a uniform fashion. Several software packages allow you to create custom forms for almost every purpose.

If you are filling out important forms—performance review forms, for instance—we recommend that you create photocopies and generate several rough drafts before completing the actual document.

DEVELOPING PERSPECTIVE

Professionals who progress in their companies usually write more every year. Even entry-level employees are expected to communicate effectively through a variety of short reports. Eventually you will supervise the writing of your subordinates. Their reports will often go out under your signature and will reflect on the quality of work done under your supervision. Clear reporting is a valuable skill for any career.

You want to develop the capacity to write fluently. Good functional writing is clear, concise, and direct. When you are asked to write something, you want to respond quickly and flexibly. Learning to write this way will save you significant amounts of time, establish your credentials as a communicator, and let you help the people you supervise.

PREPARING SHORT REPORTS: EXERCISES

1. Write a progress report using Fig. 12–1 as a model. Describe the present status of some ongoing activity in which you are involved. If you have difficulty choosing a topic, you might describe your progress in becoming an effective writer and presenter.

2. At some point in your life, you have probably been involved in an accident where there was some sort of physical injury. Write an accident report about the event, making sure to provide specific details. If you are unable to remember specific times and places, you can use your imagination. Include a brief section of ways to avoid similar accidents. You may photocopy the accident report form included in this chapter.

3. Sandy Pascal is planning to travel to Mexico City, where she hopes to negotiate a contract with a local retail firm which will act as our Mexico sales representative. Lourdes Santiago assigns you to conduct some research and prepare a report for Ms. Pascal. In particular, she wants you to provide information about the business climate, customs, and negotiating styles that Ms. Pascal might expect to encounter in Mexico City.

   This report should be three to four pages long. Headings and subheadings should indicate your organization of the information and make it easily accessible to Ms. Pascal.

4. Interview three people who work as business professionals and find out what type of reports these people write on the job. Then use this information to write a one-page report describing your findings.

5. Write a short report to your class on a new or emerging technology in your field. Include at least one table or graph to convey key information. Where will you place the illustration for maximum effectiveness? How much explanatory text will you include?

6. Choose a country in South America or Africa and write a short investigative report in which you describe the language,

climate, population, and current political situation. Be sure that your information is accurate and concise, and acknowledge your sources in the report.

7. Design a preprinted form that collects information from your fellow students or co-workers. Decide what information you will request, and write a survey form that contains at least six questions. See the shaded box for five different types of survey questions. If you desire, you can vary the type of questions.

   Distribute the form to at least ten people, and present the information you collect in a table or graph. Make sure you explain what your graphic demonstrates.

8. Write a feasibility report to Sandy Pascal on the possibility of installing an exercise room at Pascal Business Systems. The room would be a place where employees could go to work off stress. You want to include several exercise machines and perhaps a punching bag for bad days, and any other equipment you consider appropriate. Be sure to provide a simulated budget.

Multiple Choice
   Check the box that best describes you:
   I live on campus.   ☐
   I walk to campus.   ☐
   I commute by car.   ☐
   I commute by train.   ☐
   I commute by bus.   ☐
   Other _____   ☐

Dual Alternative
   If you commute by car, do you park on campus?

       Yes ☐   No ☐

Rank Order
   Rank order the four parking facilities on campus. Use 1 to describe the safest parking lot and 4 to describe the least safe.

       East Lot _____   South Lot _____
       West Lot _____   North Lot _____

Completion
   Complete the following sentence.
   The parking facilities on campus are _____.

Continuum
   Rate the overall parking facilities on campus based on the continuum presented below. Place an *X* on the continuum in the appropriate location.

   |———————|———————|———————|———————|
   very good   good   average   poor   very poor

DESIGNING GRAPHICS AND ILLUSTRATIONS

In the past, few colleges taught individual courses in graphics and illustrations. The colleges that did teach these courses were specialized: engineering, design, and art schools. One reason for this was the difficulty of producing quality illustrations without professional-quality drawing ability or equipment too expensive for the average individual or the average small business to afford. It was assumed that most people would not need the ability to create illustrations.

Personal computers have changed all of that. Now you can generate high-quality graphics on a personal computer for a remarkably low cost. Relatively inexpensive software programs allow you to create sophisticated graphs and charts quickly and easily. You will need some time to learn a program, but once you have mastered the basics, you can produce illustrations that only professionals could have attempted 20 years ago, and

159

you can incorporate these illustrations into memos, business letters, reports, and presentations smoothly and easily. Essentially, the advantages of producing your illustrations on a computer are these:

- You do not have to do all of the calculations yourself. You can enter numbers and the software will make the calculations and figure out the correct proportions.
- The computer will produce neat, crisp lines. The quality of these lines will depend on your output source, whether it is a dot-matrix printer, laser printer, plotter, or $30,000 imagesetter. The higher the quality you desire, the more expensive the investment.
- The computer will allow you to make revisions easily. For example, you can change a number on a graph and redraw the graph effortlessly.
- With many software programs, you can easily insert a graph or illustration within a body of text. With more sophisticated programs, you can make the text flow around the graphic.
- The computer enables you to include many special features. For example, you can include *clip art* (ready-made artwork), or you can use a scanner to insert a photograph in your document. With certain programs, you can add sound, animation, or an interactive environment.

This does not mean that we recommend that you rely solely on computers for your graphics and illustrations. Computers, printers, scanners, and so forth are expensive, and not everyone has access to them. Hand-drawn graphs and tables can, when done by talented individuals, look every bit as good as and sometimes better than what an individual can do with a computer. If you have talent, you should put your talent to use. There will be times when pens and pencils are the right tools to use. You may find, however, that you can also put this talent to use on a computer, and that, when working with numbers, the computer will save you valuable time.

However you produce your graphics and illustrations, you should understand the options you have at your disposal as you work to produce good-looking, clear, and accurate tables, charts, graphs, drawings, and other illustrations. As an aid to understanding what you write and what you say, or standing on their own, good illustrations are invaluable.

Many people understand material better when they can see it. Words do not help these individuals as much as pictures do. Actual and symbolic representations allow us to grasp concepts. So include illustrations to support your text and clarify concepts for your audience.

APPLYING SOME BASIC PRINCIPLES

This chapter covers a variety of different kinds of illustrations, and yet we have not covered all of them. With so many possibilities, building general rules that apply to all of the different kinds of graphics and illustrations is difficult, but there are indeed a few. Fig. 13–1 offers some basic principles that you should be aware of whenever you plan to include an illustration.

six rules
for illustrating your documents

- Consider the audience.
- Keep illustrations simple.
- Illustrate one main point.
- Title each illustration.
- Label each illustration.
- Add a caption.

 **figure 13–1** This is also an example of a bulleted list.

When you construct an illustration, remember this: tables, charts, graphs, and other illustrations tell a story. You must tell the story in such a way that your audience can read and appreciate its full message. A graph that is unclear, incomplete, or inaccurate, no matter how nice it looks, is virtually useless and sometimes harmful. Try to arrange the material as a hierarchy of information, with the most important data receiving the primary focus.

Thus, you should design your illustration for your readers. Follow the document design process step by step with each illustration; that is, consider your purpose, audience, data, deadlines, style and strategy, and format with each illustration. After you have composed the illustration, edit and test your output before you produce the final copy. You can find the document design process in Chapter 1 and in Appendix C.

The vast majority of the time, your illustrations will accompany a longer document: a chart in a formal report, a graph as part of an oral presentation, a drawing as part of a sales document, an illustration in a marketing proposal. Let your graphics enhance the full document. Position each illustration in such a way that your readers will be led to it from the text, and so that it will lead readers to the text if they read the graphic first.

MAKING DISTINCTIONS AMONG YOUR OPTIONS

The choices may seem overwhelming. You know that your document or presentation needs a graphic, but which one? What should it look like? This section examines a number of options available to you so that when you are confronted with a choice, you can make an informed decision.

Tables

Tables are particularly effective ways for people to visualize information. A monthly calendar is a table. Try to imagine a month without visualizing it in terms of a table. Tables are also effective ways of presenting comparisons and contrasts.

Table Number and Title

Line Description	Column Descriptions			
	Column Heading	Column Heading	Column Heading	Column Heading
Line Heading				
Line Heading		Cell		
Line Heading				

figure 13–2 A sample table layout. You can add subheadings if necessary. The column and line descriptions are optional and depend on what your audience needs to know.

Fig. 13–2 shows a typical table format. The *rows* (horizontal) and *columns* (vertical) allow you to present a great amount of information, particularly numbers, in a condensed form that is easily understood and remembered. (The rectangles formed by the rows and columns are called *cells.*) The essential details (dimensions, specifications, capacities, and so forth) of three or more items can be quickly compared by a reader.

Tables have one clear advantage over graphs: you can put much more information into a table. Notice how much information is presented in Fig. 13–3. Imagine putting this much data into a single graph.

Sometimes the line (or row) descriptions and headings and the column descriptions are self-explanatory and therefore unnecessary. Here are some general rules to help you create clear, readable tables:

- Use lines for a grid effect.
- Make sure your rows are straight.
- Make sure you include an overall title above the table.
- Provide column headings and line headings.
- Place data to be compared in the horizontal rows, the direction our eyes move when reading. Use decimals instead of fractions.
- Convert your data to a consistent unit of measurement.
- Make the information easy to grasp.

A *ratings table* (or *matrix*) (Fig. 13-4) allows the reader to compare different items against certain established criteria, such as speed, performance, quality, price, and so forth.

A particularly effective use of this type of illustration is to create easy-to-read troubleshooting and problem-solving tables to accompany machinery, tools, and other technological products. Your readers will thank you for a table that tells them how to resolve their problem when something goes wrong, like the one shown on p. 164.

Table 1 Civilian labor force by sex and age, 1979 and 1992, and moderate growth projection to 2005

	Level (thousands)			Change (thousands)		Percent change		Percent distribution			Annual growth rate (percent)	
	1979	1992	2005	1979–1992	1992–2005	1979–1992	1992–2005	1979	1992	2005	1979–1992	1992–2005
Total, 16 years and older	104,962	126,982	150,516	22,020	23,534	21.0	18.5	100.0	100.0	100.0	1.5	1.3
16 to 24	25,407	20,454	24,127	-4,953	3,673	-19.5	18.0	24.2	16.1	16.0	-1.7	1.3
25 to 54	64,520	91,097	105,054	26,577	13,957	41.2	15.3	61.5	71.7	69.8	2.7	1.1
55 and older	15,034	15,432	21,335	398	5,903	2.6	38.3	14.3	12.2	14.2	.2	2.5
Men, 16 years and older	60,726	69,184	78,718	8,458	9,534	13.9	13.8	57.9	54.5	52.3	1.0	1.0
Women, 16 years and older	44,235	57,798	71,798	13,563	14,000	30.7	24.2	42.1	45.5	47.7	2.1	1.7

Source: Bureau of Labor Statistics. (Fullerton, 32)

figure 13–3 An example of a table.

	Criterion #1	Criterion #2	Criterion #3	Criterion #4
Product #1	√			
Product #2		√	√	√
Product #3	√	√	√	√
Product #4		√	√	
Product #5		√		

figure 13–4 A standard format for a ratings table. If all four criteria were equal in value, product #3 would be rated superior.

Problem	Analysis	Solution(s)
If this occurs	then it means	try this
x	y	z

Charts

There are many different types of charts, including organizational charts, flow charts, and time charts. Many people also refer to graphs as charts. As a guide to understanding, we intend to make a distinction between charts and graphs in this textbook; in general, charts deal less with numbers and more with abstract processes and structures. What we refer to as a bar graph in this book may be called a bar chart in another text. Both terms refer to the same thing.

Organizational charts enable us to visualize structures of complex organizations. Fig. 13–5 presents an organizational chart for Pascal Business Systems. Notice how this chart focuses your attention on the positions and their relative importance within the hierarchy of the company.

Flow charts allow us to visualize processes and systems. Flow charts are particularly valuable guides to understanding decision-making processes and technical processes where alternative paths may be taken. The symbols in a flow chart represent specific activities, such as operations, data, or material flow; for example, a diamond symbolizes a step in a process where a decision needs to be made, while rectangles represent activities in the process. Lines and arrows represent interrelationships among the components.

Time charts allow us to visualize a schedule of work to be done. They are particularly helpful when you have a large project to do that requires simultaneous efforts by many people or organizations. Time charts are an especially valuable planning tool because they make us aware of all of the tasks that need to be accomplished to complete a project.

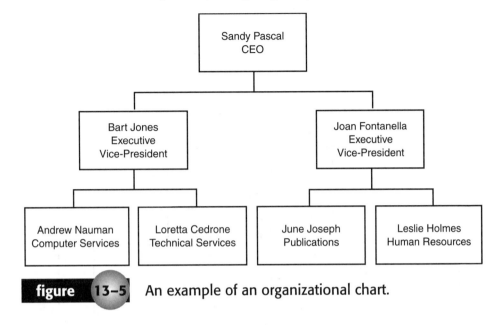

figure 13–5 An example of an organizational chart.

Gantt charts and *PERT charts* (Program Evaluation and Review Technique) depict the status of each part of a project, and are particularly valuable for project management. In a Gantt chart, each division of space represents a time interval, and bars show the work to be done during the intervals. Gantt charts can also be used to compare planning estimates and actual work done. PERT charts are much more complex, and require sophisticated computer software to compare current progress versus planned objectives with an emphasis on time performance and cost. A PERT analysis estimates the probability of a task ending on a particular date at a specific cost. A very simplified version of a PERT chart is presented in Fig. 13–9, which analyzes a six-step process, from the authorization of a new laboratory to the beginning of operations. Some PERT charts analyze thousands of steps.

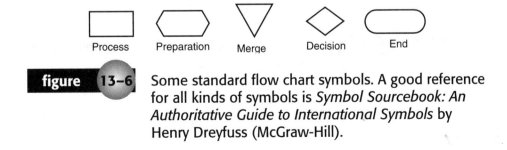

figure 13–6 Some standard flow chart symbols. A good reference for all kinds of symbols is *Symbol Sourcebook: An Authoritative Guide to International Symbols* by Henry Dreyfuss (McGraw-Hill).

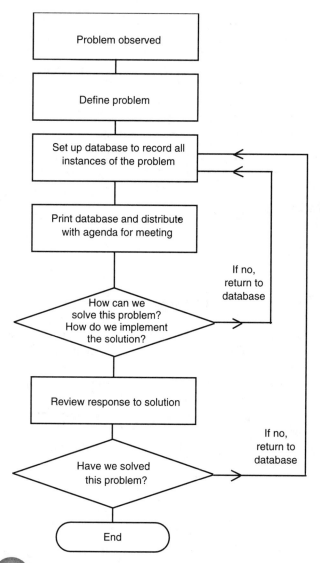

figure 13-7 An example of a flow chart for a problem-solving process.

	next-to-final day							final day						
	8:00	9:00	10:00	11:00	12:00	1:00	2:00	8:00	9:00	10:00	11:00	12:00	1:00	2:00
Decide on cover design	▬	▬												
Integrate art work		▬												
Complete contents			▬	▬										
Print document					▬	▬								
Print cover						▬								
Bind pages							▬							
Distribute copies												▬		
Mail the document													▬	

figure 13-8 An example of a Gantt chart.

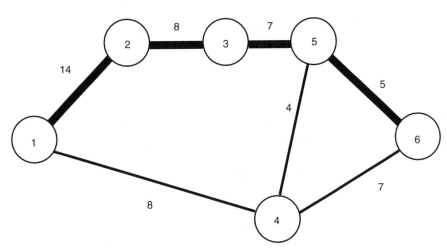

1 = Authorization of project
2 = Acquisition of equipment
3 = Installation of equipment

4 = Transfer of staff to office
5 = Training of staff
6 = Beginning of operations

figure 13-9 In this illustration of a PERT chart, the heavier black line represents the path that takes the most days from start to finish. The numerals above the lines illustrate the number of days projected to complete steps in the process. This chart does not analyze costs.

Graphs

We can visualize simple and complex relationships between numbers with graphs. We can take, for example, 21 different numbers that would be virtually incomprehensible in a list, and turn that sequence into an easily understood illustration that has great impact.

The personal computer has changed our ability to produce graphs. As previously mentioned, we can now take a complex set of statistics and rapidly transform it into a clear and accurate graph. And since creating graphs has become easier, we now see more of them. Your ability to read and understand graphs and your ability to create clear and accurate graphs will be very important in your career.

Parts of a Graph   Graphs can differ tremendously. However, some standard features are common to almost all graphs. This section examines some of these standard features.

Except for pie and column graphs, graphs have a *horizontal axis* (or *x*-axis) and a *vertical axis* (or *y*-axis). You should divide each axis into equal parts. The two axes will represent different kinds of quantities, such as months (time) versus dollars (profit), so the axes need only be consistent within themselves. In other words, you could make each division (or increment) in the *y*-axis one inch apart and make each division in the *x*-axis three inches apart. The *x*- and *y*-axes should be clearly and correctly labeled.

Every graph should have a *title*. The title is one more aid for your reader. The title should be straightforward and accurate, conveying in a few words, ideally fewer than eight, the subject of the graph. A subtitle can be included to add information to the title. If you are producing a series of graphs, you should have a cover page with an overall title.

A *legend* or *key* is needed whenever you are graphing more than one item. Whenever you are comparing two or more items, you will need to represent the items in different ways: different colors, shadings, shapes, or interior designs.

Finally, each graph should be clearly labeled. The *label* should include a figure number and some explanation of what the graph represents. This explanation is frequently referred to as the caption. Use this opportunity to direct the way your audience reads and understands your graph. Describe what the graph conveys. Remember, some of your audience may understand the words better than the visual presentation. The figures should be arranged in numerical order; for example, Fig. 1, Fig. 2, Fig. 3, and so forth, or Figure 1–1, 1–2, 1–3, and so forth.

Note: If you need to abbreviate in order to save space, make sure you use standard abbreviations. In other words, consult a dictionary.

At times, in order to save space, you may want to skip some of the numbers or other increments on one of the axes. Usually you will do this with the *y*-axis. To let the reader know that you have done this, use the symbol ⚡ or ⚡ .

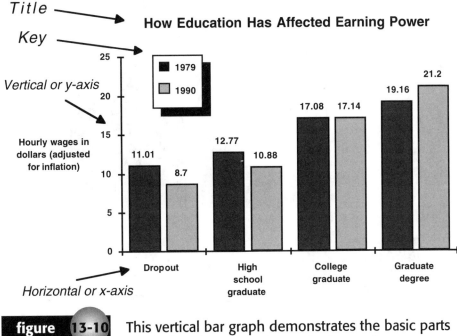

Title

How Education Has Affected Earning Power

Key

Vertical or y-axis

Hourly wages in dollars (adjusted for inflation)

Horizontal or x-axis

figure 13-10 This vertical bar graph demonstrates the basic parts of graphs. The graph shows the increasing importance of graduate degrees and the shrinking wages of high school graduates and those without a high school diploma.

Graphs Can Lie Statistics can lie. They can be presented in such a way that readers can be deceived; the readers receive an impression that may be radically different from the actual situation. In the same way, graphs can lie.

Examine Figs. 13–11, 13–12, and 13–13. Notice that the only difference between the three graphs is that the increments on the *y*-axis have been changed. In Fig. 13–11, the

ethical considerations

As both a reader and a creator of graphs, you should know that graphs can lie. As a reader of graphs, you should study the graph closely to make sure that you know exactly what it says, which may be different from what the maker of the graph wanted you to see. As a creator of graphs, you need to be aware of what you should and should not do to influence your audience in a particular way. Obviously, you want to affect the way your readers look at your graphs, but you do not want to cross over the fine line between influence and misrepresentation.

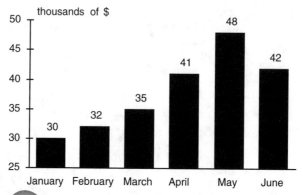

figure 13-11

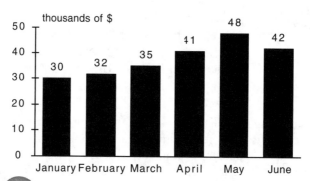

figure 13-12

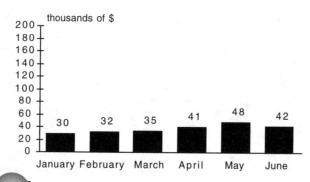

figure 13-13

y-axis goes from $25,000 to $50,000; in Fig. 13–12, the *y*-axis goes from $0 to $50,000; and in Fig. 13–13, the *y*-axis goes from $0 to $200,000. Everything else about the graphs is exactly the same. Yet if you were to take a quick glance at the three graphs, you would assume that the graphs showed completely different sales figures; sales seem to increase dramatically in Fig. 13–11, while sales seem to change hardly at all in Fig. 13–13.

Which one is the real graph? They all are. Each of the three is an accurate representation of the data. (The graphmaker should highlight the fact that the y-axis in Fig. 13–11 begins at $25,000 and not at zero.) What do the three graphs show? You must study each graph closely so that you can interpret what it says.

This is obviously not the only way to use the structure of the graph to influence your readers. Some of the things to avoid when creating graphs are:

- distorting the bars in a bar graph (for example, making a bar twice as tall and twice as wide creates a visual image four times as large)
- using a non-uniform time scale
- omitting key information (for example, Fig. 13–11 would give a very different impression if the month of June were omitted)
- using outdated data

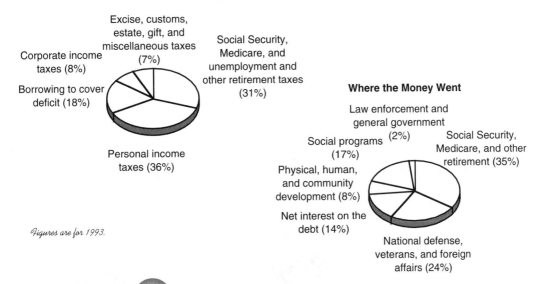

Where the Income Came From

Excise, customs, estate, gift, and miscellaneous taxes (7%)

Social Security, Medicare, and unemployment and other retirement taxes (31%)

Corporate income taxes (8%)

Borrowing to cover deficit (18%)

Personal income taxes (36%)

Figures are for 1993.

Where the Money Went

Law enforcement and general government (2%)

Social programs (17%)

Social Security, Medicare, and other retirement (35%)

Physical, human, and community development (8%)

Net interest on the debt (14%)

National defense, veterans, and foreign affairs (24%)

figure 13-14 Two pie graphs showing the money collected by the federal government in 1993 (left) and what the government did with the money (right).

Source: Department of the Treasury.

You owe it to your audience to represent the information accurately and clearly and to avoid misrepresenting the data.

Types of Graphs   This section illustrates the most basic kinds of graphs. Many other kinds exist, but if you understand the ones covered here, you have a good basis for tackling more complex kinds of graphs.

Pie graphs and *column graphs* are particularly useful in depicting the parts of a whole. Whenever you have 100 percent of something, or one unit, and you want to show parts of that whole, think first about pie and column graphs. (*Note:* Pie and column graphs are frequently referred to as charts. We are covering them in this section because they are so closely related to bar and line graphs, and because most graphing software programs allow you to do pie and column graphs. Strictly speaking, they are graph charts.)

Since each slice of the pie represents a proportion of 100 percent, pie graphs are difficult to draw by hand. You need to calculate the percentage of each slice in terms of 360 degrees. For example, a slice that represents 20 percent of the whole would be calculated as follows:

$$20/100 = x/360$$
$$x = 72 \text{ degrees}$$

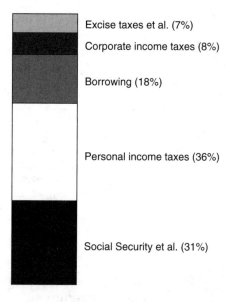

Where the Income Came From

Excise taxes et al. (7%)

Corporate income taxes (8%)

Borrowing (18%)

Personal income taxes (36%)

Social Security et al. (31%)

figure 13-15   A column graph illustrating the same data as the first pie graph in Fig. 13–14.

You will need to measure the angle with a protractor or some other instrument, and draw the circle with a compass. (When drawing a pie graph by hand, you should begin measuring the angles at the noon position on a clock.) A computer program with graphing capabilities will handle all of the calculations and the drawing of the graph in milliseconds. The same principle is true of column graphs; a computer program will calculate the correct proportions for you.

Avoid having more than twelve divisions in a pie graph. The human eye has a difficult time seeing differences in pie slices under 30 degrees.

Line graphs are good ways to show trends. Generally easy and quick to plot, they allow the reader to see the direction or progress of a variable against time or some other constraint. You can connect points on a line graph with straight lines; you can make a single line to show a trend; or, if you do the calculations, you can show a curve of the changes between points on the graph. Fig. 13–16 connects the points.

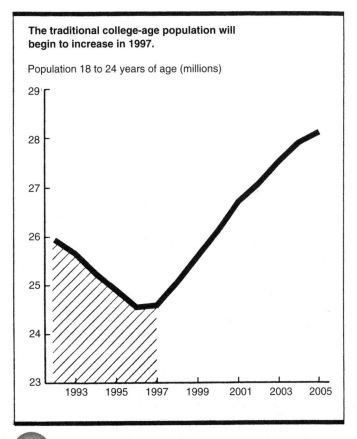

The traditional college-age population will begin to increase in 1997.

Population 18 to 24 years of age (millions)

figure **13-16** This line graph shows how the population of 18-to-24-year olds has begun to increase.

Source: Bureau of the Census.

Smoking and American Mortality

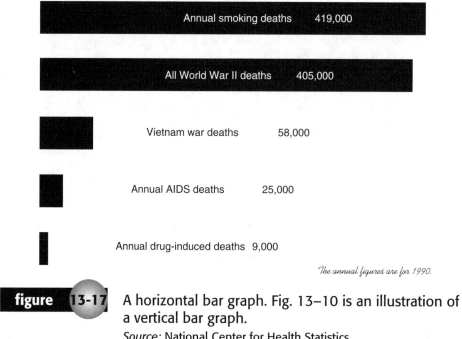

Annual smoking deaths   419,000

All World War II deaths   405,000

Vietnam war deaths   58,000

Annual AIDS deaths   25,000

Annual drug-induced deaths 9,000

The annual figures are for 1990.

figure 13-17 A horizontal bar graph. Fig. 13–10 is an illustration of a vertical bar graph.
Source: National Center for Health Statistics.

Bar graphs represent information in bars or columns. They are particularly clear ways of showing comparisons between two or more variables. A helpful feature of bar graphs is the inclusion of the values of the bar just above or inside the bar. The bars can be either vertical or horizontal. Horizontal bar graphs are preferable when the bars do not begin at 0.

Stacked bars are bars that are divided to show how different variables contribute proportionally to the whole. Each stacked bar is similar to a column graph; the stacked bars are plotted on a graph to show comparisons.

Surface graphs (or *area graphs*) depict fluctuations over time, and are particularly good for showing changes over many time periods. Use surface graphs for illustrating changes in volume and changes across a positive and negative axis. For example, surface graphs are used to illustrate financial changes, such as stock market fluctuations or profit changes. Be very careful with surface graphs when there are three or more items being compared; the magnitude of trends can be distorted.

The *Guidelines for graph decisions* on page 176 should help when you are faced with a decision about which type of graph to select. Make your decision carefully; it is not always easy to change from one type of graph to another.

Creativity plays a role in graphmaking. The limits of graphing possibilities are placed only by your imagination, and sophisticated computer programs allow you to invent new forms. *Pictographs* (pictorial graphs) are graphs that use pictures and images rather than lines and geometric shapes to represent data. Figure 13–20 is a pictograph.

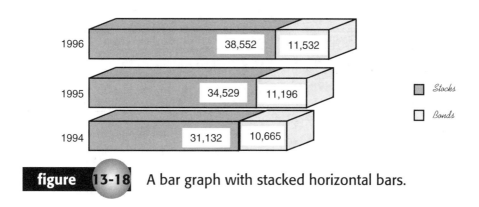

figure 13-18 A bar graph with stacked horizontal bars.

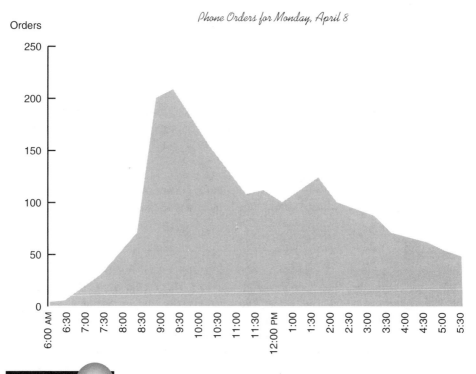

figure 13-19 This surface graph shows the number of phone orders received by Pascal Business Systems across a typical day.

Guidelines for graph decisions

If you want to show:	Then use:
Change in volume	Surface
Change over time periods	Bar/line combo
Emphasis	
on a part of a whole	Pie with cut slice
on volume	Surface
on one of several series	Line or bar/line combo
Parts of a whole	
at a specific time	Pie or column
at two different times	2 pies or 2 columns or 2 stacked bars
over a few time periods	Stacked bars
over many time periods	Surface or stacked bar
Relationships between two series	
over a few time periods	Bar or bar/line combo
over many time periods	Line
Trends	
statistical trends	Line
over many time periods	Vertical bar
over a few time periods	Line

Projections   Projecting future trends is an inexact science at best. Whenever you are projecting, you need to make this fact very clear to the reader, and you need to state the basis for your projection; this should include how you came up with the projections, how you made the calculations or, if you are basing your projections on research you have done, the source of your statistics. Note the projections in Fig. 13–21.

If your graph reports past and future situations, the exact point where the graph changes from recorded past to future projections should be clearly marked on your graph.

Drawings

Drawings, sketches, diagrams, and schematics allow the reader to picture what you are saying in your text. The typical reader can visualize the arrangement of components (*configuration drawing*) or the relationships of the parts of a system (*schematic diagram*) much more easily when the information is presented visually. Whether you work with an artist or draw an illustration yourself, there are a number of things to remember:

- Plan the illustration carefully.
- Construct a rough draft. Evaluate this draft and make the necessary changes.
- Keep the illustration simple.

The Perceived Value of Vacations

figure 13-20 An example of a pictograph.
Reprinted with the permission of Edith Twining.

Projections Vary

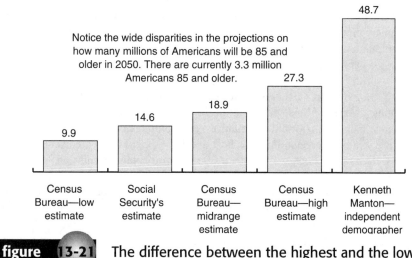

figure 13-21 The difference between the highest and the lowest projections is almost 39 million.
Source: National Institute on Aging.

Freehand Drawings The ability to draw accurate representations of products, processes, technical parts, and machinery is a very helpful one. If you have it, by all means use it. You should also realize that not everyone has artistic talent; if you do not, you need to find another way to illustrate your work. Many organizations have professional artists on staff for important documents, and you can find freelance artists in the phone book and by inquiring at art supply stores.

The artists will need your technical expertise to guide them in completing the illustrations you need. Make sure you provide specific written instructions that express exactly what you want. Another way is to utilize a computer design program.

Computer-Aided Design CAD (computer-aided design) and CADD (computer-aided design and drafting) software have revolutionized the design process. Knowledge of a CAD program will enable you to present readable and accurate drawings and diagrams. The programs are expensive for an individual to purchase, and they can take some time to learn, but the results are worth the effort. Some of the programs enable you to do three-dimensional modeling. Knowledge of a CAD program is viewed as a very valuable commodity by technical industries. The knowledge alone may get you a job.

Other Kinds of Illustrations

New technology allows us access to a wide spectrum of graphic applications. We can do just about anything we can think of if we have the right equipment. This section suggests some graphics you can use to enhance your documents and get your message across.

Clip Art Many software programs allow you to take a predrawn image and place it anywhere in your document. You can size the image to your liking, and with some programs you can change the proportions of the clip art. (Some programs also allow you to manipulate the image.) The images include drawings, symbols, icons, and other artwork that may enhance your documents.

Maps Don't underestimate the importance of placing your readers within a geographical locale. Maps show relationships of elements in space. Some clip art programs include maps of major cities, countries, and continents. Topographical, astronomical, historical, nautical, economic, and a host of other types of maps are excellent communication aids. If you photocopy a map, make sure that you obtain permission to do so.

Photographs Although not everyone is a great photographer, any clearly focused representation is indeed worth a thousand words.

Scanned Images Until recently, most of us thought that the only way to incorporate a photograph into a document was to paste it in. Scanners digitize a page and import the image into a picture format. Once imported, it can be manipulated, scaled, rotated, or reversed before it is included in a document.

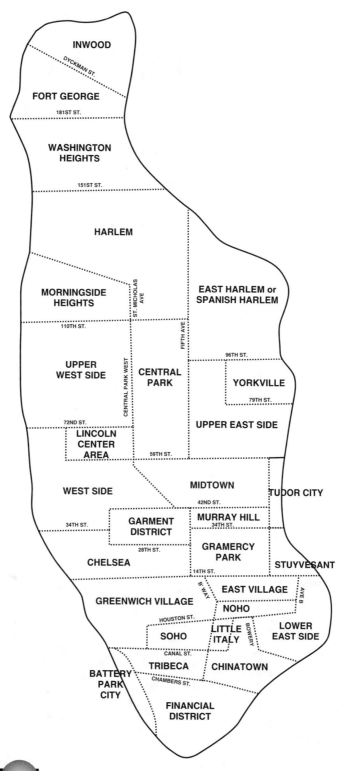

figure 13-22 This map offers a new perspective on an old subject.

map sites on the web

University of California–Berkeley Library Collections in Maps and Cartography
http://www.lib.berkeley.edu/EART/MapCollections.html
The Perry-Castañeda Library Map Collection, University of Texas at Austin
http://www.lib.utexas.edu/Libs/PCL/Map_collection/Map_collection.html
Cartography and Graphic Services, Florida State University
http://cartlab-www.freac.fsu.edu/

Lists You certainly do not need high-tech equipment to accomplish one very basic and very helpful illustration for your readers. Making a list of important material in a series puts the items in an easily understood frame of reference for your reader.

Positioning Graphics and Illustrations

When most people look at a page that has both text and an illustration, their eyes are immediately drawn to the illustration. If you can, you should try to position the illustration within, or surrounded by, the text. If you send a reader to an appendix or to another page, it is highly unlikely that the illustration will have a forceful impact. It may not even be seen. Illustrations are easily viewed as blocks because they are usually rectangular in nature. Carefully place the illustrations on the page where readers will see them. Don't force the reader to manipulate the page to see the graphic. Positioning should be part of your overall design plan.

figure 13-23 The image on the left was distorted to form the image on the right.

some rules for positioning your illustrations

- Place your illustrations near the first reference in the text.
- The size of the illustration should be roughly equivalent to its importance.
- Consider enclosing your illustrations with a border. There may be times when it is best not to use a border, but think about the possibility first.
- Avoid having your readers rotate the document whenever possible. If you must include an oversize illustration, have readers turn the document 90 degrees clockwise.
- Try to balance your illustration blocks on the page.
- If possible, position an illustration in the top right-hand area of the first page of a section of your document, slightly below your heading.

Your purpose in most of the illustrations you create in your business career will be to inform rather than to attract attention and provoke an atmosphere or feeling. Make sure that the design of the page supports your purpose.

USING SPECIAL EFFECTS

Color charts and graphs in texts, and color overheads during presentations, were striking at one time because of their rarity. Special effects are special because they have not yet become something that many people can do. Now people are impressed with interactive video and 3-D animation. You may have the opportunity to work with these and other special effects during your career. When you attend meetings and conferences, or when you see exciting graphics and illustrations in print or other media, try to learn new techniques that can improve your illustrations.

why do we use visual aids?

- To present information effectively
- To save comprehension time
- To direct the audience's attention
- To display statistical relationships
- To show comparisons
- To influence the audience *visually*

Once you have mastered the basics of the preparation of visuals, you may become very excited by what you can do. There is a danger here. Don't get carried away and overwhelm your reader with fancy visuals.

We would like to re-emphasize the second and third rules in Figure 13–1: *Keep illustrations simple,* and *Illustrate one main point* with each visual. Tell one main story with each visual, and tell that story completely.

As a general rule, assume that your readers have 10 to 20 seconds to grasp the main point of your illustrations. Don't expect them to spend ten minutes deciphering material, no matter how important it is. Most readers will not make the effort. Your task is to simplify.

DESIGNING GRAPHICS AND ILLUSTRATIONS: EXERCISES

1. Make a table based on the information that follows:

   According to Dataquest estimates as of March 1995, Apple has gained a 22.9 percent worldwide market share in terms of estimated multimedia PC shipments in 1994; Apple has shipped 2,349,000 units. Packard Bell has a 19.2 percent market share with 1,969,000 units. Compaq, at 11.9 percent (1,226,000 units); IBM, at 8.0 percent (820,000 units); and Gateway, at 5.8 percent (598,000 units), follow, while all other companies compose 32.2 percent of the market at 3,305,000 units. The total worldwide market is 10,267,000 units.

   The situation in the United States is slightly different, where Packard Bell leads with a 24.3 percent market share, which represents 1,678,000 units, compared to Apple's 20.5 percent of the market, representing 1,415,000 units. Compaq is third with 13.5 percent of the market (934,000 units), while IBM has garnered 7.0 percent of the market (483,000) and Gateway has 7.5 percent of the market (515,000 units). Other companies shipped 1,883,000 units, representing 27.3 percent of the market. The total number of units shipped within the United States was 6,908,000.

2. Create a text chart or graphic using the following information: The United States ranked fourteenth out of sixteen industrialized nations in terms of money spent on education for grades K through 12. The study calculated the money spent on education as a percentage of the gross domestic product. The source of this information is the UNESCO Center for Education Statistics (1988). *Hint:* Don't try to force a graph out of this exercise.

3. Prepare an illustration to depict the following information:

   A 65-year-old who retires today has a 58 percent chance of living to age 85, a 38 percent chance of living to age 90, and a 19 percent chance of living to age 95. (Source: *The TIAA-CREF Participant,* 1993.) Don't assume that a graph is the only way to communicate this information; a graph is one way, but there are others.

4. Create an illustration or graphic using the following information:

   According to the July 1993 *MacWorld* national survey on electronic eavesdropping, 4 percent of top corporate managers believe that electronic monitoring is a "good tool to routinely verify honesty," 12 percent believe such monitoring to be a "good tool to routinely monitor performance," and 22.6

	Total number		Number per 100 million km	
	Injured	Killed	Injured	Killed
Canada	280,575	4,285	206.8	3.1
Japan	752,845	10,344	137.2	1.9
Turkey	80,437	7,007	329.0	29.0
United Kingdom	313,400	5,050	116.0	1.8
United States	3,495,000	46,385	112.9	1.5

percent believe monitoring is a "good tool to verify evidence of wrongdoing," while 7.3 percent believe that it is a "good tool to enhance performance." On the other hand, 16.3 percent agreed with the statement that electronic monitoring is "usually or always counterproductive," and 34.6 percent responded that electronic eavesdropping is "never acceptable." (*Note:* The total may not equal 100 percent due to nonresponses.)

5. Construct a flow chart that illustrates a process that you know well. The process may be nontechnical in nature, but it should have at least seven steps before completion. Remember, you can add text to help explain material presented in the flow chart.

6. Here is your opportunity to create a visual display of information on road accidents that result in injuries and deaths. You do not have to illustrate all of the information in the table at the top of this page. Select the details that you determine make a significant statement, and create a graphic that highlights this statement.

   The number of accidents may reflect how crowded the roads are, the quality of the roads, or the impact of safety measures such as seat belts and tougher drunk-driving laws.

   These figures are for one year, *the latest available year from 1985–1988.* The number killed refers to individuals dying within 30 days of the accident.

7. According to the Boston Public Works Department and Energy Systems Research Group, the city of Boston generates an estimated 231,702 tons of trash a year. Construct a graph that illustrates the top ten categories of trash.

Category	Tons per year
1. Newspapers	21,763
2. Leaves	20,145
3. Food waste	16,999
4. Books/magazines	14,583
5. Grass and brush	14,332
6. Clear glass	13,844
7. Cardboard boxes	13,614
8. Plastic packages and containers	10,421
9. Miscellaneous scrap iron	10,375
10. Nonpackaging plastic	8,520

8. Draw a graph to illustrate the following estimated percentages of trash generated by the city of Boston in a year:

Category	Percentage
Paper and cardboard	32%
Leaves and yard debris	15%
Glass	12%
Metals	12%
Plastic	8%
Miscellaneous	21%

9. The city of Boston generates the following amounts of glass trash in a year:

Category	Tons per year
Clear glass	13,844
Green glass	7,411
Amber glass	4,816
Miscellaneous glass	2,637

(a) Construct a pie graph to illustrate this information.

(b) Now construct a pie graph that emphasizes the estimated amount of green glass generated by the city of Boston in a year.

10. On average, Americans ate 14.8 pounds of seafood in 1992, according to the National Fisheries Institute. Here are the top five categories:

Species	Pounds per capita
Tuna	3.5
Shrimp	2.5
Alaskan pollock	1.2
Salmon	1.0
Cod	1.0

Draw an illustration that highlights this information. Your caption should lead the reader to a conclusion about the information: What does the illustration show? Draw your own conclusion, but make sure that your illustration emphasizes this conclusion.

11. Most colleges monitor the percentage of their students who graduate within five years of entering. According to the American College Testing Program, students who scored over 1100 (combined) on their SAT were the most likely to graduate within five years; the figures at the bottom of this page are for students who entered college in 1987.

Create a graph to display this information.

12. Use color or some other special effects to construct an illustration highlighting what you consider to be a significant point, one that you want other people to understand and appreciate.

13. Choose an appropriate format to illustrate the following information, all of which involves the typical loudness range of some common sounds.

Sound	Range (in decibels)
Clothes dryer	50–73
Vacuum cleaner	60–84
Automobile	60–89
Train	72–92
Power lawnmower	80–94
Motorcycle	80–110
Snowmobile	84–109

Include in your illustration the following information: Prolonged exposure to noise of 85 decibels causes light hearing loss. Prolonged exposure to noise of 90 decibels causes mild to moderate hearing

Average combined SAT score of students accepted in 1987	Graduation rate of students attending private colleges	Graduation rate of students attending public colleges
over 1100	82%	66%
931–1099	66%	52%
800–930	55%	45%
700–799	45%	40%
under 700	43%	38%

loss. Prolonged exposure to noise at 95 decibels causes moderate to severe loss. Short exposure to noise at 100 decibels can cause permanent hearing loss. *Hint:* Consider a horizontal bar graph as one possible way of graphing this information.

14. The town of Stanfield, Oregon, is attempting to monitor its water use more closely. Prepare a series of appropriate illustrations for a presentation based on the last four years of water usage. See the figures below.

15. If you have the technology available to you, present a demonstration to the class on how computers can manipulate images. Scan an image from a popular magazine, manipulate the image (for example, you might distort the image, take the head off one individual and put it on another, or radically change the color scheme), and print the new image. Bring both the original and the manipulated image to class. The class may want to discuss the ethics of such manipulation. Under what circumstances is it acceptable? When is it morally unacceptable?

	Year			
	1	2	3	4
Total*	76.62	83.59	73.42	96.61
Maximum Day	0.35	0.40	0.35	0.95
Average Day	0.21	0.23	0.20	0.26

* all figures in millions of gallons

DELIVERING PRESENTATIONS

14

In this chapter we examine how to prepare and give presentations that work. As you advance in your career, you will be called upon to present your ideas in front of groups more and more frequently.

The more details you can prepare beforehand, the better your presentation will be. Imagine how you want the presentation to go. Imagine the reaction of the audience. Visualize the presentation being a complete success. As you become more comfortable with public speaking, your ability to visualize your presentation will improve.

For our purposes, we will define a *presentation* as any event where your primary purpose is to speak in front of an audience. In truth, there is very little to distinguish a meeting from a presentation, and there are times when the two words are used interchangeably. We may be able to distinguish a presentation and a meeting by noting two differences.

The focus of a presentation is usually on the presenter, while the focus of a meeting is usually on the group. A second key distinction has to do with the audience; the leader of a meeting usually has control over who will and who will not attend, but a speaker in a presentation rarely has complete control over who attends. For a presentation, a general announcement is usually made within an organization or to the general public, and interested parties become the audience.

Given that you have little control over who attends, presentations tend to be more formal than meetings. In a positive sense, you are putting on a show for your audience, who have come to hear what you have to say; in other words, your task is to communicate a certain amount of information. You may be curious about what the audience has to say in response, but primarily you want them to absorb your message. In contrast, the leader of a meeting is frequently very concerned with getting feedback from the audience; the leader may encourage participation, sometimes to the point of generating a discussion and then standing back and letting the participants determine the direction of the discussion.

PREPARING FOR A PRESENTATION

Presenting information before an audience demands that you consider how your audience will receive your message, and that means that you need to think about the ways that a speech is different from a written document. Look at the presentation evaluation form on the next page for a list of some of the factors that make a presentation successful.

This presentation evaluation form certainly does not take into account every factor that is important in a presentation, but it should give you some ideas about areas on which to concentrate. As you give more presentations, your sense of presence before an audience improves. You project more, you remember to make eye contact with the audience, you feel more comfortable being on stage. With the added confidence, your posture improves, your gestures become more natural, and your transitions become smoother. This is why it is so important to get experience by making presentations, and learning what works and what does not work for you. (If you are serious about gaining experience and have few opportunities, investigate joining a Toastmasters club or a campus organization.)

The most important advice we can give you is to conceptualize the presentation beforehand. Try to imagine your audience, and give the presentation aloud. The following list gives some more advice:

- Speak to the back row.
- Look at your audience.

Presentation Evaluation Form

Speaker _____

Topic _____

1 = needs improvement	2 = satisfactory	3 = good	4 = excellent

		1	2	3	4
Content	Knowledge of topic				
	Organization				
	Introduction				
	Body				
	Conclusion				
	Clarity				
	Awareness of audience				
	Transitions				
Delivery	Voice projection				
	Eye Contact				
	Posture and gestures				
	Visual aids				
	Optional – enthusiasm				
	vocal variety				
	language use				
	credibility				
Q and A	Content of responses				
	Rapport with audience				

Overall Evaluation

What did the speaker do most effectively? _____

_____

What areas could be improved upon? _____

_____

General Comments: _____

_____

_____

- Pick out three different individuals in the audience and speak to them.
- Practice different postures and speaking positions.
- Work out the timing of the different parts of your presentation.
- Write down the transitions between sections.
- Test the equipment you will be using.
- Imagine the questions from the audience.

Overcoming Anxiety

First and foremost, you must come to grips with one basic proposition about your presentation: You may be nervous before your speech. And you are not alone. Many people experience anxiety before making a presentation. So it is perfectly possible that your pulse rate will increase, you will sweat more than usual, your mouth will become dry, and your memory will become hazy.

If this happens, accept it. It is normal, and the odds are that it won't affect your presentation. As soon as you get through the first minute, you will be fine, and you will build momentum as it becomes obvious that your worst fears haven't come true. Avoid reacting to your nervousness negatively: "I expected to be nervous and now I am. It's going to ruin my speech. Now I'm even more nervous. I can't do it." Instead, channel your nervousness. Realize that being nervous also means that you have more adrenaline to channel into your presentation. Make the added energy work for you: "I expected to be nervous and now I am. But that's to be expected. Many presenters are nervous, and I'm no different. I've prepared well, and so my speech will go well."

From our experience—we have seen hundreds of individual and group student presentations—presentations that do not have a positive energy do not go over well with the audience, no matter how knowledgeable the presenters are. A poor presentation actually drains an audience and makes the audience feel uncomfortable. On the other hand, when the presenters are enthusiastic, the energy is transferred to the audience. Therefore, being slightly nervous can have positive consequences.

Analyzing Your Audience

As we mentioned before, you may not be able to control who attends your presentation. However, you can still prepare for your audience. Know as much as you can about their point of view, know their positions within their company or organization, know their responsibilities, and know their history.

Knowing as much as you can about your audience will help you determine the best ways to bring your point across. You will decide how much detail to include and how sophisticated you can make your explanations.

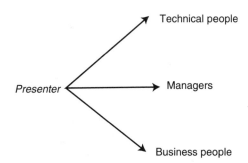

A presenter may be speaking to three different groups, each of which may focus on seperate issues.

- What will get the audience's attention?
- Are you influencing a decision? How?

DISCOVERING YOUR PURPOSE

As we have tried to stress, the nature of your audience influences your purpose. In the document design process, we placed knowing your purpose before knowing your audience. Here, however, because your audience determines to a great extent your message, once you have analyzed your audience you can begin to understand your purpose. In truth, audience and purpose are so interrelated as to be united. It is difficult to think about one without the other.

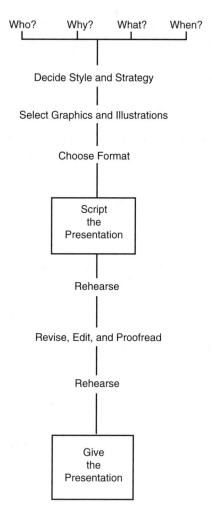

| Who? | Why? | What? | When? |

Decide Style and Strategy

Select Graphics and Illustrations

Choose Format

Script the Presentation

Rehearse

Revise, Edit, and Proofread

Rehearse

Give the Presentation

figure **14–1** The presentation design process.

Your presentation will generally have one of a few basic purposes: to propose, to report, to motivate, to inform, to instruct, or to persuade. However, you may want to accomplish a combination of purposes.

You need to decide your primary purpose before you begin. As a way of testing yourself on your purpose, complete the following sentences:

The purpose of my presentation is to _____ my audience *to* (or, if your purpose is to inform, substitute *about*)

_____ .

At the conclusion of my presentation, I would like the audience to

_____ .

Since your audience will have to receive information at your pace and they will not have the opportunity to backtrack to clarify important points as they could if they were reading your writing, it is a good idea to state your purpose a number of times in your presentation. Remember, many people do not retain information presented to their ears as well as they retain information presented visually. So make certain that your audience understands your message:

- State your purpose early and explicitly.
- In the middle, review your purpose.
- Return to your purpose in your closing.

If you follow this advice, you have already completed the first step toward organizing your presentation.

ORGANIZING YOUR PRESENTATION

This is truly simple advice, essentially the King's admonishment to the White Rabbit in *Alice in Wonderland:* "Begin at the beginning and go on till you come to the end: then stop." What could be simpler? All you need to do is to figure out what should be in the beginning, the middle, and the end. Unfortunately, sometimes it isn't quite so easy.

Here is a sample rough outline of some areas covered in many presentations. You need to work out a logical order for the material you want to present. Notice the structure of the sample outline:

1. Title
2. Introduction
3. Overview
4. Background and History

  5. The Main Issue or Issues
  6. The Alternatives
  7. Recommendations
  8. Cost Analysis
  9. Closing
  10. Question-and-Answer Session

This organization is not intended as a one-time, all-purpose organizational plan. Let your structure fit your presentation. The important thing is to have a clear and logical sequence for the ideas you present. Here are some sequences for you to consider:

- *problem→solution*—Use this pattern when your task is to solve a problem.
- *theory→plan of action*—Similar in nature to the problem→solution approach, this pattern emphasizes an abstract concept that you or your team has developed.
- *cause→effect*—Use this pattern to analyze the possible outcomes of a strategy.
- *first event→last event* (chronological order)—This pattern works particularly well when you are analyzing the history of a process. This pattern is often employed when a business experiencing problems is attempting to determine what went wrong.

Whatever pattern of development you choose, the end of your presentation should always emphasize *closure:* a note of finality or a sense that you have successfully covered your main points.

PLANNING YOUR PRESENTATION

A main aspect of planning for a presentation involves considering how much new information you need. Once you know this, you can figure out where you need to go to get it, and how much advance time this will require. Time to get the information can be costly if you have failed to plan ahead.

Ways of Presenting

Somewhere between reading a speech and speaking "off the cuff" lies a middle ground that we recommend for presentations. (If you are a relaxed extemporaneous speaker, you don't need to read this section.) We suggest that you write down your first three sentences on a notecard and read these sentences. This ensures that you will get off to a good start. Now you can switch to using an outline of the main sections of your speech. Obviously, you may want to write down particularly complex ideas or statistics and read these directly, and you may want to read your conclusion from a prepared notecard.

There are some strategies you can employ to reduce the risk of forgetting information or becoming tongue-tied. One is to prepare visual aids to emphasize key elements of your presentation. Visual aids allow you to deflect attention away from yourself and direct the audience to a chart, graph, or bulleted list. You can point out the relevance of specific items in your visual aids, and you can elaborate on other items. If you are speaking to a large audience, you can hide notes to yourself (which the audience is unable to see) between the lines of a chart or poster. (Write these lightly in pencil.) If you are speaking from a podium, you can have a prepared text ready in case you need help. If you do not need the assistance, the audience need never know that it was there. Finally, you can use a mixture of media (for example, slides and overhead projections) with each one serving as a prompt for you to discuss another aspect of your main approach.

As a general rule, the more often you speak in front of an audience, the more comfortable you will become. You will be able to determine what works best for you. And, by all means, learn from others. If you see a presenter employ a technique that works well, adapt it to your own presentations.

The Arrangement of the Room

Do not overlook the importance of familiarizing yourself with the location of your presentation.

Whenever possible, visit the site before your presentation. Locate the outlets and the light switches. Set up your equipment and arrange the room to your needs (see Figure 14–2). This gives you a sense of control and allows you to create a particular atmosphere. For example, if you can move the chairs in the room, you can create intimacy or distance between yourself and the audience.

The final thing you should do before the audience arrives at the site of your presentation is this: Visualize success in the room. Picture yourself performing successfully in front of the audience. Imagine the positive response you will receive.

Rehearsal

We would like to emphasize just how important we think this is: REHEARSE! The time you spend going through the process will pay off—you will smooth out rough spots, you will improve your transitions between sections, and you will have a good estimate of how much time you will need to deliver your presentation. This is particularly important if you are working with a group; everyone in the group needs to understand completely the pacing, the cues, the transitions, and each other's roles before the presentation begins.

When you rehearse, you will make your major errors in front of no one, or in front of friendly faces. Finally, if you are unable to turn on the overhead projector, you will be able to figure it out without becoming flustered and risking disaster.

UTILIZING AUDIO AND VISUAL AIDS

The rationale behind visual aids is this: many people comprehend ideas better when they see them. Visual aids can enhance your presentation by allowing your audience to see your ideas as well as hear them. Visual aids can also help you by giving you something concrete to refer to during your presentation.

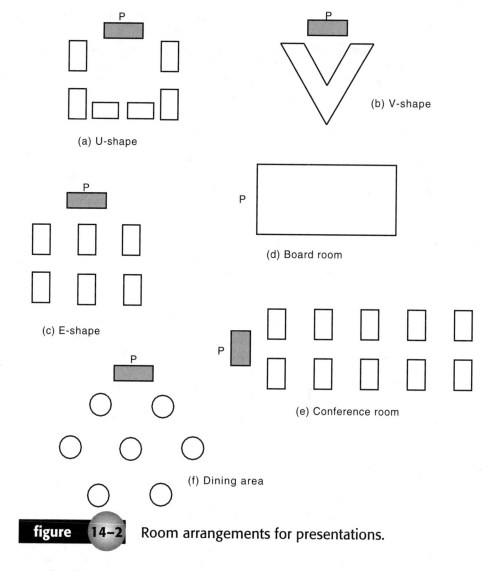

figure 14-2 Room arrangements for presentations.

See Chapter 13, "Designing Graphics and Illustrations," for more information and examples on preparing your visual aids. Also see the following list for some specific advice on including visual aids in your presentations:

- Keep visuals simple.
- Use large type—large enough to be seen clearly in the back of the room.
- Give your audience time to digest the data.
- Count to ten before you begin talking.
- Work on making smooth transitions between your visual aids.
- Talk to the audience, not to the screen where your visuals are projected.
- Be prepared to refer back to a visual if a question arises from the audience.

Sound can now be incorporated into many presentations. You need an appropriate speaker system to meet the needs of your room, but music can be a major influence on your audience. (Imagine a major motion picture without a musical score to gain a sense of the impact of music on our emotions.)

Equipment

Modern technology allows us a wide variety of possibilities for our presentations. In this section we summarize some of the more popular media and some of the advantages and disadvantages of each.

Overhead Projectors   Still the most common medium employed in presentations, overhead projectors have one big advantage over other media: virtually every conference

Guidelines for selecting a visual medium

	Flip Charts	Overheads	Slides	Computer Graphics
Audience size	Under 20	10–75	10–250	10–250
Degree of formality	Informal	Informal or formal	Formal	Formal
Materials	Easel and paper	Projector and screen; window shades	Projector and screen; window shades	Computer screen; hookup to projector
Production costs	Inexpensive*	Inexpensive*	Relatively expensive	Expensive at startup

*Unless drawn by a professional.

Source: This is a modified version of a table in Marya Holcombe and Judith Stein's *Presentations for Decision Makers.*

room has one. If you are traveling somewhere to give your presentation, you can be reasonably confident of finding an overhead projector. Transparencies are relatively easy and inexpensive to make, usually requiring only a photocopy and a thermofacsimile machine. (*Note:* Most transparencies are smaller than a standard $8\frac{1}{2}$-by-11-inch sheet of paper.) Cardboard frames can be put around the transparencies for easy handling. Make sure you can locate the light switch, since you will need a darkened room.

Slide Projectors   A sequence of good-quality color slides is an excellent way of telling a story to your audience. You can organize your slides with a carousel tray and advance the slides at your pace. Slides do require some expertise with a camera, and enough lead time to get the film developed; sometimes you have to reshoot certain pictures.

Computer Projections   The capacity to project the image from a small computer screen to a large audience is costly and requires extensive setup. You need a large-screen projector and a conversion system. (The conversion may take the form of an interface cable or a signal splitter, among other options.) Portable computer projection panels work with overhead projectors to create a dynamic large-screen image.

Since you can do so many things with a computer, the possibilities for enhancing a presentation are as great as your imagination allows you. Make sure you test the system in the location of the presentation before the audience arrives. If you combine voice, video, text, and graphics (multimedia), realize that more can go wrong. Set aside more time for setting up and testing in the room and under the conditions of your presentation.

Videocassette Players   A television screen can be comfortably viewed by a small group of people. If your audience consists of more than ten people, you will need a large-screen projector. A well-planned and well-executed recording can be a very effective way of capturing an audience's attention.

New Technology   Within the next ten years, we will see a staggering number of new media. Keep an open mind to these new media and their possibilities for enhancing your presentations. (For example, an electronic "blackboard" is available that turns what you write on it into a handout to give to members of the audience.) You can enhance your presentations by integrating recorded speech and music, and by importing still and moving images into your computer from videodisc players, CD-ROM players, and image scanners. Hypermedia systems can control the integration.

While we advise you to explore the new technology, we don't want you to lose sight of the "old" media.

Posters   A well-designed poster is a most effective way of conveying your message to your audience. Lettering machines allow you to make crisp, large text that can be viewed from the back of a room.

Flip Charts   A very portable means of communication, flip charts allow you to illustrate your ideas and write text in rooms with no media equipment. For example, if you are asked to present at a luncheon meeting in a restaurant, you should consider flip charts as an option.

Microphones   For large presentations where more than about 125 people will be in attendance, it may be necessary to use a microphone. We advise you to practice; be particularly aware of how close you need to be to the microphone.

Pointers   These pointers are so convenient and so helpful, we wonder why they are not used more frequently by presenters. Pointers are inexpensive and portable, and they allow you to clarify your visual aids. But be careful: Don't play with the pointer as you speak.

Handouts   By distributing key information to the audience, you allow your listeners to be readers, to follow along with the presentation, and to have some hard copy to take out of the room with them. Too much information can overwhelm the audience and become a distraction, so limit your handouts to essential information.

Chalkboards   An option in a small or medium-sized room, chalkboards are rarely seen in the business world.

Some Advice on Using Equipment

- Test the equipment. Make sure that it works and that it works in that particular location. Very few things are more embarrassing than being unable to turn on a machine in front of 150 people. Find the outlets in the room, and check on whether you will need an adapter to plug in your equipment.
- Don't get carried away. Not everyone will be impressed by flashy visuals. Content is the crucial factor. A great-looking presentation enhances the message, but it does not take the place of your message.
- Mixing media requires good timing. You cannot afford delays while you switch from one medium to another. Work on your transitions. Try to practice them, the way a relay team practices passing the baton. The smoother your transitions, the better your presentation.
- Have options in case something does go wrong. Even if you prepare thoroughly, something could still go wrong. Don't panic. Have a backup plan so that you can continue with your presentation. If the problem is out of your control, you will find that your audience will be very forgiving.

MAKING QUESTION-AND-ANSWER SESSIONS WORK FOR YOU

It is important to have a positive perspective on questions from the audience: view them as an opportunity to make your case one final time. Handle the questions as a way of emphasizing the points you are trying to make. Do not become defensive.

---

whenever you receive a question, there are a few simple rules to follow:

- *Restate the question.* This allows the entire audience to hear the question and provides you with valuable time to frame your response.
- *Break down the question.* If a series of questions has been asked, answer them one at a time. If a single question is lengthy or involved, break the question down into its parts.
- *Don't argue with the audience.* Even if an individual is obviously wrong, let the audience decide who is right. You have nothing to gain and the respect of the audience to lose by entering a heated exchange. If the questioner persists, suggest that he or she meet with you after the end of the presentation.
- *Try to predict questions from the audience.* This is a main aspect of preparing for a presentation.

Some presenters prefer the audience to break in whenever they have a question, believing that this practice makes for a more spontaneous interaction between them and their audience. The drawback is that the presentation may be taken away from its intended course by a question that opens up a new area. The audience may follow this new path and make it difficult to bring the presentation back on track. If you as a presenter fear that this may happen, we recommend that you ask that all questions be held until the end and that you do this in your introduction. You want to make this request before someone asks a question; otherwise you may be seen as evading a question.

As with the other parts of a presentation, you will become more skilled at responding to questions as you become more experienced. Even skilled presenters can antagonize people if they fail to maintain a positive attitude toward their audience.

GAINING CLOSURE

The concept of closure is important enough to mention again. You need to give your audience a sense that the presentation is coming to an end and that something has happened during the presentation.

You can refer back to your statement of purpose or you can return to the first sentences of your presentation. Either approach is a clear signal that you are coming to the end. (For example, you can say, "When I began my talk, I asked you to consider four factors in approaching this problem. . . . ") Remember, frequently the last impression an audience has is the strongest one.

As part of our closure of this chapter, we have included a list of items to consider when making a presentation.

- Prepare to be nervous.
- Find out as much as you can about your audience.
- Complete this sentence: The purpose of this presentation is to _____.
- Get all of your audiovisual equipment ready well before you speak.
- Rehearse. Rehearse all of your presentation.
- Speak to your audience, not at them.
- Stay within yourself. For example, don't try telling a joke if you are not comfortable telling jokes.
- Keep to your time limit. An excellent presentation may be ruined by excessive chatter.
- Prepare for questions from the audience.
- End on a positive note.

Another way of gaining closure in a presentation is to give the audience a suggestion of things to do to follow up with the ideas you have presented. For example, in closing this chapter, we suggest further reading to be done, such as the monthly magazine *Presentations: Technology and Techniques for Better Communications* published by Lakewood Publications. Or you could give the audience a task; for example, our task for you is to find a videotape of any of the presentations of Tom Peters, the author of *A Passion for Excellence* and numerous other works, to see an enthusiastic and informative speaker in action.

DELIVERING PRESENTATIONS: EXERCISES

1. Locate a short videotape of a presentation. Use the presentation evaluation form shown in this chapter to rate the presentation. After you have completed the evaluation, write a list of five things you have learned.

2. This exercise is called "The Press Conference," and it is modeled after the standard press conference we see on television. The audience, role-playing members of the media, asks questions of a volunteer who stands in front of the room and tries to respond spontaneously. The volunteer should begin with a very brief introduction and then invite questions from the audience. The audience should attempt to elicit as much biographical information as possible from the person in seven minutes. (Seven minutes may seem to be a short time until you try it.)

   At the end of the press conference, the audience should discuss only the positive aspects of the way the volunteer handled questions. In other words, you are to give positive feedback. Focus on the good things that the individual did.

3. Divide into groups of three or four individuals. Take fifteen minutes to discuss the following: What could be done for under $1,500 to improve the facilities on campus? Focus on one improvement. Then discuss how you intend to present your proposal to the class. At the next class meeting, be prepared to make a presentation of your idea.

4. Sandy Pascal comes to you with a request. She would like you to investigate the possibility of establishing a videoconferencing link between the home offices of Pascal Business Systems in Houston and a major supplier, Quest Computers, in Chicago. In the last fiscal year, PBS employees logged 23 separate trips to visit Quest Computers; although Sandy does not feel that the organization can eliminate trips to the supplier completely, she would like to cut the number of trips to five.

   Assume the cost of one trip to be $620, which includes employee time, airfare, transportation to and from the airport, hotel accommodations, and meals. (The average length of stay is two days, one night.)

   Research the cost of videoconferencing. Obviously, both PBS and Quest already have computers. Compare the different videoconferencing options in the marketplace. Estimate the requirements and cost savings of the different possibilities. Prepare to make a ten-minute presentation in two weeks.

5. Prepare an outline for a ten-minute informational presentation on ergonomics. Your audience is a group of ten managers who supervise secretarial pools.

6. Conduct a survey of all of the equipment potentially available to you at your school. Write a list of what you have discovered. If you could purchase one new piece of equipment, what would it be? Write a memo to your instructor in which you request the purchase of the equipment. Be sure to provide a rationale for your request.

7. Conduct an investigation of computer projection systems. What are some of the different technologies currently available? How much do they cost? Prepare a

ten-minute presentation to your class on the subject. At the end of the presentation, make a recommendation to the class on what purchases your institution should make within the next year.

8. Develop a one-page questionnaire to be given to an audience to elicit feedback at the end of a presentation.

section 4
WORKING ON TEAM PROJECTS

· · · · · · · · · · · · · · · ·

When you are attending college, you are frequently encouraged to produce work by yourself. On an exam, for example, asking another student for the correct answers is considered cheating, and it can get you an F in a course, or worse, expelled from school. Colleges need to test you for how much of the contents of a particular subject you understand so that you can be given a fair grade; in the business world, however, working with others is the regular way to accomplish tasks. An employee who communicates well with co-workers and who can collaborate is a valuable asset.

In college, you will have many opportunities—group presentations, team reports, peer review groups, study groups, and lab partners, to name a few—to work as a team. These experiences will be excellent preparation for the workplace.

In many organizations, the responsibility for the completion of projects is delegated to working groups of specialists assembled for specified periods of time from different parts of the organization. Once the project is finished, the team members return to their home bases. (Morrison and Schmid, 199) This section deals with the kinds of large projects where many individuals are responsible and share the praise or blame. The three chapters in this section—"Collaborating on Long Reports," "Preparing Sales and Marketing Proposals," and "Designing Office Manuals"—all emphasize team building and cooperation.

COLLABORATING ON LONG REPORTS

Producing long reports involves collecting, organizing, and distributing written information. Your audience will use your report to decide what to do or how to do it.

Business organizations regularly use long reports as decision-support tools. Complex decisions require a careful analysis of all available research and factual data. A formal written report provides a database for this sort of activity. Readers will expect to use your long report as an information source that will provide them sufficient background material to make involved decisions.

Skillful writers of long reports recognize that productive reports must be useful. The people who use the reports have to find the information they need quickly and efficiently.

At the same time, they need to be confident of the facts upon which they are basing their decisions. Your reports need to be both accurate and credible.

DEFINING THE LONG REPORT

A *long report* is a formal document with three basic parts: the front materials, the body (containing information and analysis), and the end materials.

Long reports are more widely distributed than short reports. They are reviewed and used by more people and they stay in circulation for extended periods of time. Long reports are often kept and referred to for future decisions and action.

Long reports serve a variety of functions within technical organizations, and they are sent outside the organization when a formal written document is appropriate. Some of the functions of long reports include:

- presenting research
- forecasting future plans
- reviewing projects
- analyzing products
- supporting recommendations

In other words, long reports are used when the decision is important and all available information needs to be considered, often by many different people.

Thinking clearly about your audience is particularly important when working on long reports. You need to remember that a long report will have many different readers and each will bring specific interests to your document. Busy managers, for example, may

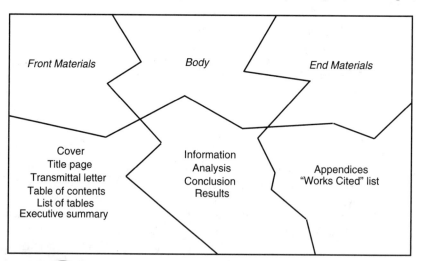

Front Materials	Body	End Materials
Cover Title page Transmittal letter Table of contents List of tables Executive summary	Information Analysis Conclusion Results	Appendices "Works Cited" list

figure 15–1 Putting together the pieces of the three major parts of the long report.

not have time to go through the whole report. They will focus on the summary and recommendations. Other individuals, especially those who will have to carry out the recommendations, may have a strong interest in the exact details of the report.

When you are thinking about the purpose of the report, think about the following:

- What were you asked to do?
- Who will use the report? How? Why?

Since long reports may have several different purposes and since your readers will bring their own purposes and interests to the document—not all readers will want to read your entire report—your task is to help them use the document efficiently.

Formal in appearance and style, long reports attempt to provide readers with enough background, data, and other information to support informed decision making. Readers expect to use these reports to determine a course of action. Your report should be helpful to them in making this choice.

Some Types of Long Reports

Feasibility reports are used to consider whether a course of action is practical. These reports assemble information that is used to decide whether an idea is workable and suitable, and whether to go ahead with it.

Research reports describe the results of investigations, studies, and experiments. Empirical information resulting from actual test data is an important product for technical organizations in an information economy.

Field reports describe the findings of on-site investigations, in which information is collected directly from its source, categorized, and sent to the organization for further analysis.

Failure analysis reports are used to explain why something broke down or didn't work as expected. These are very important to business organizations because technology learns from its failures and mistakes. Every plane crash, for example, is investigated and a cause determined. This information is presented in formal reports and used for future technical decisions.

Progress reports are used to describe how a complex project is going. Generally these will be short reports, but the more complex the project, the more complex the reporting requirements.

Periodic reports provide information at regular intervals on the activities and conditions of organizations or projects. Annual reports, cost/schedule status reports, accounting statements, and other types of calendar-scheduled documents qualify as periodic reports.

Parts of the Long Report

Long reports are generally designed in three sections, each with a number of different parts. Some of these parts are optional and others necessary. You should be aware of all of these parts so that you don't overlook something which would improve your own report's credibility and usefulness.

We are going to describe these parts from front to back, the order in which they would usually occur in a long report. We do not mean to suggest, however, that this is the order in which they should be written, assembled, or prepared. The front material will often be written last. It would make no sense, for example, to write a transmittal letter before you write your report. The purpose of the letter is to direct the attention of the readers to the report itself, to focus their interest, and guide them efficiently through the document. The report needs to be written first.

On the other hand, some material can be prepared or assembled before long reports are actually written. Some of the appendix information can be collected with the idea that it will be used to provide detailed data in future reports.

Front Materials   Your report begins at the cover. You should use the *cover* and *binding* of your document to create interest and a positive impression. Base your selection on how the document will be used. Considerations such as your audience, length of the report and number of copies, and the need for users to photocopy sections are some of the factors that should influence your decision.

Expensive covers are not always the best idea. The message they convey can be interpreted as extravagance. An attractive cover invites the reader to continue, but it can be

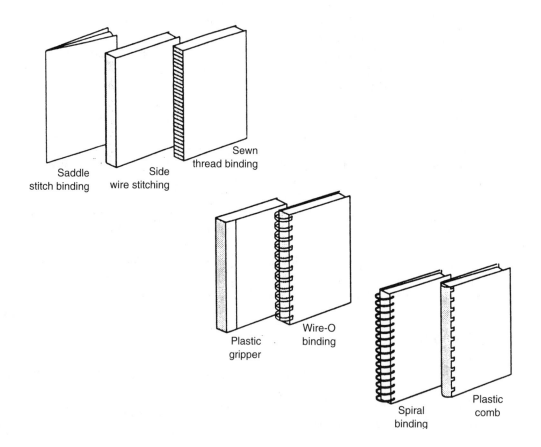

Saddle
stitch binding

Side
wire stitching

Sewn
thread binding

Plastic
gripper

Wire-O
binding

Spiral
binding

Plastic
comb

reasonably priced. When you are choosing bindings, think about whether people will need to remove or insert new pages, and especially consider whether they will need to photo-copy sections.

Your *title page* should draw readers into the report. Professional reports are not re-quired to have dull titles, so you should attempt to be informative. Subtitles can add inter-est by providing detail or motivation for the reader.

The *transmittal letter,* sometimes called a *cover letter,* presents the report to a reader. (Sometimes the transmittal letter is placed before the report, in front of the cover.)

A Framework for Global Electronic Commerce

President William J. Clinton
Vice President Albert Gore, Jr.
Washington, D.C.

"We are on the verge of a revolution that is just as profound as the change in the economy that came with the industrial revolution. Soon electronic networks will allow people to transcend the barriers of time and distance and take advantage of global markets and business opportunities not even imaginable today, opening up a new world of economic possibilities and progress."

Vice President Albert Gore, Jr.

 **figure 15–2** This is an example of a hypertext title page from a long report on the World Wide Web.

Any report that you do not deliver personally should have an explanatory memo or letter attached. Within the organization, a memo is usually sufficient.

Begin with a paragraph explaining what is being sent and to whom. Specify the title and purpose of the report. Depending upon your communication strategy, you may want to direct the reader to a recommendation, conclusion, or other information you think is important to the reader. You should not repeat the summary or abstract.

A carefully prepared *table of contents* is a map that provides your readers with ac-cess routes to the specific information they are looking for. The more detailed you are, the easier it will be for the people using your report to find the facts they need. A table of con-tents is necessary for any report longer than ten pages. This table should list all of the headings used in the report along with their location. Attached materials should also be listed and located for immediate access to readers. A *list of tables* or *list of exhibits* is sometimes useful in a major report. You want to tell the readers where to find figures and tables so these can be referred to quickly and easily. This is particularly important if your report has many illustrations.

Table of Contents

BACKGROUND

PRINCIPLES

ISSUES

I. Financial Issues
    1. Customs and Taxation
    2. Electronic Payment Systems

II. Legal Issues
    3. Uniform Commercial Code for Electronic Commerce
    4. Intellectual Property Protection
    5. Privacy
    6. Security

III. Market Access Issues
    7. Telecommunications Infrastructure and Information Technology
    8. Content
    9. Technical Standards

A COORDINATED STRATEGY

figure 15-3 The table of contents for the Web page shown in Fig. 15–2.

Perhaps the most important thing that you write will be the *executive summary.* This will be the most frequently read section of your report. Many readers will form their judgment of the whole report from this one page. You need to convince potential users that reading the report will be worth their time. The executive summary, used to compress the main points of the report, is very important to busy technical professionals who need to use their reading time productively. The summary uses the same organization as the report itself, stating results and recommendations in the same sequence. Provide only enough information for the user to determine whether to read the report itself.

The Body The body of the report needs to be carefully planned. Your report discussion needs to be complete, containing your conclusions and recommendations. The text of your report needs to fully describe the background, purpose, and technical detail.

Begin by telling the user how the information in the report was collected. Describe the sources of the data and the technical processes used to obtain the information. Your reader needs to know where the information comes from. This step is particularly important if the report uses survey or laboratory data.

The organization of the discussion section should reflect the strategy you have chosen to communicate your information. For example, if you are asked to produce a recommendation report, in which your task is to choose among alternatives, you need to use a

A FRAMEWORK FOR GLOBAL ELECTRONIC COMMERCE
EXECUTIVE SUMMARY

The Internet has the potential to become the United States' most active trade vehicle within a decade, creating millions of high-paying jobs. In addition, Internet shopping may revolutionize retailing by allowing consumers to sit in their homes and buy a wide variety of products and services from all over the world.

Many businesses and consumers are wary of conducting extensive business electronically, however, because the Internet lacks a predictable legal environment governing transactions and because they are concerned that governments will impose regulations and taxes that will stifle Internet commerce.

"A Framework for Global Electronic Commerce" outlines the Administration's strategy for fostering increased business and consumer confidence in the use of electronic networks for commerce. The paper reflects widespread consultation with industry, consumer groups, and the Internet community.

The paper presents five principles to guide government support for the evolution of electronic commerce and makes recommendations about nine key areas where international efforts are needed to preserve the Internet as a non-regulatory medium, one in which competition and consumer choice will shape the marketplace. With respect to these areas, the paper designates lead U.S. government agencies and recommends international fora for consideration of each issue.

figure 15-4 The executive summary of the Web page shown in Fig. 15-2.

learning about organizing

Brainstorm first. Make a list of all the ideas and concepts you want to put into the document. Make sure you get input from everyone responsible. Now you need to prioritize your list: find out which items are vitally important, which items support other items, and which ones are relatively unimportant.

As you prioritize, look for connections. Is it possible to group certain items under the same heading? Do other items form a sequence or pattern? Which items need to be placed first? Which items would be appropriate at the end of your document? Use notations or symbols to mark your organizational thoughts. Make preliminary decisions about which topics you consider to be primary, which you consider to be secondary, and which you consider to be tertiary. Try to think of headings (primary topics) and subheadings (secondary topics) that would capture the nature of these topics for your readers.

Now turn your list into an outline.

There are many ways to outline. You can employ a Roman numeral outline, a numerical outline, or an outline where distinctions are made by different headings and typefaces. Observe the three possibilities here:

I. Introduction	1.0 Introduction	INTRODUCTION
A.	1.1	First major topic heading
B.	1.2	Second major topic heading
II. Development	2.0 Development	DEVELOPMENT
A.	2.1	First major topic heading
B.	2.2	Second major topic heading
1.	2.2.1	First subtopic heading
a.	2.2.1.1	First sub-subtopic heading
b.	2.2.1.2	Second sub-subtopic heading
2.	2.2.2	Second subtopic heading
C.	2.3	Third major topic heading
III. Conclusion	3.0 Conclusion	CONCLUSION
A.	3.1	First major topic heading
B.	3.2	Second major topic heading

Whatever system you choose, make the outline consistent; the kind of information provided at each level should be equivalent. Each lower level should break down the higher level into separate but equivalent pieces. The entire outline should allow a reader to see the logical progression of the ideas to be presented.

Working from your outline, you can now begin to write your draft. By viewing the draft as a preliminary stage in the process, you can relieve some of the stress of having to "get it right." Changes can be made later, and you can concentrate on getting all of the material into the document. Polishing and perfecting will also come later.

A significant advantage of this way of writing is that it allows you to review your writing after time has passed. You may come to see that a different approach or format is appropriate for your document, and the draft allows you to "play with" a variety of potential products. Rewriting is much more than copying over your work with a few minor changes. You need to challenge what you have written, evaluate the strong and weak points, and revise accordingly.

Many writers like to put their thoughts down on paper well before a deadline so that their unconscious mind can ponder what they have written. Without being aware that they have been thinking about the writing task, they return to the work some time later with a whole new set of ideas. A draft allows them to do this.

Remember also to write down the sources of your statements, facts, statistics, quotations, and expert opinions. You may need them for the final version of your document. You need to acknowledge your sources with footnotes, endnotes, or some other accepted format within your field.

comparative strategy. Use graphics to compare and contrast your selection criteria and your conclusions.

Make the report interesting with lots of visual support. Diagrams and drawings can help to make your meaning clear. Remember to use well-written, informative captions for the illustrations in your report, because many readers will just skim the document, glancing at the pictures and captions.

You may want to include a conclusions and recommendations section. Although you may have mentioned your outcomes in the summary, introduction, and body of the report, this allows you to restate your recommendations and provide general reasons for them.

End Material   The *appendix* or appendices contain all types of information which would interrupt the flow of the report. Letters of support, computations and data sheets, interviews, and questionnaires should be provided when appropriate; use separate appendices to organize such information for your readers. You should include information that people might want to refer to immediately in order to verify a claim or computation.

A *"works cited"* list or bibliography is necessary to give credibility to verbal and secondary data. Most of us judge the validity of information by its source. Your readers want to know where your information comes from. You do not, however, want to interrupt your text. If you want to acknowledge a source within the text, use a *parenthetical citing*. Mention the source briefly and clearly in parentheses:

> The United States is a member of the ATA Carnet system, which allows business travelers to temporarily bring commercial samples and scientific/technical equipment into other countries without paying duty. (U.S. Council of International Business, 1212 Avenue of the Americas, New York, NY 10036)

Your bibliography or "works cited" section needs to follow standard formats. The people who use it are looking for information, and they do not want to have to figure out your system. Let them look where they expect to find things.

ORGANIZING THE LONG REPORT

The format of a long report is the logical arrangement you use to assemble the various parts of the document. Your format will depend on which strategy you choose to present your information. In turn, your strategy will depend on two things: your assignment and your audience.

For instance, if you have been asked to provide recommendations, then you need to do so. If you believe your audience will not be pleased with these recommendations, however, you may choose to lead up to them rather than stating them at the beginning. Before you can begin to outline the report or start to write the different sections, you need to decide how your document will be structured. Two basic patterns are *particular→general* (induction) and *general→particular* (deduction).

Use induction when you need to build a case for a general rule or guideline for action; start by establishing a number of specific cases until you have constructed a general rule. For example, if you want to explain why company profits exceeded expectations in the last quarter, you could look at each individual account and build toward a general rule.

Use deduction when you have an established rule; apply a specific case to the general rule and draw your conclusion. If, for example, you had already established that all of your computer software clients need an upgrade after fourteen months, you could apply a specific case, Company X, and conclude that you need to supply them with an upgrade in November.

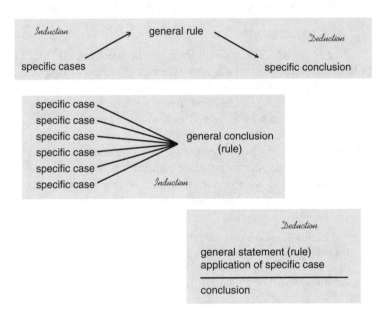

The most common structure for recommendation reports is *problem→solution*. Begin with the problem, stating it as exactly as you can. Then describe your method of investigating the problem and propose a variety of solutions, demonstrating that you have given thorough consideration to the issue. Finally, discuss the solution you recommend and explain your reasons.

Many companies provide formats for long reports. If this is true in your company, it is essential that you follow the company format closely. If you are designing the format, however, you must make sure that it is complete and useful for its various readers. The logical arrangement of your material should reinforce what you say in the report by making it easy for all of your readers to find what they need.

DISCOVERING SOME USEFUL TECHNIQUES

We have discovered that most effective report writers begin by considering the preparation of a long report as a carefully planned and scheduled activity. In most instances long reports aren't simply written; they are deliberately and closely managed documents. Many people are involved and their activities must be coordinated.

Collaboration

Long reports are commonly created by teams of professionals. This type of writing is a collaborative activity where many people work together to create reports that represent their combined information, viewpoints, and decisions. A business project team, for example, might have an accountant, a human resources expert, an environmental engineer, a lawyer, and a variety of specialists, all working on the same activity. Who will write the report? Every one of them will be involved in the crucial activity of reporting.

Performing this task means working in a group environment where you will be required to brainstorm, share assignments, search out and evaluate alternatives, and package your information in an attractive and useful format. If you are going to do a good job, you need to work well with others.

Outlining

Careful document design is essential to the process of creating effective long reports. This means outlining. You need to keep the whole report in mind at each step, through research and data collection, writing and editing, and the preparation of front and end materials. When you are writing a long report, you are assembling a complex structure with many parts. As with other types of building, you need to consult your blueprint at each stage of construction.

An Outline of a Sample Business Plan

Section	Description
I	Executive Summary
II	Mission and Strategy
III	Market
	Background
	The Target Customer
	Product Description
	Competitive Analysis
	Business Classifications
	Strategy and Approach to the Market
IV	Pricing, Profitability, and Break-Even Point
V	Operations
	Merchandising
	Costs
VI	Management and Staffing
VII	Contingency Plans
VIII	Financial Projections
	Background and Assumptions
	Application for Loan with Repayment Conditions
	Projected Revenue and Financial Statements

You don't want to leave out important information. At the same time, you don't want to clutter your report with irrelevant details. Detailed information that will interest only a few people can be included in the end material as an appendix. Material that is unnecessary should be left out. This is why you need to keep your audience firmly in mind and create your document for their use.

An *outline* is a tool that lets you work with the structure of your document before you begin the actual writing. A *topic outline* uses short phrases to indicate the order and importance of different sections. *Sentence outlines* use complete topic sentences to summarize each section. These sentences are explained and elaborated to provide the paragraphs for the rough draft.

Complex writing projects such as long reports often involve the creation of two outlines. First, a topic outline is brainstormed; then the sentence outline is developed from this beginning. At the outline stage, you can easily change the pattern or structure of your document. As you add detail and revise the outline, you can experiment with the order and placement of your information, and review your document blueprint for balance and organization.

Scheduling

A complex formal report will often require that the efforts of many different people be coordinated. Schedule these efforts carefully. Create a writing plan that lays out all of the tasks and assigns responsibilities and deadlines. Use the schedule to maintain these deadlines.

The final version of the agreed-upon schedule should be expressed graphically so that participants can see what they are agreeing to provide and when. Flow charts, activity charts, and work breakdown schedules (WBSs) all provide ways to understand visually what will be expected and when.

Storyboarding

Storyboarding is an effective method for coordinating multiple authors in designing, planning, and editing successful reports. This is a graphics-driven approach to document design, an elaborated version of the cut-and-paste technique used by many writers.

A *storyboard* is a visual blueprint in which you create a model of your entire document before the majority of writing is done. You begin by breaking your report topics into information passages of about five hundred words each. Each passage is treated as a module or series of specifications that can be reviewed before the final text and graphics are completed.

Each module has four elements. The *headline* is a phrase that describes the contents of the spread. The *summary* provides a brief abstract of the module content and enough information for the reviewers to verify the accuracy and importance of the module. Finally, you should leave a place for *notes* by the review team where they can leave comments, questions, and suggestions. *Exhibits* supplement the text. These can include tables, drawings, bulleted lists, photographs, or any other type of graphics. You can simply describe your exhibits or provide a rough sketch.

A. Section of Document	D. Exhibits
B. Headline	Smoking and American Mortality Annual smoking deaths — 419,000 All World War II deaths — 405,000 Vietnam war deaths — 58,000 Annual AIDS deaths — 25,000 Annual drug-induced deaths — 9,000
C. Summary	
E. Notes	

figure **15–5** An illustration of a storyboard for a long report.

At this point, with all the modules drafted, you should schedule a walkthrough or review session. All the members of the team need to participate. The modules should be taped to a wall and the team should carefully consider each one. Look at the order of the modules and the amount of information included in each one. Determine whether the graphics support the text. Is your information accurate and complete? The purpose of this session is to make changes before the draft report is written.

Group Revision

Everyone makes mistakes. When many people are working on the same writing project, there is an even greater chance for mistakes to slip into a document. The whole team needs to be involved in revision. Mistakes cost credibility. Even simple mechanical errors can create the impression that your report is careless and flawed. Be sure that you carefully proofread every section of the report. Review captions, the numbering, table of contents, the index, and the appendices. Every reader will look at something different and every section needs to be error-free.

Software tools can make revision and editing simpler. Some word processors have a helpful feature called *redlining mode,* in which comments and new text are highlighted to distinguish them from the original. Other programs allow dated and initialed comments to be inserted throughout a document. In the end, however, you are responsible for the report your team provides. The only way to be sure that your work is perfect is to check it yourself.

Some writing teams choose a designated proofreader and editor, a person whose responsibilities include assembling and proofreading each circulated revision. Some sort of head writer or editor will be necessary to maintain the schedule and complete the final report. This person will manage the writing project.

GAINING PERSPECTIVE ON LONG REPORTS

Long technical reports are information products, created for specific audiences. To design useful reports you need to know how the product will be used, who will use it, and for what purposes. No one will read your report for enjoyment. Your audience is working. They want a product that is easy and quick to use.

---

long report on the web

You can look at the long report we use as an example—A Framework for Global Electronic Commerce—at this web site:
http://www.iitf.nist.gov/eleccomm/ecomm.htm

Easy reading means hard writing. Report writers need to anticipate what various readers already know and what they will need to find out. The needs of your audience will determine the design of the report. Some of your audience will simply glance at the report, some will study it, and others will use it on a regular basis. This means writing for all of them. Your ability to communicate effectively and your technical competence will be judged by your business reports. This means writing, editing, testing, and rewriting. Business reports must be designed to explain technical information to a wide variety of audiences. Don't confuse your interest in the technical task with your need to produce a report that addresses these multiple users.

COLLABORATING ON LONG REPORTS: EXERCISES

1. Design two different title pages for a long report. The report describes the abilities of Pascal Business Systems to provide an ergonomic work environment for a small desktop publishing business. This publishing business employs four people: two graphic designers, a photographer, and an administrative assistant. Make up any details you need. Discuss the different impressions the titles create with your work group or classmates.

2. Create a table of contents for a book about your life. Try to organize it with some consistent patterns or categories, such as time, work roles, or personal interests.

3. Prepare the following parts of a long report:

   Title page

   Table of contents

   Table of illustrations

Executive summary

Transmittal letter

For the purpose of this report, assume that some organization of your own choosing, such as the school you attend, has asked Pascal Business Systems to solve a problem. (You can find out details about PBS in Appendix A.) Your report should contain an analysis of the problem, its causes, and its effects; a discussion of possible solutions and their advantages and disadvantages; and the supporting evidence for your recommended solution.

You do not have to write the entire report, but you will need to think through the problem before you begin. Your table of contents must be complete, with at least two levels of headings. If a topic is not listed in your contents, it can be assumed that you did not intend to introduce that topic in the report.

4. Conduct a survey of use of fax technology within your company (or class). Write an outline for the body of a long report based on the results of your survey; discussion, results, recommendations, and conclusions should all be written up in a sentence outline.

5. Write a memo to the people in your office or classroom describing and explaining some ways in which appendices can be designed so that people will be more likely to read them.

6. Prepare a letter of transmittal, a list of tables or figures, and a glossary that defines five related terms with which you are familiar. What do these documents tell you about the imaginary report upon which they are based? How do these support elements influence the way that readers will view the report itself?

7. Using the advice in this chapter, write a long technical report of at least ten pages on some topic that you find interesting and are currently involved with at work or in another course. Be sure to include all of the parts of the long report; do not overlook graphics and illustrations.

8. Working with a group of at least three people, create a topic outline for a long report. Then turn the topic outline into a sentence outline. Discuss the difficulties you encountered, both with the outline formats and in collaborating with other writers.

PREPARING SALES AND MARKETING PROPOSALS

16

Formatting Sales and Marketing Proposals
  Types of Proposals
  Parts of the Proposal

Coordinating the Proposal Writing Process
  The Team
  The Plan
  The Outline
  The Storyboard

Selling Solutions

Editing the Proposal

The ability to write successful sales and marketing proposals is one of the most valuable business writing skills you can develop. This is true whether your business is small or large, or whether your proposals are one page or hundreds. Successful proposals mean sales. Every proposal sells something: a product, a service, or an agreement.

A proposal is a bid for business, a report written for the special purpose of selling something: an idea, a product, or a service. Its chief function is to persuade a very special audience to make a decision. Successful proposals are designed to help these readers arrive at a positive decision.

A business organization's ability to respond to Requests for Proposal (RFPs) and Invitations for Bid (IFBs) may become the key factor in its profit base. Your ability to contribute to this important process will be noticed and appreciated.

FORMATTING SALES AND MARKETING PROPOSALS

Appropriate formats for sales and marketing proposals are extremely varied depending on your audience, the type of proposal, and the detail of the offer. Some proposals will be very short: a one-page letter, for example, bidding on replacing a porch. Other proposals offering to provide complex services or closely specified products may contain dozens of pages providing exact details of the offer. This chapter will focus on these longer, more formal sales documents, which are frequently the result of a group effort.

Whether you are collaborating with colleagues or writing by yourself, you need to consider the type of proposal you are preparing, and you need to consider your audience: specific decision-makers, people who will award the contract. Solicited sales proposals often carry exact specifications for their preparation. With an unsolicited bid, you need to give your audience careful consideration. What are they expecting? What will persuade them?

Types of Proposals

Proposals are sometimes defined in terms of their audience. *Internal proposals* are made within an organization and are usually designed to solve some immediate problem. Typical in-house proposals might recommend the location of a new facility or the purchase of new equipment. They are directed to individuals higher up in the organization for decisions and funding.

External proposals are sent outside of the organization to potential clients. Both government and sales proposals represent an offer to provide goods or services. Such proposals are strategic documents that define an organization's offer to deliver these items.

---

proposal writing sites on the web

Greco Research Engineering (GRE)
A nine-year-old small business focused on government technical proposals
http://www.itribe.net/greco/proposal_preparation.html
Business Financing Listings & Proposals
http://www.cfonline.com/cfo/opps/opps.html
Federally Funded Research in the United States
http://cos.gdb.org/best/fed-fund.html

Sales, marketing, and grant proposals—whether internal or external—all share this feature: the proposal needs to persuade the audience. Winning proposals need to be comprehensive organizational, technical, and business plans that will persuade your audience that yours is the best offer. Thorough, persuasive, and competitive proposals bring business and contracts.

Your primary writing task is to make your offer look good to the people who will make the decisions. This means that you must stress benefits to the readers.

Many different formats can be used for proposals, but in general you are designing a persuasive report. Some potential clients provide no specific guidelines for proposal content. Many, however, have very specific instructions for formatting and organizing your proposal. Follow these directions exactly.

Some companies and government agencies put out a *Request for Proposal* (RFP) or *Invitation for Bid* (IFB). These documents describe in detail the conditions of the agreement; they often contain very precise directions for responding. Solicited proposals will not be successful if they do not follow these directions exactly. The proposal team's first job is to know what the audience is looking for; once you know what your audience wants, you can work to provide it. Generally, a small business will have fewer specifications than a large one. Government (local, state, and federal) has numerous requirements on bidding for awards, contracts, and grants.

Parts of the Proposal

Sales or marketing proposals, whatever the scope of work or size of the project, basically contain the same functional parts:

- Introduction and summary of conclusions.
- Statement of the problem you propose to solve.
- Statement of the work you will perform.
- Your management approach and performance schedule.
- Your capabilities and qualifications for the job.

The *front matter* of a proposal generally includes a title page, a table of contents, a list of illustrations, and a list of tables. This front section should be used as a map to help readers quickly discover and cross-reference the information they are seeking. Very often a *notice of proprietary information* states that the proposal information should not be given to other organizations.

Transmittal letters often accompany government and sales proposals. Make sure that your letter references the RFP you are responding to by name, date, and number. Point out that the proposal is in compliance with all procurement requirements. Do not expect the letter to accompany the proposal through the evaluation process.

Your *table of contents* needs to support the entire proposal. It is there to help your audience. You must make sure that it is sufficiently detailed, with meaningful headings and subheadings. This is one of the access points to your proposal and it should provide both substance and direction to the readers.

The *summary* must be concise and responsive. Often this will be the only section of your proposal that is reviewed. Your summary must communicate the essential message by identifying key points and focusing the readers' attention on results, conclusions, and recommendations. Busy readers want to get enough information from your summary to know what is significant and what decisions need to be made. Try to understand the information needs of your audience and then arrange your summary to be clear, focused, and helpful.

Your *introduction* provides a description of your qualifications and ability to deliver what you offer. Use this section to relay your understanding of the problem and your responsiveness to the request. Substantiate any claims you make for technical expertise, key personnel, or unique facilities. In other words, support your sales proposal with as much evidence as you can.

A *compliance matrix* (a table directing the reader to specific pages) helps your audience complete their evaluation. Essentially this is a cross-reference page that visually displays your compliance with the request. What you are trying to do here is make it easy for your readers to see that you have met all of the conditions they have required. Make sure that you list all of the deliverables and number the objectives for discussion purposes.

The next section is frequently a problem for proposal designers—the technical *discussion*. Here's where you get down to the details of your business. You don't want to lose your audience at this point. Remember to include enough background so the evaluators can analyze the scope of work and your anticipated difficulties, alternatives, and solutions.

Trade-off standards must be explicitly stated, and reliability considerations have to be clear. Other issues, including safety and quality control, have to be addressed. Testing requirements, evaluation procedures, and other measurements may need specification. Service conditions, subcontractor and supplier roles, and milestones and decision points all need to be arranged.

Successful proposals usually contain a graphic illustration of the management organization, frequently a chart that displays team access to decision-level managers. You need to illustrate a management control plan. (PERT and Gantt charts allow you to visualize what must be done to accomplish a desired objective on time.) Outline your reporting procedures, and describe your *management experience.* Very often your organization's qualifying past performance serves as a key to your selection.

All of your customers will be interested in *schedules.* When will the project be completed? How will progress be monitored? Work breakdown schedules, frequent reporting requirements, and quantitative scrutiny of the completion steps all provide assurance to the client.

Accounting is another area of client concern. The *costs* section provides the reviewers with evidence that your level of expertise, supervision, and accounting methods will ensure completion of the contract on the delivery schedule. Travel, options, and alternative cost implications must be discussed. Costs are usually kept separate from the main body of the proposal because they are considered incidental to the plan of work.

You need to show your readers what you mean, to let them see what you are saying. Appropriate *illustrations* break up the monotony of plain text, provide support for your words, and help the readers see your main points. Strong graphic support is essential to a successful proposal.

Marketing Proposal for
CAPE DESIGN ASSOCIATES

Section 1:   OVERVIEW

Section 2:   FINDINGS

Section 3:   CUSTOMER NEEDS OUTLINE
                        Quality Requirements Outline
                                    Materials
                                    Delivery
                                    Installations
                                    Project Management
                        Design Services
                        Insurance Guarantees

Section 4:   CUSTOMER SERVICE PROPOSAL OUTLINE
                        Quality Assessment
                                    Materials
                                    Delivery
                                    Installations
                                    Project Management
                        Design Services
                        Insurance Guarantees

Section 5:   FEE OVERVIEW
                        Materials
                        Delivery
                        Installation
                        Project Management
                        Design

Section 6:   POLICIES OVERVIEW
                        Terms of Payment
                        Contracts
                        Retainers
                        Change Orders
                                    Additions to Contract
                                    Changes to Contract
                                    Impact on Scheduling

Section 7:   SCHEDULE OVERVIEW
                        Proposed Scheduling
                        Schedule Changes

Section 8:   MARKET ANALYSIS
                        Remodeling
                        New Construction

Section 9:   FIGURES & ILLUSTRATIONS

Section 10:   COMPETITOR SUMMARY

figure 16–1 An example of an outline for a marketing proposal.
With permission of and thanks to Janet Rustin.

Tables, charts, spreadsheets, work breakdown schedules, even equations—all of these can be displayed visually. Many proposal teams try to achieve a ratio of 60/40 between text and graphics. Whenever you can support your text with an illustration, it is a good idea to do so.

For long proposals, an *index* can provide assistance to your readers. Cross-references lead them from topic to related topic. The index should be a useful entry point to your proposal, guiding the leader who is looking for a particular section.

The main index entries repeat your headings and subheadings and emphasize the points that you have already made. You need to ask yourself where you would look for a term if you were unfamiliar with the subject. Be careful not to scatter your references under a variety of synonyms that are not cross-referenced.

COORDINATING THE PROPOSAL WRITING PROCESS

Both sales proposals and government proposals are generally created by teams of business professionals. Performing this task means working in a group environment where you will be required to brainstorm, delegate tasks, search out and evaluate alternatives, and package your research into a persuasive presentation.

Sales and marketing proposals have become an increasingly popular way for business and government organizations to seek the information they need to make purchasing decisions. Competitive procurement markets ensure that written proposals will become increasingly important as a method of gaining new contracts and business.

Successful proposals will come from organizations that prepare themselves for a team effort and for a continued effort. Collaborative writing teams, good document design, and a competitive business position can be coordinated to produce winning proposals.

Your tasks—and your opportunity—are to work effectively with your team, pay attention to the process, and contribute whatever you can through careful analysis of the client's needs. Every opportunity you have to participate in the proposal preparation process will increase your ability to contribute to the next proposal.

The Team

Management, human resources, accounting, design, and technical personnel are often assigned to proposal writing teams. Preparing winning sales proposals is a collaborative activity in which many people work together to create documents that represent their combined information, viewpoints, and decisions.

The team, no matter how many members it contains, necessarily fills a number of different roles—proposal manager, contract officer, text editor, graphics editor, writer, and production editor. Sometimes these roles may be filled by only one or two people, but all of these jobs need to be done.

The Plan

A systematic approach with specific stages and steps is necessary to move a detailed sales proposal toward completion. Most marketing proposals are complex group efforts which need to be managed very carefully. Research, writing, graphics, and production responsibilities need to be assigned to competent people. RFP deadlines are inflexible; a schedule must be created and maintained.

Good proposals require good planning. This means that serious planning is an essential element in the preparation process. Competitive proposals need to contain a careful and thoughtful inventory of your business goals and objectives, methods and quality-control processes, personnel, and abilities. Assembling this material, editing it through multiple drafts, and seeing it through production all require commitment and a detailed writing plan.

A *writing plan* lays out all of the tasks, assigns responsibilities and deadlines, specifies the number of edits, and, in general, describes the procedures for preparing and producing the proposal.

The final version of the agreed-upon schedule should be expressed graphically so that participants can see what they are agreeing to provide and when. Flow charts, activity charts, and work breakdown schedules all provide ways to understand visually what items will be expected when.

The Outline

The first stage of proposal preparation is the creation of a detailed outline. The outline needs to be consistent, using the same lettering or numbering system throughout. This outline will be the framework for the writing, assembly, and production phases and will provide continuity to the collaborative efforts of many different people.

	Day one							Day two						
	8:00	9:00	10:00	11:00	12:00	1:00	2:00	8:00	9:00	10:00	11:00	12:00	1:00	2:00
Receive RFP	■													
Analyze RFP		■												
Sketch initial plan		■												
Form teams			■											
Form proposal team				■										
Establish data bank				■										
Outline proposal								■						
Decide on strategy										■				

figure 16–2 An example of part of a proposal schedule.

The Storyboard

Storyboarding, discussed in detail in Chapter 15, is an effective method for coordinating multiple authors in designing, planning, and editing successful proposals. *Storyboarding* is a graphics-driven approach to document design, an elaborated version of the cut-and-paste technique used by many writers.

---

incorporating the four C's

Generally a C performance is only adequate and something to be avoided, but when you are writing a proposal, four C's can be a perfect score. Trying to achieve four C's can be a successful strategy if you can match your client's need for clear understanding, conformity, competence, and above all, credibility.

- **Comprehension** Your clients need to know that you understand exactly what their problem or need is. There is only one way to do this: Explain it back to them while weaving your solution into their story.
- **Compliance** These same clients want to make sure that your offer exactly matches their specifications, procedures, and expectations. They want this exactly, no matter how carelessly they have defined what they want.
- **Capability** Occasionally, and too frequently, companies propose to carry out activities for which they do not have the capability—defined simply as the facilities, personnel, equipment, detailed plans, and appropriate people to carry out the work. Be realistic! Don't take on jobs that you can't do. This is not the way to build an organization.
- **Credibility** Last, and most important, your offer needs to be believable. When you are doing business with strangers, the last thing they want to do is make a mistake. Try being very clear: Use words that can be measured.

SELLING SOLUTIONS

When you write a marketing proposal, you are selling something: an idea, a service, or a product. You are providing solutions for your clients' problems. This means you are designing a persuasive document. The following are some suggestions to make your writing more effective.

Make It Readable

Design your sales proposal to be used. The few people who read it need to make a decision. Anything you can do to help your readers arrive at a positive decision is good design. This means your offer must be neat, attractive, and readable. Careful and thoughtful document design is an essential part of your planning process.

This includes providing your readers with a transmittal letter, a table of contents, detailed headings, illustrations, glossaries, charts, figures, checklists, summaries, appendices, and an index. All these devices are used to make sales and marketing proposals more readable, interesting, and persuasive.

Use Headings to Label Your Ideas

Every page in your proposal must be visually attractive. Headings can break up solid chunks of text, provide white space on the page, and give your proposal a professional appearance. Most readers develop an attitude toward your document from the way it looks, even before they begin reading. Appearance can assist clear writing in appealing to the people who will evaluate your proposal.

Headings and subheadings make information easier to find. Proposal readers are often looking for specific information, and it is up to you to help them with plenty of tables. Readers can skim and find the sections in which they are particularly interested. Headings make your proposal more accessible and useful to busy readers.

Include a Compliance Matrix

We recommend that you prepare a compliance matrix for solicited marketing proposals. This should list each subsection of the RFP and next to it the part of your proposal that responds to that section. This guarantees that your document is fully responsive to the RFP.

Compliance Matrix

Requirement	Section	Reviewer's Comments
Subline Item 01 AA	2.2.1	*(left blank for reviewer)*
Subline Item 01 AB	2.2.2	
Subline Item 01 AC	2.2.3	
Specific Content		
(a) Statement of available plant, equipment, and test facilities proposed for use on this contract.	4.1.1	
(b) Statement of additional plant, equipment, and test facilities required for this contract.	4.1.2	

Take a Positive Approach

Hard-luck stories will impress on your readers that you have needs, not competence for the task. You need to present a positive message that demonstrates your capacity to deliver what you are offering.

Remember, people are looking to choose a successful applicant, not a source who cannot complete the task or provide the product. An organization's reputation for success is based on the ability to choose applicants who will accomplish what they set out to achieve.

EDITING THE PROPOSAL

Editing a lengthy proposal is a group effort, as is the writing. A series of proposal reviews should be scheduled at various stages of the preparation process. All of the parties to the proposal should be involved in the editing. You don't want to jeopardize the proposal's credibility because of poor writing or business mistakes.

creating a cumulative effect

Preparing a comprehensive sales proposal is a costly way to market your services and products. It is a time-consuming and labor-intensive process that requires a great deal of effort, particularly the first time through. However, there is a cumulative effect that makes subsequent proposals easier to put together.

Even an unsuccessful proposal can improve the quality of a company's goals, result in better planning and financial management, and improve credibility and business management structures. Preparing a written marketing proposal can help your organization assess its operating strategies. This effort will contribute to the next proposal you prepare because much of this process will not need to be repeated.

Learn from your mistakes. Many companies and agencies will discuss your unsuccessful proposal with you. You can ask why you did not win the award or contract, and frequently you will get an answer. Use this information to improve your next effort.

Another useful outcome from the cumulative effect is *electronic boilerplate:* reusable text that can be stored on a computer for future sales efforts. This text describes your business management structure, for instance, or your related experience.

Some parts of all proposals can be prepared ahead of time and simply plugged into subsequent sales proposals. These include personnel abilities, company accounting policies, and other details that change very infrequently. As you prepare each sales proposal, you should be accumulating a library of reusable text, illustrations, and supporting materials that can be used again and again.

You need to edit for compliance as well as for grammar, but remember, both can cost you the contract. The source selection board or evaluators may mistake your mechanical errors for larger incompetence. Simple errors cannot explain themselves because you are not present while the proposal is being reviewed. Every detail needs to be checked and rechecked.

We recommend a formal proposal review process in which all parties to the process are brought together to review the finished document, page by page. Only about one in five proposals is accepted, and winning government proposals generally score above 95 on the 100-point scale that is used to determine awards. The closer you are to zero defects, the greater your chances of success.

PREPARING SALES AND MARKETING PROPOSALS: EXERCISES

1. Find a Request for Proposal (RFP) in your local newspaper or in *The Federal Register.* Write a letter requesting a copy of the RFP.

2. Prepare an internal proposal to persuade Sandy Pascal to purchase a color scanner for the documentation team. You want the scanner as soon as possible so you can begin to add digitized images to the company's reports and proposals. Use a *problem→solution* strategy to put forward the benefits of your idea.

3. Prepare an Invitation to Bid that will be circulated among minority vendors and manufacturers. Pascal Business Systems wants to assure federal contractors that we are sincerely and actively searching for minority and female subcontractors. You have been asked to produce a two-page document that will encourage mi-nority- and female-owned businesses to participate in these contracts.

4. Use the World Wide Web address

   http://www.
      cfonline.com/cfo/opps/opps.html

   which provides Business Financing Listings & Proposals, to choose a proposal that you think might interest Pascal Business Systems. Be prepared to explain why you think this is a good proposal or a bad one.

5 Use the World Wide Web address

   http://cos.gdb.org/best/fed-fund.html

   to find examples of federally funded research in the United States. Review some of the abstracts for successful proposals and bring one that you like to class.

DESIGNING OFFICE MANUALS

- **Defining the Office Manual**
- **Formatting the Office Manual**
  - *Types of Office Manuals*
  - *Parts of the Office Manual*
- **Writing Office Manuals**
- **Reaching Administrative Decisions**
  - *Policies*
  - *Procedures*
  - *Consistency*
  - *Readability*
- **Editing and Testing Office Manuals**
- **Maintaining Office Manuals**

Many businesses today spend a great deal of their time changing data into information. To accomplish this they use various equipment—hardware and software—to collect data and transform it. Cash registers, bar-coders, and inventory spreadsheets are simple examples. The two most important and often neglected parts of this process, however, are people and procedures.

If the data a company collects is not consistent and the information it creates is not reliable, then the whole effort loses its value. To achieve reliable, consistent data collection, people must follow the same rules and procedures in all similar cases. In turn, this means that people need to be informed and aware of company policies and procedures, the rules and regulations that they are expected to follow.

DEFINING THE OFFICE MANUAL

Office manuals are task-oriented documents that provide detailed rules and operating instructions for complex business systems, services, and products. In this chapter we use the general term *office manuals* to describe a variety of documents that contain instructions, specifications, rules, and procedures for employees and customers.

These information devices, often called *employee, operating, style,* or *procedure manuals,* fill two important functions: instruction and reference. In either case, the purpose of office manuals is to provide rules and information for people who need to find facts and do things in a common way.

Complex systems need detailed and elaborate explanation. A well-designed office manual is an information device, an important part of a business system. Office manuals should be engineered for use. This means that the design considerations must emphasize the viewpoint of the people who will be working with the manuals. Carefully designed office manuals can increase employee and customer satisfaction, improve training, and increase productivity.

Providing written support material for a business system requires a lot of effort, but it is an important part of a business system's performance. All types of manuals—reference, employee, safety, and procedure manuals—are used by people who need to find some information or do something. These manuals need to be designed, written, edited, tested, maintained, distributed, and used.

FORMATTING THE OFFICE MANUAL

Since they will be widely distributed throughout the organization, office manuals need to be carefully planned. Know what kind of manual best fits your purpose, and work to present the information clearly and effectively.

Types of Office Manuals

Operations manuals tell people how to do things. These documents are used to instruct users. This means demonstrating how to operate products and how to follow the procedures in complex systems. Operations manuals are organized according to the tasks that the reader will carry out. Complex plans for involved activities, for example, require very elaborate procedures (sets of activities in sequence) that must be followed exactly.

Reference manuals provide users with information they might want to have but do not need in order to use the system or product. Typically, these documents will contain detailed business information. Inventories, parts lists, and catalogs are examples of reference manuals that require complete, current, and accurate information.

Style manuals are used by many businesses to ensure consistent, uniform standards for designing documents. Many companies consider it important for all documentation to maintain consistent standards. Consistent style standards convey an image of uniformity and strict control, an image that many companies seek.

Quality assurance, safety procedures, service, and *training manuals* are all used by business and industry to establish standards and specifications for products, services, and response systems. People need to know what to expect from the other people with whom they interact in complex organizations. Standards, expectations, product codes, and safety steps are all detailed in various types of office manuals.

Whatever the function, office manuals exist for users. Their styles and strategies should be transparent, so that readers don't even notice the document. Users are interested in meaning more than in style. Good manuals should come equipped with search tools. The people who use your manuals want to know about something or how to do something, and they need to find this information quickly.

Parts of the Office Manual

Your *cover* and *title page* should draw readers into the manual. Indicate the purpose of the manual in the title. This means that the title must be informative in a few short words. Practical considerations such as printing and binding costs will affect your choice of cover, but it should be attractive and appropriate. Durability may also be an important design factor.

A carefully prepared *table of contents* is a map that provides your readers with access routes to the specific information they are looking for. The more detailed you are, the easier it will be for the people using your manual to find what they need. It is also a good idea for you to provide a detailed table of contents at the front of each chapter or section.

Begin by describing the product or system and then explain how to use the manual. The *introduction* provides background and special information that the reader will need to perform operations and use the manual effectively. It provides an overview so that readers will know how to locate what they need. Establish a friendly, helpful tone with clear, direct statements.

Overviews at the beginning of chapters and *summaries* at the end help readers find and keep their place. Remember, your chapters are lessons. You are teaching people what to do and how to go about it. They will be using your manual for self-instruction and you need to respect their learning.

As with sets of technical directions, you must include *warnings* and *cautions* when there is any danger of damage to people or property. This is a legal as well as an ethical obligation. People who use the product carefully will rely on the manual, so you need to protect them from possible harm. Include *notes* when you want to provide the reader with some useful information that does not involve any danger.

Provide *lists* of simple steps, one action in each step, numbered for easy use and carefully sequenced. In other words, present the steps in the order in which the readers will perform them. Organize your material according to what users will want to do. Then tell them what to do. Each step should be a command.

Reference sections will be more useful if you organize your materials in *table* format. Rows and columns make information easy to locate. Again, your task is to help the reader. Use standard formats for bibliographic information and other reference materials.

A *glossary* will provide definitions for users who do not want to search through the index and manual. If your manual will be used by people who are not familiar with many of your technical terms, then prepare a glossary. Select a list of terms that need to be defined and explained. Don't assume, however, that all readers will use your glossary to teach themselves definitions and terms. Many people will never consult the glossary, so also include definitions of key terms within your text.

You may want to include an *index.* This is an alphabetical listing of all the major topics discussed in the manual, along with their location. Some users always begin at the back with the index. Others will judge your book by the entries in the index. Try to include all of the major topics in the manual and include common synonyms so that the reader does not have to use your preferred term to find a topic.

WRITING OFFICE MANUALS

Long documents such as office manuals require a systematic approach and a structured design. A systematic approach views the entire process (design, writing, assembly, and production) as a single complex operation that you need to manage carefully. The efforts of many people need to be coordinated and combined into a coherent manual.

Structured design leads to structured documents. You want to place your message in an accessible and reliable sequence so your readers can quickly extract the information they need. The organization of your manual must be clear and easy to follow. Multiple writers can use the structured design to connect their individual contributions to an organized plan.

some office manual categories

- General
- Organization
- Operation of the Board
- Personnel administration
- Leases and rentals
- Fees and charges
- Budget
- Accounting controls
- Legal matters
- Public relations

- Procurement of materials, supplies, and equipment
- Control of materials, supplies, and equipment
- Maintenance of equipment
- Repairs to equipment
- Facilities planning, alterations, and construction
- Facilities maintenance and upkeep
- Merchandise sales
- Safety, security, and emergencies
- Systems control

Essentially, office manuals are long reports designed for a very specific audience: people who need to know how to locate, do, or learn something. If you are involved in working on a manual, you should read Chapter 15, "Collaborating on Long Reports," for advice on scheduling, collaboration, and other issues of creating a complex document with multiple authors, audiences, and editors.

Use outlines to build models of the document before you create the document itself. The outline is a blueprint that can be reviewed and revised. It is easier to rework models than to change the completed manual. Your outlined model provides a complete, precise description of the manual. This is used as a basis for writing and assembling the finished document.

If a structured outline is going to be effective, it must be substantive and detailed. The outline must provide enough information for the editing/testing process, in which team members and users examine the model to see whether it is what they want. Remember, it is important to include users in the review of the model, because their needs should determine the final design.

Begin this complex writing project by defining your audience. Who are they and what will they need to know? What tasks will they want to perform? Design your manual by considering their needs first. Try to develop an overall plan that will unfold its details on the readers' schedule.

Organize by what users need to do. If you use your product or system as a framework, users will have to jump all around the document, looping and branching to get what

**the five stages
of office manual design**

1. Needs analysis
2. Design
3. Assembly
4. Editing
5. Maintenance

they need. If you pattern your manual on the logical sequence of user activities, your audience will recognize that your design has them in mind.

Writing office manuals is a five-stage process. You begin with a *needs analysis,* defining and deciding what documents or publications will be needed. You are providing your audience with information devices and it is important to determine exactly what they might need, what you can afford, and what you can produce in time for product or service delivery.

Your second stage is *design,* in which you develop a structured outline in complete detail, including headings and subheadings. You need to develop and polish your outline or storyboard so that it can be presented for technical verification and approval to proceed.

The third stage is *assembly,* in which a whole variety of elements, including tables, graphs, charts, text, and illustrations, have to be pulled together and connected in a draft document. This means coordination of a planned schedule in which many people work together, difficulties are anticipated, and resources are provided. Keeping many people working together on the same writing project is like directing a symphony—a whole lot of hard work.

Editing is a group process when a document is created by several people, but even if you are the only editor, you need to consider the views and needs of different people who will be using the document. Accuracy and clarity are the most important things you can contribute to this process.

The final stage of office manual design is *maintenance.* Outdated, unreliable information will cause problems for users, and every new edition multiplies the number of versions in circulation. Maintenance needs to be a part of the original design considerations. A plan for keeping the user documents current and accurate is an essential part of customer service.

REACHING ADMINISTRATIVE DECISIONS

To develop consistency, avoid problems, make operations run efficiently, and help employees avoid guesswork, organizations formulate and distribute policies and procedures. The larger the organization, the greater the need for clearly defined policies and procedures. While you may not set far-reaching administrative decisions until you have advanced to an executive level, you may be responsible—usually in collaboration with other employees—for setting local policies and procedures within your department or within an area of your expertise.

Policies

Policies are statements of fundamental principles and objectives. They are long-term guidelines. Policy statements define broad objectives and directions. (Heyel, 201) They will most likely be set by high-level executives.

Procedures

Procedures are detailed statements specifying actions to be taken to perform tasks and achieve objectives. Procedures are ways of implementing policies; they guide day-to-day actions to conform to the general principles of the organization. Thus, procedures, as commonly defined in business and industry, are descriptions of how trained people, already familiar with their individual tasks, cooperate to complete an operation. The procedure writer outlines what individuals within the organization need to do to follow the policies of the organization.

Here is a sample policy statement from a Pascal Business Systems office manual:

"The Customer Credit File is our most important record in customer negotiations. This file records the data by which we accept the customer's business. We use this file to determine whether to continue, change, or discontinue a customer's credit. Keep this file current and complete. Base all credit recommendations on the data from this file."

Consistency

Your readers should not have to deal with sudden and unexplained changes in the office manual, which is frequently their only source of information. Careless inconsistencies can confuse your readers, frustrate them, and cause them to improvise. New words should not appear while readers are puzzling out how to do something. You don't want your readers confused by inconsistent terms. Users should not have to branch, loop, switch volumes, or move around the document unless it is unavoidable. Use familiar formats so readers can find information quickly.

Office manuals, whether their purpose is reference or instruction, need to be consistent throughout. Everything has to match. This includes vocabulary, cross-references, structure, and design. When one of these elements changes, readers expect that the change means something. Continual changes will confuse and discourage your readers. Stick to the same format.

Repetition works very well in real life. Look at advertising and engineering. In advertising, important messages are repeated several times to verify that they have been communicated correctly; redundancy of systems is an accepted engineering principle. Double your chances by saying it twice.

Frequently, there are different ways to describe the same process. *Inputting, keyboarding,* and *entering* are all words that describe the same function. Every effective office manual establishes a consistent and simple style for itself. Don't use synonyms. Choose a term and stick with it.

Keep your manual consistent with its own design and structure. Don't wander from one design to another. Don't vary the way you organize the chapters or sections unless there is a very good reason. Develop document standards and keep to them.

The most important consistency is with the product or system itself. You should actively field-test the manual by trying it out with novice users. No matter how elegantly your manual is written, it is a device that needs to communicate complete, accurate information to beginners. It is better to discover problems *before* the manual is produced or distributed than after.

Readability

Many businesses and organizations use readability scales to measure the level of reading difficulty of their customer-oriented documents, especially employee and training manuals. The U.S. military, for instance, uses a revised version of the Flesch reading scales. These indexes, which attempt to provide some objective measure for text analysis, use various formulas to determine how much effort will be required to read a particular document.

At the least, try to improve the readability of your manuals with wide margins, varied type sizes, repetition of key points, frequent illustrations, and an overall professional appearance.

---

a list of useful ideas

- *Include lots of illustrations.* Probably every section of your manual could use some sort of illustration. Often your graphics will duplicate the information that is in your text. This kind of repetition ensures that your message is received.

- *Add definitions.* Don't assume that your readers know what you mean or intend by what you say. Define your terms. Let your readers know exactly what you are talking about. Explain by giving thoughtful definitions to your words.

- *Prepare summaries.* Include plenty of summaries—short, condensed versions of key material. Frequent summaries allow readers to review and consolidate what they have learned.

- *Tell your audience where to go for further information.* Direct your audience to sources of further information. This is very important if they are likely to need details that you do not provide.

- *Include examples.* One of the best ways to communicate difficult concepts is to include examples where you model applications and problems that the typical user might encounter.

EDITING AND TESTING OFFICE MANUALS

Reliable office manuals are the result of reliable testing. What many involved authors forget is that the purpose of testing is to cause failures that can be corrected. We'll say it again. *The purpose of testing is to cause failures!* The more failures you discover and correct, the better you are doing your job.

It is difficult work trying to explain complex procedures to people who know a lot less than you do. You need to think of your readers as confused, error-prone, and dependent. You have to adapt to the vocabulary and skill levels of your readers. Users are looking for clarity and reliability. Good manuals provide both.

At every step of the design and writing process, you should check for factual accuracy. This is essential. If your facts are wrong, the manual is useless and possibly harmful. Every factual statement should be verified.

Search your draft document for places where the users could lose their way. Watch out for detours. You don't want your users to become confused and set out on their own. During your first review of the office manual, revise language, identify inconsistencies, and clarify content. You are trying to discover and remove misleading information. Watch out for the ripple effect. Changing one section of the manual can have surprising and unanticipated problems.

learning about information problems

There are three kinds of information problems that turn up in manuals and cause trouble for users. The first is **missing information.** Your audience has a right to expect that the manual on which they rely will be thorough and complete. New users will not know that the information is missing until they are required to carry out a task or procedure. Unnecessary telephone support, service and warranty complaints, and customer aggravation will be the result.

Incorrect information can lead to even more damage. You have an important professional responsibility and a legal obligation to provide accurate and correct information, as well as complete information. People and property can be injured by careless misinformation. Simple proofreading errors can multiply into endless hours of explanation and apology. Make sure that it is correct the first time.

Ambiguous information, which confuses the audience and produces unintended options and choices, is quite common. Clarity, almost as important as accuracy in business messages, requires that you make your meaning as clear as is reasonably possible. Office manuals create a special obligation for direct, understandable, and well-crafted language. Your audience is dependent on your ability to anticipate problems and explain procedures in ways that cannot be misunderstood. This is a design task of the first order.

Edit for mechanical errors—grammar, spelling, and punctuation. If you want your manual to have credibility with users, find your mistakes and fix them. It may be an unfair perception, but readers will equate errors with incompetence.

MAINTAINING OFFICE MANUALS

How easily can your office manuals be corrected, updated, or improved? This is an important question. What many people forget is that office manuals need to be maintained. They need to be kept up to date constantly. If they are not current, they will not be used. A well-crafted manual can be easily supplemented and modified as the product or system changes.

Designing an office manual should always include planning for future modifications. If your document will need frequent revisions, for example, consider using a loose-leaf binder. Try to include variable information in the appendices. Date your documents and supplements clearly to avoid confusion.

Usually some person is assigned the task of maintaining the office manual over time, making sure that it changes as the product or system does. This means changing the document when the product is modified or new features are added. Changes in policy or system procedures also need to be communicated as they occur. Often the upkeep costs of office manuals will be more than their development costs. This means that you should consider how the document will be maintained and modified while you are in the design stage. It is too late to think about this when the manual is complete.

Remember that poorly designed products or systems will not be compensated for by the wonderful manual your team creates. A poor procedure will be difficult to follow, no matter how carefully you write it down. A bad product, clearly explained, is still a bad product. Well-designed business systems and products need less documentation than their inferior counterparts, and the writing problems you experience may be a reflection of what is in your mirror: the product or system your manual supports.

Well-written office manuals return more than their costs to the companies that make the effort to create and maintain them. Good documentation can reduce expensive customer services, including field and phone support, training, and error adjustments. Good writing can also add value to a product, service, or system by making things easier for users. Your office manual should be a friendly, user-oriented publication designed for the convenience of your audience.

DESIGNING OFFICE MANUALS: EXERCISES

1. Pascal Business Systems specializes in creating ergonomic office environments. It is particularly important, therefore, that PBS offer an ergonomic environment for its own personnel. Create a policy statement and three procedures for creating an ergonomic working environment at Pascal Business Systems.

2. Decide on a standard format for every assignment in the course you are now taking. Design a sample assignment using this standard format. Write a policy and procedure statement that will introduce this standard format to your classmates.

3. Write two descriptions of a procedure, one for a general audience and one for an

expert audience. Review your document with members of your group to determine whether you have met the needs of your audience.

4. Have every person in your group bring an office manual of some sort to a meeting where you will rank order the different manuals and the appropriateness of their design.

5. Assume you are working for Pascal Business Systems. Create a short report in which you suggest three reporting procedures for field marketing representatives to keep the home office informed and up to date. You may want to consider having standard progress reports. Discuss dates, formats, and distribution, among other possible procedures. Send your report to executive vice-president Joan Fontanella.

6. Find an office manual that visually appeals to you. Establish criteria, such as page layout, visual aids, style, and strategy, to defend your selection of this particular manual. Now write a short report to recommend this format to your co-workers. Attach samples from the manual to your report.

7. Write a short report in which you specify the maintenance requirements for a projected reference manual. Assume that the manual is for a software product that is revised on a six-month schedule. In other words, you need to design a set of procedures for bringing the manual up to date every time there is a scheduled change in the product. (*Hint:* Determine what will need to be updated, then determine the order of the updates.)

8. Prepare a manual for your college or school that details policies and procedures for student use of the computer equipment. Look at hours of availability for the different labs on campus, access to the Internet, use of and payment for printing, and whatever other issues exist at your school. Consider assigning priority for classes and class projects and whether users are allowed to bring food and drinks into the labs. Make sure you include illustrations for your readers.

Your school or college may already have a manual. When was it last updated? What improvements could be made to this manual?

section 5
LOOKING DOWN THE ROAD

· ·

In this final section of *Communicating for Future Business Professionals*, we encourage you to think ahead, beyond your first career job to a time when you have achieved a measure of success in your field. Perhaps by peering this far into your future, you may be able to affect it. Many college students have only a vague, hazy notion of where they want to be in midcareer. Given the pace of technological change, it has become extremely difficult to predict what the future will hold.

In Chapter 18, we take you down the road of your future, examining some of the signposts along the way. While your path will follow its own unique course, there are some general principles that will apply to virtually everybody. One is that you will need to be flexible, for the world of the 21st century will demand that you adjust to change. What you learn in college will provide a basic foundation for the work you will do, but you will have to learn continuously. The path you choose today may change directions many times over the course of your career, and each change of direction will require new knowledge and skills.

PREPARING FOR YOUR FUTURE

Starting Now

Seeing New Horizons

Assessing Your Progress

Coordinating and Supervising People

Leading Meetings

Designing Your Career

You may have found yourself changing during the course of the semester. Your time horizons may be longer, and, if this book has been successful, you are thinking more about your career and are able to picture what certain aspects of your career may be like. In this chapter we take this process one step further.

As we learn more about ourselves, we define our identity, and our working situation has much to do with helping us define ourselves. While we certainly do not advocate that you define yourself solely by your career choice, we do recognize that a significant percentage of your adult life will be spent working; inevitably, you will come to see yourself partially in terms of what you do for a living. By planning ahead for your career, you can have a direct impact on the person you become. By setting goals, you can structure your time more productively.

STARTING NOW

As we have emphasized previously, you need to build a network of contacts within your field; now is the time to begin. If you haven't constructed a résumé as part of the course you are taking this semester, do so now. Do it on a computer so that you can update it easily.

Are there any glaring weaknesses in your résumé? Now is the time to begin filling those gaps. Join clubs. Volunteer. Gain experience. Make a list of individuals who are in your field and who have knowledge. Since most jobs are never listed in the classified ads, these are the people who will help you find jobs, now and later. You may find that after you have some experience in your field, the organization you are working for offers little opportunity for advancement—perhaps your path is blocked by a number of young executives who seem destined to retain their positions for a long time, perhaps you are ready for a new challenge—and your network can keep you informed about developments in your field as well as job opportunities. In some fields you need to move out of an organization in order to move up. Yes, it may seem risky, but if your ultimate goal is advancement, you may need to assume some risks.

Keep a list of your professional highlights: projects you work on, publications, important contracts, grants and government proposals—in short, anything that you consider significant and that employers would be looking for.

SEEING NEW HORIZONS

In college, we can barely see beyond the next exam. Many students, and you may be among this group, learn to survive by cramming for an exam, pulling all-nighters to complete a major paper for a course, working until the early morning and skipping classes for a week to complete a large project. And it frequently works! However, this may not be the best strategy for survival within an organization.

You may need to think not in terms of the next exam or the end of the semester, but in terms of the completion of a project, or the end of the fiscal year (usually June 30). In some organizations there are no clearly marked time periods; work simply continues, week after week. In such cases, it is up to you to create individualized time horizons.

Because of the continuous nature of most work environments, consistency is rewarded. You need to focus on your responsibilities and not fall too far behind in your projects. Deadlines are important. Work completed after a deadline may cost the organization; in fact, a contract may be lost because a proposal is submitted five minutes after a deadline. You may be a stellar employee, but if you cause the organization to lose this contract, the rest of your performance may be overlooked. So determine which projects need your immediate attention and complete these first.

As you settle into the routines of the workplace, it is easy to lose sight of the future. You may become focused on short-term commitments, completing projects and reports and then quickly beginning a new project. If you think in terms of larger blocks of time, however, you may avoid the pitfall of becoming stagnant.

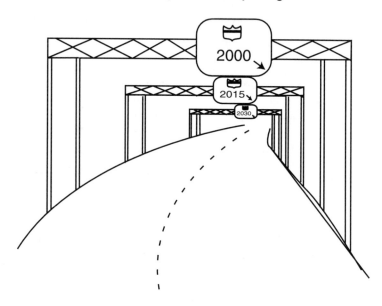

Here are some general guidelines to follow:

- *Stay positive.* Confront whatever problems develop on the job—and there will be problems—openly and with humor.
- *Get to work on time.* Get to meetings on time. File your reports on time. Know what your duties are and fulfill them. You may want to make a list of priorities so that you know which tasks you need to do first.
- *Watch for subtle shifts of policy within the organization.* The grapevine is an excellent source for this. Keep your finger on the pulse of the grapevine, realizing as you do that you cannot accept everything you hear on the grapevine as the absolute truth. In general, stay out of power struggles unless you are sure that you have correctly assessed the future direction of the organization.
- *Wait six months to one year before you ask for more money.* Once you have gone through a few positive performance reviews, then you can initiate a salary discussion.

ASSESSING YOUR PROGRESS

You have now worked in the organization for a period of time, let's say a year. You have begun to understand how your organization works, you know your co-workers and your supervisor, you have begun to feel comfortable with your position, and you have received at least one performance review. Now it is time to evaluate your role within the organization.

At one extreme is the perfect fit—you are energized by the organization and your role in it and you are happy with your responsibilities and duties, your relationships with co-workers and supervisors, your salary and benefits package, and your opportunities for advancement. The other extreme is an untenable work situation—you are in conflict with the organization's people, goals, philosophy, or business practices to the extent that you are miserable.

Take the following test to determine your happiness.

---

do you like your job?

Here's a test you may want to take as your career develops, suggested by Carol Kleiman in her book *The 100 Best Jobs for the 1990s and Beyond*:

1. Do you look forward to going to work each day?
2. At the end of the day, do you have a sense of accomplishment?
3. Do you respect your employers, and their goals, ethics, and professional expertise?
4. Are you doing what you do best, using the skills and knowledge you have acquired for the profession of your choice?
5. Do you feel you are being paid fairly, including salary, benefits, and other perks?
6. Are you positioned to move ahead in the next two to three years?
7. Does your organization have a commitment to continuing education and training to keep you up to date in your field and in the new technology?
8. Does your employer know your professional goals and discuss with you on a regular basis the skills you need to move into the next job level?
9. Is your present employer concerned about issues such as flexible hours, parental leave, job sharing, and child and elder care programs?
10. Are you satisfied with the balance between your time commitment to your personal goals and responsibilities and your professional goals and responsibilities?
(Kleiman, 128–129)

If you finish this test with a sinking feeling in the pit of your stomach, you need to look for another job. Start by preparing your résumé, letting your network know that you are looking for a new challenge, and reading. You may want to consider a professional headhunter, a trained job-finder who will search for a fit based on your career goals and qualifications. Some other good sources include the *National Business Employment Weekly*, published by *The Wall Street Journal*, and the *Executive Employment Guide*, published by the American Management Association.

However, don't quit your job until you have something definite lined up as a replacement. Resist the temptation to lash back at your employers; describe the causes of your unhappiness at your exit interview as calmly and honestly as possible.

Another possible source of displeasure in a working situation occurs when employees feel that they must behave in a way that conflicts with their religious, ethical, or personal codes of conduct. You may find yourself pressured into behavior that does not agree with you. This can make for a very stressful work environment, where the part of you that wants to do well in a job can be in conflict with your sense of self-worth.

While we cannot offer a hard and fast rule here, consider this: Don't risk your health. Don't let the stress become so unbearable that you dread going to work each day. You may need to consult your network and find a less stressful working environment.

---

ethical considerations

As you move up within an organization, you may find a gradually increasing pressure to conform. For some companies, what is "politically correct" can be defined in very unusual ways. And there are political and emotional barriers to taking a stand that may be difficult to confront. For example, executives may find it risky to speak in favor of affirmative action, mandated parental leave, increased government spending, higher taxes, and national health care. What is an acceptable position in some conservative companies? Perhaps only "Let the free market work."

(Solomon, 45, 49)

Ultimately, realize this: It's your life. You must determine whether you can live within a particular organization. In the same way that not every college is right for every student, not every organization is right for every employee. Changing jobs need not represent failure. You may need to change jobs, even career paths, two or three times before you find the situation that is right for you. If you are flexible and persistent, and if you continually upgrade your skills and knowledge, you may find yourself in a satisfying and rewarding work environment.

If you decide to look for a new position, activate your network and update your résumé, but you need not inform your employer until you have accepted another job offer. Customarily, give your employer two weeks' notice before you leave the organization.

If you are fired from an organization, resist the temptation to feel self-pity. Understand that many organizations terminate employees on a regular basis; activate your network, get references from co-workers before you leave, update your résumé, and send out prospecting applications. You may have to go through the job application process a number of times before you find the perfect fit.

COORDINATING AND SUPERVISING PEOPLE

Now let's project even further into the future: You have been promoted. You find yourself leading a department, managing people, and planning long-term projects.

With the promotion comes more money, better benefits, more prestige—perhaps a longer vacation, use of a company car, profit sharing, use of a credit card, executive lunches—but more decision-making responsibilities, more pressure, more risk, and possibly, longer hours at work. The organization has expressed its confidence in you, but it also expects more from you.

Accept the responsibility. You may have to revise the way you think about yourself, and the people you supervise may look at you a little differently, but if you handle situations honestly and fairly, you will retain the trust of the people with whom you work. When confronted with a decision, don't allow the pressure to affect who you are; weigh all of the variables, make your decision honestly and fairly, and then do all you can to follow it through.

For many people, supervising others is difficult. They do not want to criticize others and find it hard to confront someone who is not living up to expectations. Supervisors need a blend of skills; you need to treat people with respect and motivate them to work at their best. You need to build teams and develop a sense of commitment within the people you supervise. The best approach is honesty, directness, rewarding people for their work, keeping them informed, allowing them to make key decisions that affect them, and creating a positive, secure atmosphere. Learn from the supervisors you most admire as you move through the organization.

As a manager, you will need human skills and conceptual skills as well as technical skills. In this case, *human skills* refers to the range of behaviors required to lead a unit of an organization and to collaborate with peers and superiors. *Conceptual skills* involve a way of thinking about an enterprise: that is, always considering "relative emphases and priorities among conflicting objectives and criteria; relative tendencies and probabilities . . . ; and relative correlations and patterns among elements." (Katz, 44) Don't assume that technical competence will ensure success. You need to be able to deal with the people you supervise and allow them to succeed, and you need to be able to balance all of the conflicting information at your disposal and make decisions based on your ability to weigh all of the factors.

LEADING MEETINGS

When you move into your first position after college, you will most likely attend meetings but rarely lead them. As you advance within the organization, the chances are greater that you will have the opportunity to lead meetings. There are some simple rules to follow, some of which have already been presented in Chapter 6, "Encountering People on the Job."

As the coordinator of the meeting, you are responsible for making meetings productive and, to a certain extent, enjoyable for the participants. You can develop a style that is efficient but not stifling, moving meetings forward yet allowing individuals to have their say. Watch those leaders who have success in meetings and learn from them.

If you are responsible for planning meetings, you can follow this checklist to help in the preparation stages:

---

a checklist for meetings

Answer each of the following questions before you hold a meeting. As you answer, check off each question.

Do we really need to meet about this?	☐
What should the meeting accomplish?	☐
What should occur after the meeting?	☐
Who should attend the meeting?	☐
How long should the meeting be?	☐
Where should we meet?	☐
How can we prepare the site?	☐
What special equipment is needed?	☐
What is the agenda?	☐
When should the agenda be distributed?	☐
Who will keep the minutes?	☐

According to a survey conducted by the Annenberg School of Communications (University of Southern California), the typical meeting:

- is a staff meeting
- is held in a conference room
- lasts one hour and 55 minutes
- has no written agenda distributed in advance
- occurs after two hours' notice
- is attended by nine people
- involves the participation of most of those in attendance
- uses handouts (*Modern Office Technology,* June 1990, p.100)

We hope that you can see some ways of improving on this typical meeting profile. If you regularly lead meetings within your organization, spend at least some time analyzing the meetings. You may want to put such an analysis on your agenda for an upcoming meeting.

DESIGNING YOUR CAREER

In the end, it's your career. We hope that we have given you a better perspective on how to design your career so that it conforms to your needs and desires, but ultimately it is up to you, and you need to measure your success by your standards and goals. And even when the dominant culture measures success in materialistic terms, it is not necessary that you do so. We hope that you live a rich, full life, however you define *rich* and *full.*

Finally, we'd love to hear from you, particularly any reports of work experiences that you would like to share with us. Please write to us:

Michael Greene and Jon Ripley
   c/o Editor, Career and Technology Division
   Prentice-Hall
   Upper Saddle River, NJ 07458
   Current (1997) e-mail addresses
   GreeneM@wit.edu
   Ripley@wit.edu

PREPARING FOR YOUR FUTURE: EXERCISES

1. Interview three people over age 50. Try to find out as much as you can about their careers without probing too deeply into areas that they would rather not discuss: How did their careers evolve? What were the high points? The low points? Did their education and training prepare them for the world they have encountered?

2. Define *success* in your own terms. Prepare for a group discussion of the meaning of success by pinpointing two individuals you believe are successful.

3. How long do you expect your working life to be? Discuss with the class your expectations about the length of time you plan to spend at work. Do you think this will involve any career changes?

4. Form a pact with your closest college friends that you will stay in touch via the Internet after graduation. Follow through by exchanging Internet addresses and keeping your friends informed about your progress. These individuals will become a part of your network.

5. Discuss with your group whether you would like to be a leader, supervisor, or decision maker after graduation. Explain your reasons. You may find a wide range of aspirations, and this may lead to an interesting discussion.

6. Write to the authors of this book, sharing experiences from your postcollege years.

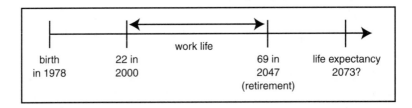

APPENDIX
PASCAL BUSINESS SYSTEMS

Many of the exercises at the end of the chapters and some of the examples within the text are based on Pascal Business Systems. This appendix is an overview of PBS.

Pascal Business Systems began in 1981 when Sandra Pascal left her job as a client service representative with a Houston-based computer company and began a consulting company specializing in working with small organizations who could not afford large mainframe computer systems. Gradually, the company grew and evolved into Pascal Business Systems. In 1983, Sandy Pascal realized that personal computers would soon replace mainframes for virtually all small businesses. By 1987, Pascal Business Systems had made major inroads into the direct order business for computers and computer supplies. By 1990, the organization was committed to offering solutions to the growing number of individuals suffering from repetitive stress injuries involving computers. This added specialization created a tremendous growth spurt within the organization in the early 1990s.

Pascal Business Systems is now engaged in the sales, distribution, and installation of business hardware and software and office automation systems. The company uses computers to automate the routine tasks confronted by its customers. The company is, fundamentally, in the office supply business, catering to small organizations and the growing number of individuals who work at home. Most orders are placed by phone.

Besides hardware and software, the organization specializes in ergonomically designed office equipment, including chairs, computer desks, keyboards, headphones, screen filters, anti-static equipment, and a host of other add-ons. Pascal Business Systems markets a full range of wrist rests, computer gloves, foot rests, ergonomic keyboards, mouse pads, noise control headsets, indirect lighting, phone supports, monitor glare shields, pads, and braces to control the work environment.

Ergonomics is the study of human characteristics for the appropriate design of the living and work environment.

The organization markets internationally, although most of its clients now reside in the United States. The customer list is growing rapidly both within the United States and internationally. More and more, the clients of Pascal Business Systems recognize that working full-time with a computer necessitates that they consider health issues.

Although carpal tunnel syndrome (CTS) has gotten the most attention from the media, there are many other repetitive stress injuries (RSIs) and cumulative trauma disorders (CTDs) that result from the continuous use of computers. Such injuries can be painful and, in some cases, so debilitating that the individual who suffers is unable to work at all. A severe case of carpal tunnel syndrome, for example, can cost $100,000 in medical expenses and lost productivity. (Furger 1993, 120) In 1990, there were 185,000 CTD diagnoses; the estimated $10 billion in lawsuits is now larger than asbestos-related payments. (Scheer, 43) Computers also put severe stress on the human visual system. The close focusing on monitors causes eyestrain, headaches, and itching or burning eyes. (Tessler, 103) Pascal Business Systems employs a team of specially trained custom workstation consultants who go to the client's office, analyze all of the potential health problems, and design an ergonomic environment.

Here is a partial list of the products contained in the Pascal Business Systems catalog:

Main hardware	Software	Accessories
computers	databases	desks
photocopiers	spreadsheets	tables
fax machines	word processors	printer tables
answering machines	home accounting	file cabinets
telephone accessories,	desktop publishing	in/out baskets
including headsets	graphics and illustrations	stationery
storage systems	presentations	business cards
printers		printer cartridges and ribbons
modems		toner cartridges
		beepers, mobile radios
		cellular phones

Besides the lucrative direct-order business, Pascal Business Systems also consults with customers, offering a manual on how to set up a home office. The previously mentioned consultants will come into a home office and offer recommendations on how to better utilize equipment, space, and materials.

Orders are the crucial element. The entire business is geared toward helping the customer place orders and get the products quickly. Many people who work in home offices won't buy a product until they need to complete a job. Then they need it immediately. The task is to get it to them as quickly as possible. The organization requires an excellent, readable, informative catalog, so it needs to test products. The product line has to be the best, even though it will need a variety of products just in case a customer wants something the product testers don't recommend as the best.

Currently, Pascal Business Systems employs 245 individuals in a variety of tasks. Here is a partial list of the positions and the tasks employees do:

product testers

customer sales reps (place orders, take customer complaints, achieve customer satisfaction)

accountants

collection-letter writers

custom workstation consultants

database engineers

buyers

merchandise experts

shipping/receiving warehouse personnel

software experts

hardware experts

technical writers

photographers

graphic designers

phone system engineers*

As the organization grew and became more complex, Sandy Pascal gave up more and more of the supervision of day-to-day operations. She is now the chief executive officer. She hired Bart Jones and Joan Fontanella in 1982 to oversee the business end of PBS; both are now executive vice-presidents. Ann Smith supervises the telephone staff. The ergonomic consultants function as a team, with Stan Cohen serving as the coordinator. Here are some of the other employees that you may meet in examples and exercises throughout this book:

Herman Tannebaum	Human Resources
Leslie Holmes	Human Resources
Andrew Nauman	Computer Services
Ruth Zhu	Computer Services
Loretta Cedrone	Technical Services
Nguyen Wei	Technical Services

*The phones can't go down; the entire company depends on it. Each order is filled within an hour, is shipped that day, and arrives at the customer's office the next day. Immediacy and accuracy are the bywords of the organization.

Yong Moon Han	Product Testing
Abdulhakeem Al-Hussein	Product Testing
Mike Benevento	Account Representative
Won Lee	Computer Graphics
June Joseph	Publications

Any rapidly expanding organization has its problems; a number of areas concern the leaders of Pascal Business Systems. Given the pace of change within the computer field, it is difficult to keep employees current. Training on new systems is absolutely necessary, but training is expensive and time-consuming. A second problem involves the catalog. It is growing as quickly as the number of products offered. The catalog is expensive to produce every month and expensive to mail. (Last month's issue was 132 pages.) A third problem involves the nature of PBS's business: How does a company that sells ergonomic products provide a safe and healthy environment for its employees?

Despite these problems, Pascal Business Systems has carved out a significant market niche for itself. The company projects a growth rate of 33 percent in the next fiscal year and intends to fill at least 75 newly created positions within the next twelve months. With a well-trained, well-rewarded workforce, the company sees many reasons to be optimistic about the future.

THE FIVE TYPES OF STYLE

Appendix

B

As human beings who are engaged in the complex activity of communication with all of its rhythms, rules, and confusions, we are constantly making style changes—shifts in language and expression that signal subtle differences and perspectives.

All of us change styles. We use different words and ways of expressing our message, depending on our audience. Certainly it is easier to write a note to a good friend than it is to write an article that will appear in the newspaper where everyone can read it.

What is the difference between these two messages? Quite simply, it is more difficult to talk to people we don't know, people with whom we don't share space and information. We are constantly adjusting our speech and writing styles to our listeners and our imagined audiences. For example, the city cop who "collars the punk" writes it down as "apprehending the suspect." The ways we use language change with the situation, the subject, and our relation to the audience.

Imagine yourself at the center of a series of circles, each of which shows the increasing distance between you and the people to whom you can speak or write, as shown in Fig. B-1. These circles represent five styles that we all employ.

INTERNAL STYLE

The first style we need is internal. This is for inner communication. Whether we talk to ourselves or view things in our mind's eye, each of us develops unique and powerful ways of communicating within ourselves.

This internal style is solid-state communication. It takes place inside us. We can jump from one subject to another as quickly as we want. Any type of shorthand or mental indexing will do. This style is immediate and impossible to censor. As soon as we think something, we know what we are thinking.

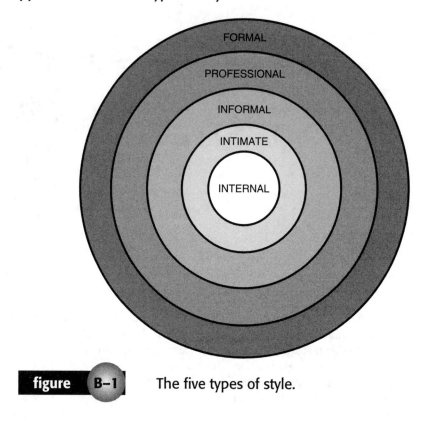

FORMAL

PROFESSIONAL

INFORMAL

INTIMATE

INTERNAL

figure **B-1** The five types of style.

INTIMATE STYLE

We use an intimate style when communicating with the people closest to us. These people—family, lovers, our closest friends—are the people who share our space, our personal history, and our experience.

The intimate style is close and quick, marked by shared signals, thoughts, and experience with language. It is free and open, spontaneous, unconstrained, and casual.

Even a few words will communicate a great deal of information when people share the same close and intimate background. A single word can contain a great deal of meaning because of shared personal associations. This type of language is a restricted code, however, known only to those who have participated in the same experience.

INFORMAL STYLE

Informal style is what we choose when we are communicating with friends and acquaintances. Since we are comfortable and familiar with these people, we can use language without being cautious, careful, or rehearsed. We can be relaxed and unceremonious and say what we intend without worrying about how we say it.

You could write a memo in an informal style to one individual within your organization with whom you have developed a close working relationship as long as this memo won't be read by others, now or in the future. To write in an informal style in a work setting, you need not be extremely close friends outside of work. Occasionally, a business letter to a close acquaintance is written in the informal style.

Again, like the intimate style, the informal style is marked by shared personal associations in which a word or signal may carry a great deal of meaning. If you know someone quite well, you can communicate a lot of information by referring to shared experience. When you say, "You know," to your friends, they probably do understand what you mean. If you and an associate have been working on the Baxter account for five years, a simple message such as "Baxter again" will communicate quite a lot.

PROFESSIONAL STYLE

A professional style is more elaborate than either the informal or the intimate style. Great care is taken to explain things fully. This style is cautious, deliberate, and marked by strong concern for the audience. In business and industry, it is essential that we are understood when we speak and write to each other.

Often this means preparation and rehearsal. A professional style is not spontaneous and immediate; rather, it is expected to be careful and deliberate. Collection letters, progress reports, and prospecting applications are just some of the tasks that require a professional style. Such documents and presentations are designed ahead of time, reviewed, and then revised to be precise and exact.

---

style site on the web

Strunk and White: Elements of Style
http://www.columbia.edu/acis/bartleby/strunk/

This does not mean that your professional writing and speaking styles cannot be conversational and easy to understand. However, even if your writing resembles offhand conversation, you need to take extra care to explain things completely to avoid the chances of misunderstanding.

Using a professional style means taking responsibility for the successful transfer of the message. This means clarifying, explaining, defining, demonstrating, illustrating, making things clear, and spelling them out.

FORMAL STYLE

Documents that you would want your attorney to review will almost certainly be in a formal style. Leases, annual reports, contracts, marketing proposals—these types of documents frequently require very exact formats, which are rigid and inflexible. Legal and contractual specifications call for precise and particular forms of language and design.

The best advice we have is to follow the specifications exactly. If your document needs to be single spaced, then make sure that it is. One of the things you can do is to make up a list of the specifications, then check them off as each is completed. When your audience supplies you with an exact format, you are saved the trouble of doing this yourself. So, the same as with a coloring book: Stay within the lines.

In the formal style, a single word or decimal point out of place can cause serious complications. You need to proofread very carefully or have someone do this for you. Careful review is essential when your document functions as a contract and obligation.

---

style guidelines

- Choose shorter words over longer words, when you have a choice, but always opt for precise words.
- Place only one major idea in each sentence. Develop this idea fully, then proceed to the next idea.
- Phrase each sentence so that it conveys your meaning precisely.

THE DOCUMENT DESIGN PROCESS

Appendix C

The *document design process* is a basic underlying set of procedures you can use whenever you have a document to write, whether it is a résumé, a memo, a business letter, a report, a marketing proposal, or an office manual. Once you have some practice, you can incorporate the process into any communication task, including oral presentations. As you become more familiar with the process, you will find that you need spend only a few minutes going through the early stages before you begin your draft.

Why? The first question you need to ask is "What is my purpose?" You may want to *propose* a course of action or behavior for the future; *report* on behavior that occurred in the past; *document* or record information for future reference; *persuade* other people concerning your ideas, qualifications, and products; or *instruct* them on how to follow procedures or processes. You may have a primary and a secondary purpose, or you may have multiple purposes. Write down your purpose: The purpose of this document is to _____. My secondary purpose is _____. When the reader finishes reading this document, I would like the reader to _____.

Who? You need to develop a profile of your audience. Here are five questions to get you started:

Who is my audience? (What do I know about my audience?)
What is my relationship to this person or these people?
Under what circumstances will this document be read?
What are the expectations of my audience?
What does my audience need to know?

Why?   Who?   What?   When?

Decide Style and Strategy

Select Graphics and Illustrations

Choose Format

Draft
the
Document

Revise, Edit, and Proofread

Test Your Output

Revise, Edit, and Proofread

Finish
the
Document

 **figure C-1** The document design process.

What?   When you approach any communication task, you either (1) know all you intend to communicate or (2) need to find out something to include. If you know all of the message, you simply have to make sure all of it is included in your document. If you need to find out something, you have to conduct research. This research may mean gathering information in a variety of ways: interviewing people, conducting a survey, searching through company records, or utilizing all of the different reference options available in a library or on the Internet.

When?   You need to schedule your time to complete a task successfully. Deadlines actually help us by establishing limits. First, discover exactly how much time you have, then work backward, leaving enough time for each step in the document design process.

Develop an outline for long documents. Contact all of the people—collaborators, artists, your sources, and so forth—who will be involved in the preparation of the document. Develop a time chart and let everyone know their deadlines. Stick to your schedule.

Decide Style and Strategy   *Style* refers to the ways you express your message, or the specific words and phrasing you use to convey your ideas. Choose a professional style—cautious, deliberate, and concerned about the audience. Clarify your message; choose words that will convey your message precisely. *Strategy* refers to the approach you take to a communication situation and the way your readers understand and react to the context of the situation. You want to skillfully manage the reactions of your audience to your message.

Select Graphics and Illustrations   New technology allows us to enhance our documents with strong visual images. We cover how to create tables, charts, graphs, drawings, and other visuals in Chapter 13, "Designing Graphics and Illustrations."

Choose a Format   Organize your information by enhancing the design of your pages. Follow standard formats, but add creative touches to make your document distinctive. As you read through this text, you will see standard formats for many different kinds of documents.

Draft the Document   A draft is more than a rough sketch of a document; it is a nearly complete version that needs polishing. Very important documents may require multiple drafts. All of the decisions you have made should be reflected in your draft.

Revise   *Revising* refers to the process of examining and improving the content and design of your document; *editing* refers to the process of examining and improving grammar, mechanics, and style; and *proofreading* refers to the process of eliminating typographical and other errors from your document. You need to do all three processes, at times simultaneously, as you work to create the best possible document.

Test Your Output   The more important and the more complex the document, the more you need to get feedback from others, even if this means asking others to evaluate what you have written. You need readers who can offer constructive criticism, and you need to respond to this feedback positively; don't be defensive, but hear what your test audience has to say.

Revise   Make sure you do a final check of your document just before you produce the final version. Errors may creep into your document as you rewrite your draft.

Finish the Document   In the final stage of the document design process, you are assembling all of the pieces of the document, preparing the final copy, and delivering the document. Given the many possible forms your document may take—hard copy, electronic mail, fax, and so forth—you need to consider how your audience will receive your message.

Appendix

INTERCULTURAL COMMUNICATION

The purpose of this appendix is to describe some techniques and strategies that can be useful in designing business communications for a global audience. English is used to communicate important information to people all around the world, yet very few business writers or company managers recognize the difficulties in communicating across cultures, even in the same language.

Many business writers, for example, use local idioms and culture-bound references in an attempt to make their documents user-friendly and more accessible. To international readers whose command of English is not strong, these attempts to be friendly can make business documents confusing and hard to understand.

Increasingly, business documents will need to be designed for a world audience whose English is global rather than local. English is the primary language of commerce and industry in such diverse places as Nigeria, Singapore, Canada, and Guyana. Business communicators need to consider these distinct cultures and their different varieties of English, and design documentation for a world audience.

Cross-cultural communication involves the sending and receiving of messages within the context of different cultures. As cultural differences increase or decrease, the difficulty of these tasks increases or decreases. In other words, it may be relatively simple for you to design your message for a Canadian audience, but it will be substantially more difficult to design the same message for your business contacts in Saudi Arabia.

If your audience is similar to you, then you can refer to common experience, use language that you both understand, and communicate freely because you can be confident about how your message will be received. When your audience is from another culture, particularly one that is not familiar to you, then you will be less certain about how to design a message that is clear and effective.

Culture influences people's self-identities, values, and patterns of language. It affects the way they communicate and the way they understand. People from other regions or different countries may communicate differently than you do, and may respond differ-

---

A number of books can help you understand other cultures and gain specific information about customs and business practices. Among them are:

The Do's and Taboos of International Trade: A Small Business Primer
by Roger E. Axtell.
Published by John Wiley & Sons.
Do's and Taboos around the World
by Roger E. Axtell.
Published by John Wiley & Sons.
The Economist Business Traveller's Guides.
Published by Prentice-Hall.

---

ently to what you write or say. Your own culture seems normal and correct to you from the inside, and the behavior of people in other cultures will often seem strange to you. Whatever puzzlement you might feel, however, you want to design your international communications with particular care and respect.

You must learn to recognize, understand, and appreciate other cultures if you want to be successful in international communication. Foreign businesses and firms will frequently have different practices and perceptions than U.S. companies. Your abilities to understand and interact with different groups and cultures will have a significant effect on your career.

Business communications always take place in a context of human cultures: national, regional, ethnic, even cultures within a community. Culture is a complex set of social attitudes and behaviors that make up the distinctive way of life of a people. A culture reveals itself in many different ways: language, social organization, economic and political systems, technology, education, the role of sexes and age groups, religions, values, and attitudes. All of these dimensions blend together in a set of expectations about what is appropriate, acceptable, and natural behavior. When we encounter members of different cultures and communicate with them, we need to be aware of alternative ways of behaving and thinking. Business is a global enterprise and you will very likely find yourself working with people from many different cultures.

Every culture offers certain cues or clues about its beliefs and attitudes. Styles of food, clothing, and architecture can give you useful insights. Body language will keep you informed about what is going on. Attentive observation will alert you to obvious norms; there are also many books and training opportunities to prepare you for interacting with people through formal correspondence.

You do not want to burden yourself with cultural stereotypes—ready-made images that are frequently wrong and incorrect: "People from England are cold and formal," "Italians are demonstrative," and "the French are rude." Every nation has its stock adjectives, but they simply do not convey the complexity of various national cultures.

the four P's of international protocol

Punctuality is one business behavior that varies from country to country and culture to culture. Here in the United States, punctuality is considered very important. You are expected to arrive on time and not to keep people waiting. In other cultures, however, time is perceived much more fluidly. A one o'clock meeting schedule may in fact indicate that the meeting will take place sometime in the midafternoon.

Patience is often a difficult quality for Americans to develop. We are an action-oriented, results-focused culture that likes decisive, short-term outcomes, quickly achieved and easily measured. There are many other cultures, however—the Japanese, for example—who do business very slowly and carefully and whose planning and strategies are aimed at long-term results.

Presents or small gifts are viewed differently by different cultures. Strict ethical codes often set clear limits on what presents you may or may not offer, but you should try to find out what attitudes are shared by the persons you are dealing with. An inexpensive gift, carefully and thoughtfully selected, can provide evidence of your interest and respect.

Preparation is always the key to success when you are dealing with people from different cultures. Genuine curiosity will be perceived as a compliment to almost everyone. Indications that you have prepared ahead by reading books and articles, viewing films, and talking with foreign visitors will show your interest in and respect for the other person's culture. The fact that you are familiar with a literary figure, an athlete's latest achievement, or local art history can demonstrate your regard and gain you the goodwill which is essential to successful professional relationships.

As easy as it is to generalize about different cultures, it is particularly important to remember that cultures are made up of individual people who exhibit the whole range and variety of human behaviors. There are boisterous Britons, shy Italians, and polite French. Simple judgments based on biased perceptions will not lead to more effective communication.

International commerce is critical to the economy of the United States and to the future of many technology enterprises. We need to export our technical products and services around the world. Technical development creates global interdependence and increased international communication. Your ability to communicate directly and accurately with overseas clients will be an important asset.

Individuals who can handle the complex task of cross-cultural communication will have a significant advantage in their careers. Perhaps the single most effective step that you can take to improve your skills in this area is to learn another language. The ability to speak and write someone else's language is invaluable. If you cannot learn another language, then take the trouble to learn a few words. You should always learn how to say "thank you" in the language of the people with whom you are dealing. Common expressions, including a toast or a folk saying, show that you have approached the culture with respect and that you are interested in the language of your audience.

BIBLIOGRAPHY

BOLTER, JAY DAVID. *Writing Space: The Computer, Hypertext, and the History of Writing.* Lawrence Erlbaum Associates, Hillsdale, New Jersey: 1991.

BRICKLEY, DAVID, and BRONWYN FRYER. "Publishing & Presentations Makeover." *PC World,* September 1993: 260–261.

BURGER, JEFF. "Presentations: Step by Step." *NewMedia,* April 1994: 93–97.

CAMPBELL, JEREMY. *Grammatical Man: Information, Entropy, Language, and Life.* New York: Simon and Schuster, 1982.

CARROLL, LEWIS. *Alice in Wonderland and Other Favorites.* New York: Washington Square Press, 1969.

CASE, JOHN. "The Question We All Wonder About: 'For Whom Do You Work?'" *Boston Globe,* 29 December 1993: 44.

CASE, JOHN. "Hey, Managers: Get out of the Way." *Boston Globe,* 6 October 1993: 48.

CROWE, ELIZABETH P. "Job Hunting in Cyberspace." *Computer Currents,* October 1994: 40–43.

DEAL, TERRENCE E., and ALLAN A. KENNEDY. *Corporate Cultures: The Rites and Rituals of Corporate Life.* Reading, MA: Addison-Wesley, 1982.

Directory of Online Databases. Cuadra/Elsevier. 11.1. January 1990.

DREYFUSS, HENRY. *Symbol Sourcebook: An Authoritative Guide to International Symbols.* New York: McGraw-Hill, 1972.

DRUCKER, PETER. "The Age of Social Transformation." *Atlantic Monthly,* November 1994: 53–80.

FULLERTON, HOWARD N., JR. "Another Look at the Labor Force." *Monthly Labor Review,* November 1993: 31–40.

FURGER, ROBERTA. "Danger at Your Fingertips." *PC World,* May 1993: 118–124.

FURGER, ROBERTA. "Time Is Running Out for Ergonomic Standards." *PC World,* March 1995: 29–30.

GHITELMAN, DAVID. "Visual Reality." *Meetings & Conventions,* June 1995: 66–72.

GREENE, MICHAEL, and JONATHAN G. RIPLEY. *Writing by Design.* Englewood Cliffs, NJ: Prentice-Hall, 1993.

FISHER, BUBBLES. *The Candy Apple: New York with Kids.* New York: Prentice-Hall Trade Division, 1990.

HEID, JIM. "Working Smart: Graphs That Work." *MacWorld,* February 1994: 155–56.

HEYEL, CARL. "Policy and Procedure Manuals." In *The Handbook of Executive Communication,* ed. John Louis DiGaetani. Homewood, IL: Dow Jones–Irwin, 1986, 200–214.

HOFSTETTER, FRED T. "Is Multimedia the Next Literacy?" *Educators' Tech Exchange,* Winter 1994: 6–13.

HOLCOMBE, MARYA, and JUDITH STEIN. *Presentations for Decision Makers: Strategies for Structuring and Delivering Your Ideas.* New York: Van Nostrand Reinhold, 1983.

KATZ, ROBERT L. "Skills of an Effective Administrator." In Levinson, 32–46.

KAWASAKI, GUY. "The Macintosh Guide to Fax Etiquette." *Macworld,* November 1993: 306.

KIECHEL, WALTER III. "How We Will Work in the Year 2000." *Fortune,* 17 May 1993: 38–52.

KLEIMAN, CAROL. *The 100 Best Job$ for the 1990s & Beyond.* Chicago: Dearborn Financial Publishing, 1992.

KOSSLYN, STEPHEN M., and CHRISTOPHER CHABRIS. "The Mind Is Not a Camera, the Brain Is Not a VCR." *Aldus Magazine,* September/October 1993: 33–36.

LASHER, WILLIAM. *The Perfect Business Plan Made Simple.* New York: Doubleday, 1994.

LEBLANC, PAUL J. "Re-inventing Writing in the Virtual Age." *Educators' Tech Exchange,* Winter 1993: 6–13.

LEVINSON, HARRY, ed. *Designing and Managing Your Career.* Boston: Harvard Business School Press, 1989.

MICHELI, ROBIN. "A Few Key Items in an Annual Report Can Tell You a Lot." *Money,* March 1988: 181.

MORRISON, IAN, and GREG SCHMID. *Future Tense: The Business Realities of the Next Ten Years.* New York: Morrow, 1994.

NORDGREN, SARAH. "Chicago Aide Is Dismissed over Flooding." *Boston Globe,* 15 April 1992: 3.

Occupational Outlook Handbook. 1994–1995 edition. U.S. Department of Labor.

PETERS, THOMAS J., and ROBERT H. WATERMAN, JR. *In Search of Excellence: Lessons from America's Best-Run Companies.* New York: Harper & Row, 1982.

PETERS, TOM. *Liberation Management.* New York: Knopf, 1992.

PILLER, CHARLES. "Bosses with X-Ray Eyes." *MacWorld,* July 1993: 118–123.

POWERS, JOHN. "The $100,000 Question." *Boston Globe Magazine,* 13 June 1993: 12, 38–47.

POWERS, JOHN. "Great Expectations." *Boston Globe Magazine,* 12 March 1995: 18, 31–38.

RAMEY, ARDELLA, and CARL R. J. SNIFFEN. *A Company Policy and Personnel Workbook.* Grants Pass, OR: Oasis Press, 1991.

RUST, H. LEE. *Jobsearch: The Complete Manual for Job Seekers.* New York: American Management Association, 1991.

SAMUELSON, ROBERT J. "How Our American Dream Unraveled." *Newsweek,* 2 March 1992: 32–39.

SCHEER, LISA. "High-Tech Agony." *Lear's,* May 1993: 42–43.

SHAW, WILLIAM H., and VINCENT BARRY. *Moral Issues in Business.* Belmont, CA: Wadsworth Publishing, 1992.

SOLOMON, JOLIE. "Taking a Stand." *Boston Globe,* 21 July 1991: 45, 49.

SPROULE, J. MICHAEL. *Communication Today.* Glenview, IL: Scott, Foresman, 1981.

"Survey Helps Pinpoint Ways to Improve Meetings." *Modern Office Technology,* June 1990: 100.

TESSLER, FRANKLIN N. "Safer Computing: How to Stay Healthy While Working on Your Mac." *MacWorld,* December 1994: 96–104.

TUFTE, EDWARD. *Envisioning Information.* 2nd ed. Cheshire, CT: Graphics Press, 1991.

WAEGEL, JANET. "6 or 8? Fax Publishing Follies." *Business Publishing,* March 1992: 36–40.

INDEX

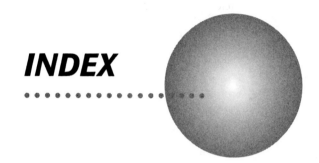

W

warnings, in office manuals, 231
writing process, 233–234
World Wide Web, *see* Internet

X

x-axis, in graphs, 169

Y

y-axis, in graphs, 169